Rethinking Authority in Global Climate Governance

In the past few years, numerous authors have highlighted the emergence of transnational climate initiatives, such as city networks, private certification schemes, and business self-regulation in the policy domain of climate change. While these transnational governance arrangements can surely contribute to solving the problem of climate change, their development by different types of sub- and non-state actors does not imply a weakening of the intergovernmental level. On the contrary, many transnational climate initiatives use the international climate regime as a point of reference and have adopted various rules and procedures from international agreements.

Rethinking Authority in Global Climate Governance puts forward this argument and expands upon it, using case studies that suggest that the effective operation of transnational climate initiatives strongly relies on the existence of an international regulatory framework created by nation-states. Thus, this book emphasizes the centrality of the intergovernmental process clustered around the United Nations Framework Convention on Climate Change (UNFCCC) and underscores that multilateral treaty-making continues to be more important than many scholars and policy-makers suppose.

This book will be of great interest to students and scholars of global environmental politics, climate change, and sustainable development.

Thomas Hickmann is a Research Associate at the Chair of International Politics, University of Potsdam, Germany.

Routledge Research in Global Environmental Governance

Global environmental governance has been a prime concern of policy-makers since the United Nations Conference on the Human Environment in 1972. Yet, despite more than nine hundred multi-lateral environmental treaties coming into force over the past forty years and numerous public-private and private initiatives to mitigate global change, human-induced environmental degradation is reaching alarming levels. Scientists see compelling evidence that the entire earth system now operates well outside safe boundaries and at rates that accelerate. The urgent challenge from a social science perspective is how to organize the co-evolution of societies and their surrounding environment; in other words, how to develop effective and equitable governance solutions for today's global problems.

Against this background, the *Routledge Research in Global Environmental Governance* series delivers cutting-edge research on the most vibrant and relevant themes within the academic field of global environmental governance.

Series Editors

Philipp Pattberg, VU University Amsterdam and the Amsterdam Global Change Institute (AGCI), the Netherlands.

Agni Kalfagianni, VU University Amsterdam, the Netherlands.

Improving Global Environmental Governance
Best practices for architecture and agency
Norichika Kanie, Steinar Andresen and Peter M. Haas

Global Governance of Genetic Resources
Access and benefit sharing after the Nagoya Protocol
Edited by Sebastian Oberthür and G. Kristin Rosendal

How Effective Negotiation Management Promotes Multilateral Cooperation
The power of process in climate, trade and biosafety negotiations
Kai Monheim

Rethinking Authority in Global Climate Governance
How transnational climate initiatives relate to the international climate regime
Thomas Hickmann

Rethinking Authority in Global Climate Governance

How transnational climate initiatives relate to the international climate regime

Thomas Hickmann

Routledge
Taylor & Francis Group
LONDON AND NEW YORK

First published 2016
by Routledge
2 Park Square, Milton Park, Abingdon, Oxon OX14 4RN

and by Routledge
711 Third Avenue, New York, NY 10017

First issued in paperback 2017

Routledge is an imprint of the Taylor & Francis Group, an informa business

British Library Cataloguing-in-Publication Data
A catalogue record for this book is available from the British Library

Library of Congress Cataloging-in-Publication Data
Hickmann, Thomas.
Rethinking authority in global climate governance : how transnational climate initiatives relate to the international climate regime / Thomas Hickmann.
pages cm. — (Routledge research in global environmental governance)
Includes index.
1. Climatic changes—International cooperation. 2. United Nations Framework Convention on Climate Change (1992 May 9) I. Title.
QC903.H54 2016
363.738'74526—dc23
2015019698

ISBN 13: 978-1-138-30416-1 (pbk)
ISBN 13: 978-1-138-93605-8 (hbk)

Dissertation University of Potsdam 2014

Typeset in Goudy
by Fish Books Ltd.

Contents

Tables

Acknowledgements

I am thankful to several people for their direct and indirect contributions to this book. Special thanks go to Harald Fuhr and Markus Lederer, who were always supportive, guided me during the research process, and provided me with feedback, critical questions, and comments. Most importantly, they encouraged me to design the research project according to my own vision and beliefs. I am also grateful to my colleagues at the University of Potsdam who have been very helpful in ensuring an enjoyable working environment. Moreover, I would like to thank Karin Bäckstrand, Per-Olof Busch, Jessica Green, Matthew Hoffmann, Hannah Janetschek, Sylvia Karlsson-Vinkhuyzen, Andrea Liese, Philipp Pattberg, Nina Reiners, Ingo Rohlfing, Miranda Schreurs, Heike Schroeder, Stacy VanDeveer, and Fariborz Zelli for their useful and constructive comments on individual chapters and the general idea of the book. Beyond that, I am indebted to a number of representatives of local governments, non-profit organizations, business associations, national delegates, and international bureaucrats involved in the United Nations Climate Change Conferences for giving me some of their time. They offered me indispensable insights into the role and function of sub- and non-state actors in global climate policy-making as well as into the formal and informal relations between transnational climate initiatives and the intergovernmental process clustered around the United Nations Framework Convention on Climate Change. And last, but not least, I want to thank my partner, Janina Barkemeyer, who has given me her unconditional support, thank you for that!

Abbreviations

C40 Group	C40 Cities Climate Leadership Group
CO_2e	Carbon dioxide equivalent
GHG	Greenhouse gas
Gold Standard	Gold Standard for Carbon Offsets
HFC-23	Trifluoromethane
ICLEI	International Council for Local Environmental Initiatives *Note: The International Council for Local Environmental Initiatives was later renamed ICLEI Local Governments for Sustainability*
ICMA	International City/County Management Association
IULA	International Union of Local Authorities
IPCC	Intergovernmental Panel on Climate Change
LGMA	Local Governments and Municipal Authorities
NF_3	Nitrogen trifluoride
OECD	Organisation for Economic Co-operation and Development
UCLG	United Cities and Local Governments
UNFCCC	United Nations Framework Convention on Climate Change

Abbreviations

1 Introduction

The reconfiguration of authority in world politics

Overview

After more than two decades of inter-state negotiations aimed at addressing and managing the problem of climate change, scholars and policy-makers have become increasingly frustrated and disillusioned with the international climate regime. Although the obstacles to reaching an international agreement for collective action have largely been identified, a fundamental breakthrough in the international climate negotiations is unlikely to occur in the near future (e.g. Keohane and Victor 2011; Hale, Held, and Young 2013; Abbott 2014). Therefore, in recent years, a number of authors have begun to direct increasing attention to transnational climate initiatives launched by different types of *sub- and non-state actors*[1] (e.g. Jagers and Stripple 2003; Betsill and Bulkeley 2006; Bäckstrand 2008; Pattberg and Stripple 2008; Andonova, Betsill, and Bulkeley 2009; Bulkeley and Newell 2010; Hoffmann 2011; Pattberg 2012; Green 2014). Many of these authors claim that multilateral treaty-making has lost much of its spark, and conceive the various initiatives developed by sub-national, non-profit, or business actors as alternative governance arrangements to the instruments established at the intergovernmental level. In particular, they hold that the increasing involvement of sub- and non-state actors in climate policy-making has generated a 'shift in the centre of gravity in climate governance away from traditional state-centric multilateral processes to multilevel governance whereby diverse, decentralised initiatives (…) form the basis for the global response to climate change' (Bernstein *et al.* 2010: 171).

Taking up this thread, this book argues that while transnational climate initiatives can certainly contribute to solving the problem of climate change, the development of such initiatives by sub- and non-state actors does not imply a weakening of the intergovernmental level. On the contrary, many transnational climate initiatives use the international climate regime as a point of reference and have adopted various rules and procedures from international climate agreements. Most importantly, the case studies in this book suggest that the effective operation of transnational governance arrangements strongly relies on the existence of an international regulatory framework created by nation-states. Thus, the book emphasizes the centrality of the intergovernmental process clustered around the *United Nations Framework Convention on Climate Change* (hereafter UNFCCC) and underscores that multilateral treaty-making continues to be more important than many scholars and policy-makers suppose.

After this overview of the general theme of the book, the introduction proceeds with a review of the changing role and function of sub- and non-state actors in global policy-making. After that, I discuss major concepts within the field of international relations theory, which are of crucial importance for this study, particularly focusing on *international regimes*, *global governance*, and *authority in world politics*. Then, I provide a brief outline of the book with its principal objective, primary research question, conceptual assumptions, case studies, and main findings. And finally, I present the general structure of the work as a whole.

Sub- and non-state actors in world politics

Over the past few years, numerous scholars have pointed to the increasingly salient role played by actors other than the nation-state in world politics (e.g. Hewson and Sinclair 1999; Higgott, Underhill, and Bieler 2000; Kahler and Lake 2003; Grande and Pauly 2005; Avant, Finnemore, and Sell 2010). They contend that different types of sub- and non-state actors now perform several functions that previously rested solely with national governments or international institutions. This phenomenon is of course not entirely new. Early examples of private actors with a significant role in world politics include commercial corporations that had a major influence in the Middle Ages, financial enterprises that already possessed substantial political power in the Renaissance, and the private empires of European holdings in colonial times (Biermann and Dingwerth 2004: 14). Nevertheless, according to many authors, the growing involvement of sub- and non-state actors in world politics has lately gained a new quality and can be regarded as a response to the increasing complexity and interdependence in global politics prompted by globalization. For instance, scholars have interpreted the increasing influence of large enterprises in the global political economy as structural power of transnational corporations (Cutler 1999; Fuchs 2007; Clapp and Fuchs 2009). They have examined the critical role played by rating agencies that estimate the creditworthiness of firms and countries and maintain a quasi-legal position in the regulation of global financial markets (Kerwer 2002; Sinclair 2005; Kruck 2011). They have focused on *public-private partnerships* and private charity organizations that are instrumental in the implementation of the *United Nations Millennium Development Goals* and provide basic public health services in a number of least-developed countries (Liese and Beisheim 2011; Moran and Stevenson 2013). They have explored how transnational advocacy groups and other actors, such as firms and domestic opposition groups, promote compliance with international human rights standards (Keck and Sikkink 1998; Risse, Ropp, and Sikkink 2013). And they have dedicated special attention to private military companies that operate in several areas of the world to establish security and thereby considerably shape the international security agenda (Leander 2005; Abrahamsen and Williams 2011). These current research examples illustrate that sub- and non-state actors contribute to the provision of collective goods and have acquired several policy-making functions across different domains of world politics. Hence, it can be argued that these actors 'have left their mark on the international system and that we cannot start theorizing about the contemporary world system without taking their influence into account' (Risse 2013: 426).

Scholars have identified various reasons for the growing involvement of sub- and non-state state actors in world politics. The most common explanation is the declining financial and technical capacity of nation-states to regulate increasingly complex matters (Strange 1996). As several scholars argue, due to the ongoing processes associated with economic, social, and cultural globalization, nation-states have lost some of their earlier dominance and other actors have begun to fill the emerging regulatory gap. According to numerous authors, sub- and non-state actors play a particularly prevalent role in the field of global environmental politics (e.g. Biermann and Pattberg 2008; Dellas, Pattberg, and Betsill 2011; Newell, Pattberg, and Schroeder 2012). Since the 1970s, several environmental problems, such as acid rain, ozone depletion, climate change, desertification, and biodiversity loss, have put additional pressure on national governments by increasing the demand for new environmental abatement policies and creating new interdependencies among nation-states (Biermann and Dingwerth 2004). While these transboundary problems have traditionally been dealt with rather exclusively by national governments at diplomatic conferences, a wide array of sub- and non-state actors has emerged in recent decades that increasingly participate in global environmental policy-making. Prominent examples include environmental non-governmental organizations and business associations, coalitions of local governments concerned with common environmental problems, international environmental bureaucracies and treaty secretariats, science networks, as well as private standard-setting bodies that often focus on particular issue areas, such as forest management, climate change, or biodiversity conservation.[2]

Interestingly, the role and function of sub- and non-state actors in global environmental policy-making has advanced considerably in the last decades. In the 1990s, sub- and non-state actors were, at the global level, still primarily conceived as environmental advocacy groups aimed at influencing certain policy outcomes negotiated by nation-states at the intergovernmental level (Conca 1995; Raustiala 1997; Keck and Sikkink 1998). Later, both environmental and business non-governmental organizations adopted a different role and started to directly engage in the formation and maintenance of international environmental regimes (Newell 2000; Betsill and Corell 2001). And most important for the focus of this book, in recent years, many scholars have recognized the development of various transnational governance arrangements beyond central governments and international institutions, such as *city networks*, *private certification schemes*, and *business self-regulatory initiatives* (e.g. Betsill and Bulkeley 2004; Levy and Newell 2005; Arts 2006; Pattberg 2007; Andonova 2010; Bäckstrand *et al.* 2010; Gulbrandsen 2010; Biermann and Pattberg 2012; Green 2014). These transnational governance arrangements supply regulation or other public goods and seek to contribute to the solution of global environmental problems. The probably most prominent example of such initiatives is the emergence of climate-related partnerships between local governments (Bulkeley 2010). In the absence of a wide-ranging international climate treaty that contains ambitious targets for nation-states to reduce greenhouse gas (hereafter GHG) emissions, cities and municipalities are now organizing themselves into networks and aim at mitigating and adapting to climate change at the local level. Other prominent examples of transnational climate initiatives include non-profit organizations that create certain guidelines and standards for responsible business behavior in order to assess corporate responses to climate change as well as voluntary efforts of businesses to account and report their GHG emissions.

Against this backdrop, some authors have argued that the growing significance of transnational governance arrangements in global environmental politics and other fields of world politics has led to a relocation of authority from state-based forms of regulation to new actors and institutions that are better suited to cope with increasingly complex issues (e.g. Rittberger *et al.* 2008a: 318). These scholars contend that transboundary problems can no longer be perceived as matters exclusively addressed by national governments at diplomatic conferences. Instead, they emphasize that different types of sub- and non-state actors increasingly take on the role of 'political authorities able to design and make rules themselves, rather than merely complying with the directives of nation-states or the result of cooperation among nation-states (treaties and intergovernmental organizations)' (Hoffmann 2011: 67). This perspective challenges classical approaches to international politics and traditional concepts of authority in world politics. However, the precise nature of the relationship between the various climate initiatives launched by sub- and non-state actors and the intergovernmental level has so far not been studied in much detail. Therefore, this book aims to move beyond the debate on the emergence of transnational governance arrangements and explores the wider implications of this development for global (climate) politics.

Major concepts of international relations theory

In the past decades, the vast majority of researchers concerned with global affairs have centered their studies first and foremost on the interactions between nation-states. These authors start from the premise that nation-states are the principal actors in the international system, and argue that cross-border concerns are primarily addressed through inter-state negotiations. Scholars in this tradition assert that due to the lack of a central government at the global level, authority resides exclusively with national governments and the different institutions they create to cope with transboundary problems. Consequently, they pay much attention to the concept of *international regimes* and focus on the question of how these institutions facilitate or shape international relations.

International regimes

The theoretical concept of international regimes began to receive scholarly attention in the 1970s.[3] At that time, a number of scholars recognized the evolution of various international institutions that could not be satisfactorily explained by the then prevailing realist approach to international politics. A few years later, the concept of international regimes was the subject of a conference convened to prepare the 1982 Special Issue of *International Organization* (Hasenclever, Mayer, and Rittberger 1997: 8). At this conference, Stephen Krasner defined international regimes as 'sets of implicit and explicit principles, norms, rules, and decision-making procedures around which actors' expectations converge in a given area of international relations' (Krasner 1982: 186). In the following years, the regime concept came into common parlance in international relations theory. Although Krasner's definition has often been criticized for its lack of clarity (Strange 1982; Haggard and Simmons 1987; Stein 1993), it has been widely used by scholars studying the creation, the maintenance, and the effectiveness of international institutions in various domains of international politics (e.g. Donelly 1986; Nye 1987; Bernauer 1995; Levy, Young, and Zürn 1995; Hoekman and Kostecki 2001). In fact, the analysis of international regimes has provided powerful tools for understanding different aspects of global policy-making, especially the dynamics of intergovernmental negotiations. One of the most important contributions of regime scholars is that they 'have convincingly shown that "cooperation under anarchy" is possible and that self-interested actors can achieve stable and enduring cooperation and overcome collective action dilemmas' (Risse 2000: 3–4). According to adherents of the neo-liberal institutionalist approach to international politics, international regimes are created by nation-states to facilitate cooperation and achieve mutually beneficial gains mainly by providing information and reducing transaction costs (Keohane 1984; Axelrod and Keohane 1986; Keohane and Martin 1995). Hence, this scholarly perspective perceives transboundary problems as collective action problems and holds that they can be solved through inter-state cooperation and the establishment of international institutions.

In the past few years, however, the regime approach has come under intense scrutiny from many directions. First, as already noted above, different observers of global affairs have pointed to the limited capability and effectiveness of multilateral treaty-making in solving transboundary problems (e.g. Reinicke and Deng 2000; Hale, Held, and Young 2013). An increasing number of scholars and policymakers complain about the slow progress of international negotiations in various issue areas of world politics, especially in the field of global environmental politics (Speth 2004; Conca 2005; Victor 2011). Second, many authors contend that conventional regime analysis has largely neglected the growing significance of sub- and non-state actors in the management of cross-border issues (Rosenau and Czempiel 1992; Koenig-Archibugi 2003; Avant, Finnemore, and Sell 2010). These scholars argue that the focus on state-based international regimes as primary modes of problem-solving has largely obscured the potential of alternative governance arrangements to contribute to effective policy-making (Dingwerth and Pattberg 2006). They maintain that new tools and institutions have emerged that are needed to cope with transboundary problems, especially in a rapidly globalizing world. Thus, in short, due to concerns about the limitations of the rather state-centric classical approaches to international politics, numerous scholars have now turned to the concept of *global governance* as a means of understanding the various new developments in world politics.

Global governance

Initially, the term 'governance' was used in national debates over new forms of public management that differ from traditional hierarchical state regulation (e.g. Pierre and Peters 2000). Later, scholars focusing on global affairs adopted the term to capture similar developments in world politics. However, since scholars have not (yet) agreed upon a common definition of the concept of global governance, the term still 'means different things to different authors' (Biermann and Pattberg 2008: 279). Klaus Dingwerth and Philipp Pattberg generally distinguish between two diverging usages of the term: (i) an analytical understanding and (ii) a normative or critical understanding of global governance:[4]

> Besides its use as an analytical concept that attempts to capture the – actual, perceived, or constructed – reality of contemporary world politics (...), the concept is often used to denote a specific political program, expressing either a normative perspective on how political institutions should react to the reduced steering capacity of national political systems or a critical perspective that refers to global governance as a hegemonic discourse.
>
> (Dingwerth and Pattberg 2006: 189)

This distinction between an analytical and a political use of the term 'global governance' brings conceptual clarity to a confusing research area. The normative understanding of global governance is closely associated with the *United Nations Commission on Global Governance* and its publication 'Our Global Neighborhood' (United Nations Commission on Global Governance 1995). In this report, the Commission highlighted the need for enhanced cooperation in world politics and a stronger United Nations system in order to cope with the challenges of the twenty-first century. Some authors have developed this position further (e.g. Weiss and Gordenker 1996; Woods 1999; Weiss 2000). Basically, these authors understand global governance as a long-term project of global integration and call for the creation of new international institutions in order to keep step with economic globalization. Other scholars take a critical stance on global governance (Brand 2005; Lederer and Müller 2005; Brand *et al.* 2008; Brand and Wissen 2011). They perceive the concept of global governance as a hegemonic project that is dominated by a number of powerful market actors who propagate neo-liberal economic development. Proponents of this approach claim that the term 'global governance' is employed as an ideological term that conceals the adverse effects of the capitalist economic model. Therefore, these scholars seek to deconstruct the concept of global governance.

The development of the analytical understanding of global governance is very much tied to the work by James Rosenau. According to his classical definition, 'global governance is conceived to include systems of rule at all levels of human activity – from the family to the international organization – in which the pursuit of goals through the exercise of control has transnational repercussions' (Rosenau 1995: 13). While this definition reflects a very broad understanding of global governance, it has laid the foundation for numerous useful conceptualizations of recent developments in contemporary global affairs. These accounts have enabled scholars from various disciplines to understand how different forms of self-organization and horizontal negotiation are possible in world politics that do not necessarily rely on hierarchy and command (Koenig-Archibugi 2003: 319). In particular, this scholarly perspective has been instrumental in describing several empirical phenomena that are not captured by classical approaches to international politics. Unless otherwise stated, the term 'global governance' is understood in this book as an analytical concept that is employed by an increasing number of scholars to study the profound changes occurring in world politics in the last few years. Arguably, the concept of global governance departs from the more traditional notion of international politics in at least four interrelated ways (cf. Dingwerth and Pattberg 2006: 191–193).

First and foremost, the concept of global governance stresses the role and function of sub- and non-state actors in contemporary world politics. In contrast to classical approaches to international politics that primarily focus on the interactions between nation-states, the global governance perspective attaches equal importance to sub- and non-state actors. Under the headline of global governance, scholars analyze how different kinds of actors other than the nation-state and international institutions are involved in the governing of collective affairs (e.g. Pattberg 2007; Ougaard and Leander 2010; Amen *et al.* 2011). Second, the concept of global governance understands world politics as a multilevel system in which local, national, regional, and global levels of decision-making are closely linked to each other and commonly involved in addressing transboundary problems. Unlike the term 'international politics', which suggests that issues at the international level can be analyzed separately from issues at other levels of social interaction, the notion of global governance underlines the importance of the interconnectedness between different levels of decision-making (e.g. Welch and Kennedy-Pipe 2004). Third, the concept of global governance captures the wide range of governance arrangements in world politics and highlights the increasing importance of network-based coordination among public and private actors in world politics. While classical accounts on international politics focus principally on power relations and interest-based intergovernmental bargaining, the term 'global governance' puts emphasis on coordination processes that are generally characterized by less hierarchical and less formal modes of steering (e.g. Börzel and Risse 2005; Jordan, Wurzel, and Zito 2005; Bäckstrand *et al.* 2010). Fourth, and most relevant for the present study, the concept of global governance provides an analytical tool to examine authority structures beyond the nation-state (Zürn 2013). In fact, the core of the debate on global governance concerns the question of how authority is reconfigured and to what extent sub- and non-state actors have acquired authority in world politics. Generally, authors using the term 'global governance' share a broader conceptual thinking about authority than adherents of classical approaches to international politics, and conceive nation-states as only one of several sources of authority in world politics. This last feature of the global governance concept is crucial because it allows scholars to critically reflect traditional concepts of *authority in world politics*.

Authority in world politics

Rosenau was among the first scholars to acknowledge the need to reconsider the notion of authority in traditional state-centric approaches to international politics. Referring to the diminishing capacities of nation-states to exercise monopolistic control in a rapidly globalizing world, he puts forward the argument that various new 'spheres of authority' have emerged in world politics beyond the control of nation-states (Rosenau 1992; 1997; 2007). Rosenau emphasizes that nation-states remain central loci in world politics, but finds that they have lost 'their ability to evoke compliance and govern effectively (…) in part due to the growing relevance and potential of control mechanisms sustained by transnational and subnational systems of rule' (Rosenau 1995: 39). Similarly, several other scholars have pointed to the development of private authority structures alongside central governments and international institutions as a result of the growing importance of private actors in global affairs. For instance, Claire Cutler, Virginia Haufler, and Tony Porter focused on different cooperative arrangements between private economic actors (Cutler, Haufler, and Porter 1999a). By adopting Krasner's classical definition of international regimes cited above, they examined the institutionalization of informal industry norms and showed that nation-states not only recognize the norms and rules negotiated by private corporations, but also incorporate them into both domestic and international regulatory structures (Haufler 1995; Cutler, Haufler, and Porter 1999b; Cutler 2002). Rodney Hall and Thomas Biersteker have adopted a more general approach and provide a comparative analysis of private authority beyond the field of international political economy (Hall and Biersteker 2002a). They distinguish between market-based, moral, and illicit forms of authority exercised by accounting agencies, religious movements, and mafias or mercenaries (Hall and Biersteker 2002b). And most recently, Jessica Green studied different facets of private authority in global environmental governance and introduced the concept of entrepreneurial private authority (Green 2014). Basically, all these authors convey the idea that nation-states no longer hold the monopoly over the resolution of transboundary problems and contend that an increasing number of sub- and non-state actors have taken on various authoritative roles and functions in world politics. According to Volker Rittberger and colleagues, authority is hence 'found to be dispersed among many actors and exercised through means other than formal position' (Rittberger *et al.* 2008b: 2).

These and other theoretical accounts of the emergence of authority beyond central governments and international institutions in world politics have given rise to wider debates on various questions, such as whether sub- and non-state actors can enhance the legitimacy of global politics, how sub- and non-state actors can be held accountable for their actions, and to what extent sub- and non-state actors might deliver adequate solutions for transboundary problems (e.g. Keohane 2003; Börzel and Risse 2005; Held and Koenig-Archibugi 2005; Wolf 2006; Bexell and Mörth 2010; Jönsson and Tallberg 2010). Certainly, these ongoing debates have improved and will continue to improve our understanding of the role and function of sub- and non-state actors in world politics. However, only limited attempts have been made thus far to systematically analyze the interplay between the wide variety of initiatives launched by sub- and non-state actors and the intergovernmental level, particularly with regard to the repercussions of this relationship for the distribution of authority in global policy-making. Against this backdrop, in the following chapters, I turn to the policy domain of climate change and examine how different transnational climate initiatives relate to the international climate regime and discuss what this implies for the concept of authority in world politics.

Outline of the book

Over the past few decades, numerous scholars have used the field of global environmental politics as an illustrative example to analyze current trends in world politics (e.g. Haas 1992; Young 1997; Clapp 2003; Bäckstrand 2008; Biermann *et al.* 2009; Keohane and Victor 2011; Abbott 2012). As Bas Arts puts it, 'the environmental domain has been a laboratory for new modes of governance *par excellence*' (Arts 2006: 184, emphasis in original). This book joins this camp and approaches the issue area of climate change as an empirical testing ground for the study of the relationship between transnational governance arrangements and existing modes of inter-state cooperation. In the following paragraphs, I briefly summarize the book's principal objective, primary research question, case studies, conceptual assumptions, and key findings.

Principal objective

As indicated above, the principal objective of this book is to *analyze the reconfiguration of authority in global climate governance by exploring the interplay between newly emerging transnational climate initiatives and the international climate regime*. While the discussion of the concept of authority is used as a theoretical background, the analytical focus of this book lies on the interplay between different climate initiatives launched by sub- and non-state actors and the intergovernmental level. The evolving research field on the growing involvement of sub- and non-state actors in world politics constitutes one of the most important dimensions in the analysis of contemporary world politics (Hale and Roger 2014: 60). The present study is a relatively early contribution to this research field and will be important in three respects. First, the book delivers rich empirical findings about the relationship between different transnational governance arrangements and existing modes of inter-state cooperation, which are crucial for both scholars and policy-makers concerned with global climate governance. Second, the book is of particular interest for scholars studying governance arrangements beyond central governments and international institutions, as well as the changing role and function of sub- and non-state actors in global affairs in general. And third, the book aims to inform the greater theoretical debate regarding the question of how authority is reconfigured in world politics through the emergence of transnational climate initiatives that have been developed by sub-national, non-profit, and business actors over the past few years.

Primary research question

The emergence of governance initiatives beyond national governments and international institutions has prompted many scholars to formulate novel theoretical approaches to capture the role and function of sub- and non-state actors in world politics. Thereby, much of the current literature revolves around the question of whether the various newly emerging transnational governance arrangements can be perceived as 'alternatives' or 'supplements' to existing modes of inter-state cooperation in the field of global environmental politics (O'Neill 2009: 169). In line with this research agenda, this study focuses on the question of *how the various newly emerging climate initiatives launched by different types of sub- and non-state actors relate to the international climate regime*. Basically, this research question is addressed in three consecutive steps. First, I review how different transnational governance arrangements have emerged and acquired important policy-making functions in the global response to climate change. After that, I empirically investigate the interplay between the different transnational climate initiatives and the intergovernmental level. And finally, I analyze which insights can be drawn from the empirical analysis for the theoretical debate on the concept of authority in global (climate) governance.

Conceptual assumptions and theoretical expectations

To systematically analyze the research question formulated above, this book draws on three conceptual assumptions that reflect different perspectives on the relationship between transnational governance arrangements and the international climate regime. The first conceptual assumption suggests a *conflictive relationship* between transnational governance arrangements and the intergovernmental level. In this scenario, the different transnational climate initiatives are thought to weaken the norms and rules negotiated by nation-states in international climate negotiations. If this assumption was correct, I would expect to observe that the different transnational governance arrangements would depart from key features of the international climate regime and propagate norms and rules that are opposed to those stipulated in international climate agreements. The second conceptual assumption points to a *complementary relationship* between transnational governance arrangements and the intergovernmental level. Within this framework, the different transnational climate initiatives are supposed to strengthen the norms and rules of the international climate regime. If this conjecture were true, I would expect to see in the empirical case studies that the different transnational governance arrangements would build on key features of the international climate regime and promote the norms and rules established through international climate agreements. And the third conceptual assumption supposes a *dependency relationship* between transnational governance arrangements and the intergovernmental level. With regard to this scenario, the different transnational climate initiatives are conjectured to rely on the norms and rules established by nation-states in international climate negotiations. If this presumption were valid, I would expect to find that the effective operation of the different transnational governance arrangements would, to a large extent, rely on the nature and scope of the norms and rules of the international climate regime. These three conceptual assumptions will guide the empirical analysis and are further specified in the research design (see chapter 3).

Case studies

Due to the great variety of initiatives launched by sub- and non-state actors to address the problem of climate change, this book analyzes three typical examples of transnational climate initiatives that have emerged in the past few years. As laid out in more detail in the third chapter, the various transnational climate initiatives can be classified according to the type of actor initiating the particular arrangement. First, I analyze the relationship between the *ICLEI Local Governments for Sustainability Network* and the international climate regime (see case study in chapter 4). This case study is conceived as an instance of the interplay between a transnational climate governance arrangement and the intergovernmental level that has been developed by a group of *public sub-national actors*. Second, I examine the relationship between the *Gold Standard for Carbon Offsets* and the international climate regime (see case study in chapter 5). This case study is regarded as an instance of the interplay between a transnational climate governance arrangement and the intergovernmental level that has been initiated by *private non-profit actors*. Third, I study the relationship between the *Greenhouse Gas Protocol* and the international climate regime (see case study in chapter 6). This case study is considered an instance of the interplay between a transnational climate governance arrangement and the intergovernmental level that has mainly been propelled by *business actors*. Since the empirical analysis is embedded in a thorough theoretical background and structured through a comprehensive research design, the case studies offer profound insights into how the relationship between transnational governance arrangements and the intergovernmental level can be conceptualized in theoretical terms.

Key findings

The analysis in this book underlines that climate initiatives launched by sub- and non-state actors play an important role in global climate governance. The various newly emerging transnational climate governance arrangements perform several policy-making functions, ranging from the development of local climate policies (as shown in chapter 4) and the creation of guidelines for the evaluation of carbon offset projects (as shown in chapter 5) to the provision of instruments for the establishment of corporate GHG inventories (as shown in chapter 6). Hence, the efforts undertaken by sub- and non-state actors can certainly contribute to the implementation of the norms and rules set out in international climate agreements. Moreover, transnational climate initiatives occasionally set guidelines and standards that are more ambitious than those agreed upon by nation-states in international climate negotiations and create novel means to cope with climate change. Nevertheless, the empirical findings presented in this book also demonstrate that an international umbrella is essential for the activities of climate initiatives developed by different types of sub- and non-state actors. The case studies provide strong evidence that transnational governance arrangements have only limited operational capacities to tackle the problem of climate change *independently* from the intergovernmental level and operate largely in the 'shadow' of the international climate regime. Therefore, this book argues that the various climate initiatives developed by sub- and non-state actors can be perceived as important elements in the global response to climate change, while they, however, need to be bolstered by an international regulatory framework and incentive structure established at higher levels of government.

This central finding of the book challenges the widely held assumption that the emergence of transnational governance arrangements automatically leads to a shift of authority away from multilateral treaty-making towards sub- and non-state actors. Instead, what can be observed in the policy domain of climate change is a *reconfiguration of authority* that only reinforces the importance of the intergovernmental level. Consequently, the present analysis suggests that the *principles*, *norms*, *rules*, and *decision-making procedures* negotiated in multilateral settings have a significant and often overlooked impact on the initiatives launched by sub- and non-state actors. This conclusion points to a more nuanced perspective on the concept of authority in world politics. The changing patterns of authority in world politics cannot be conceptualized as a zero-sum game, in which the emergence of authoritative structures beyond central governments and international institutions equals a loss of authority at the expense of state-based forms of governance. In particular, this book shows that while sub-national, non-profit, and business actors have acquired various authoritative functions in global climate governance over the past few decades, the international climate regime remains the center around which these actors revolve and upon which their initiatives are built. From a practical perspective, it would therefore be highly problematic to presume that transnational climate initiatives can solve the problem of climate change without the continuous development of an overarching international regulatory framework adopted by nation-states at the intergovernmental level. In fact, multilateral treaty-making is of utmost importance for the various transnational initiatives aimed at tackling the problem of climate change. Thus, the crucial question that needs to be addressed is not whether the international climate regime is becoming obsolete, but rather how the existing modes of inter-state cooperation can be adjusted to enable sub- and non-state actors to more effectively contribute to the global response to climate change.

Structure

The book is organized as follows. After this introduction has presented the main plan and general context of this study, the second chapter reviews the current state of research on contemporary global climate governance and points to a research gap in this field. After that, the third chapter describes the theoretical background and analytical framework of the book. In particular, it thoroughly discusses relevant theoretical approaches to the concept of authority and presents the research design for the empirical analysis. Based on this, chapters 4 to 6 empirically explore the relationship between three transnational climate initiatives (i.e. the *ICLEI Local Governments for Sustainability Network*, the *Gold Standard for Carbon Offsets*, the *Greenhouse Gas Protocol*) and the international climate regime. Thereby, all case studies follow a largely identical structure. At the outset of each case study, I provide a brief overview of the specific context in which the respective transnational governance arrangement operates. Then, I investigate the interplay between one transnational climate initiative and the intergovernmental level. At the end of each case study, I summarize the main findings and derive some conclusions for the theoretical background revolving around the concept of authority in world politics. And in the final chapter, I first briefly recapitulate the general idea of the book. Thereafter, I compare across the three cases, emphasize the most important findings, draw general conclusions on the theoretical approaches discussed in the third chapter, and point to factors that merit attention in future research.

References

Abbott, Kenneth W. (2012). The Transnational Regime Complex for Climate Change. *Environment and Planning C: Government and Policy* 30 (4): 571–590.

Abbott, Kenneth W. (2014). Strengthening the Transnational Regime Complex for Climate Change. *Transnational Environmental Law* 3 (1): 57–88.

Abrahamsen, Rita; Williams, Michael C. (2011). *Security Beyond the State: Private Security in International Politics*. Cambridge: Cambridge University Press.

Amen, Mark; Toly, Noah J.; McCartney, Patricia L.; Segbers, Klaus, (eds). (2011). *Cities and Global Governance: New Sites for International Relations*. Farnham: Ashgate.

Andonova, Liliana B. (2010). Public-Private Partnerships for the Earth: Politics and Patterns of Hybrid Authority in the Multilateral System. *Global Environmental Politics* 10 (2): 25–53.

Andonova, Liliana B.; Betsill, Michele; Bulkeley, Harriet (2009). Transnational Climate Governance. *Global Environmental Politics* 9 (2): 52–73.

Arts, Bas (2006). Non-State Actors in Global Environmental Governance: New Arrangements Beyond the State In: Koenig-Archibugi, Mathias; Zürn, Michael. *New Modes of Governance in the Global System: Exploring Publicness, Delegation and Inclusiveness*. Basingstoke: Palgrave, 177–200.

Avant, Deborah D.; Finnemore, Martha; Sell, Susan K., (eds). (2010). *Who Governs the Globe?* Cambridge: Cambridge University Press.

Axelrod, Robert; Keohane, Robert O. (1986). Achieving Cooperation Under Anarchy: Strategies and Institutions. In: Oye, Kenneth A. *Cooperation under Anarchy*. Princeton, NJ: Princeton University Press, 226–254.

Bäckstrand, Karin (2008). Accountability of Networked Climate Governance: The Rise of Transnational Climate Partnerships. *Global Environmental Politics* 8 (3): 74–102.

Bäckstrand, Karin; Khan, Jamil; Kronsell, Annica; Lövbrand, Eva, (eds). (2010). *Environmental Politics and Deliberative Democracy: Examining the Promise of New Modes of Governance*. Cheltenham: Edward Elgar.

Bernauer, Thomas (1995). The Effect of International Environmental Institutions: How We Might Learn More. *International Organization* 49 (2): 351–377.

Bernstein, Steven; Betsill, Michele; Hoffmann, Matthew; Paterson, Matthew (2010). A Tale of Two Copenhagens: Carbon Markets and Climate Governance. *Millennium: Journal of International Studies* 39 (1): 161–173.

Betsill, Michele; Bulkeley, Harriet (2004). Transnational Networks and Global Environmental Governance: The Cities for Climate Protection Program. *International Studies Quarterly* 48 (2): 471–493.

Betsill, Michele; Bulkeley, Harriet (2006). Cities and the Multilevel Governance of Global Climate Change. *Global Governance* 12 (2): 141–159.

Betsill, Michele; Corell, Elisabeth (2001). NGO Influence in International Environmental Negotiations: A Framework for Analysis. *Global Environmental Politics* 1 (4): 65–85.

Bexell, Magdalena; Mörth, Ulrika, (eds). (2010). *Democracy and Public-Private Partnerships in Global Governance*. Basingstoke: Palgrave.

Biermann, Frank; Dingwerth, Klaus (2004). Global Environmental Change and the Nation State. *Global Environmental Politics* 4 (1): 1–22.

Biermann, Frank; Pattberg, Philipp (2008). Global Environmental Governance: Taking Stock, Moving Forward. *Annual Review of Environment and Resources* 33: 277–294.

Biermann, Frank; Pattberg, Philipp, (eds). (2012). *Global Environmental Governance Reconsidered: New Actors, Mechanisms and Interlinkages*. Cambridge, MA: MIT Press.

Biermann, Frank; Pattberg, Philipp; van Asselt, Harro; Zelli, Fariborz (2009). The Fragmentation of Global Governance Architectures: A Framework for Analysis. *Global Environmental Politics* 9 (4): 14–40.

Börzel, Tanja A.; Risse, Thomas (2005). Public-Private Partnerships: Effective and Legitimate Tools of International Governance. In: Grande, Edgar; Pauly, Louis W. *Complex Sovereignty: Reconstituting Political Authority in the Twenty-First Century*. Toronto, Canada: University of Toronto Press, 195–216.

Brand, Ulrich (2005). Order and Regulation: Global Governance as a Hegemonic Discourse of International Politics? *Review of International Political Economy* 12 (1): 155–176.

Brand, Ulrich; Görg, Christoph; Hirsch, Joachim; Wissen, Markus (2008). *Conflicts in Environmental Regulation and the Internationalisation of the State: Contested Terrains*. London: Routledge.

Brand, Ulrich; Wissen, Markus (2011). Crisis and Continuity of Capitalist Society-Nature Relationships: The Imperial Mode of Living and the Limits to Environmental Governance. *Review of International Political Economy* 20 (4): 687–711.

Bulkeley, Harriet (2010). Cities and the Governing of Climate Change. *Annual Review of Environment and Resources* 35: 229–253.

Bulkeley, Harriet; Newell, Peter (2010). *Governing Climate Change*. London: Routledge.

Clapp, Jennifer (2003). Transnational Corporate Interests and Global Environmental Governance: Negotiating Rules for Agricultural Biotechnology and Chemicals. *Environmental Politics* 12 (4): 1–23.

Clapp, Jennifer; Fuchs, Doris A. (2009). *Corporate Power in Global Agrifood Governance*. Cambridge, MA: MIT Press.

Conca, Ken (1995). Greening the United Nations: Environmental Organizations and the UN System. *Third World Quarterly* 16 (3): 441–457.
Conca, Ken (2005). Environmental Governance After Johannesburg: From Stalled Legalization to Environmental Human Rights? *Journal of International Law & International Relations* 1 (1–2): 121–138.
Cutler, Claire A. (1999). Locating 'Authority' in the Global Political Economy. *International Studies Quarterly* 43 (1): 59–81.
Cutler, Claire A. (2002). Private International Regimes and Interfirm Cooperation. In: Hall, Rodney Bruce; Biersteker, Thomas J. *The Emergence of Private Authority in Global Governance*. Cambridge: Cambridge University Press, 23–40.
Cutler, Claire A.; Haufler, Virginia; Porter, Tony, (eds). (1999a). *Private Authority and International Affairs*. Albany, NY: State University of New York Press.
Cutler, Claire A.; Haufler, Virginia; Porter, Tony (1999b). Private Authority and International Affairs. In: Cutler, Claire A.; Haufler, Virginia; Porter, Tony. *Private Authority and International Affairs*. Albany, NY: State University of New York Press, 3–28.
Dellas, Eleni; Pattberg, Philipp; Betsill, Michele (2011). Agency in Earth System Governance: Refining a Research Agenda. *International Environmental Agreements* 11 (1): 85–98.
Dingwerth, Klaus; Pattberg, Philipp (2006). Global Governance as a Perspective on World Politics. *Global Governance* 12 (2): 185–203.
Donelly, Jack (1986). International Human Rights: A Regime Analysis. *International Organization* 40 (3): 599–642.
Finger, Matthias; Svarin, David (2012). Nonstate Actors in Global Environmental Governance. In: Dauvergne, Peter. *Handbook of Global Environmental Politics*. Cheltenham: Edward Elgar, 285–297.
Fuchs, Doris (2007). *Business Power in Global Governance*. Boulder: Lynne Rienner.
Grande, Edgar; Pauly, Louis W., (eds). (2005). *Complex Sovereignty: Reconstituting Political Authority in the Twenty-First Century*. Toronto, Canada: University of Toronto Press.
Green, Jessica F. (2014). *Rethinking Private Authority: Agents and Entrepreneurs in Global Environmental Governance*. Princeton, NJ: Princeton University Press.
Gulbrandsen, Lars H. (2010). *Transnational Environmental Governance: The Emergence and Effects of the Certification of Forests and Fisheries*. Cheltenham: Edward Elgar.
Haas, Peter M. (1992). Banning Chlorofluorocarbons: Epistemic Community Efforts to Protect Stratospheric Ozone. *International Organization* 46 (1): 187–224.
Haggard, Stephan; Simmons, Beth A. (1987). Theories of International Regimes. *International Organization* 41 (3): 491–517.
Hale, Thomas; Held, David; Young, Kevin (2013). *Gridlock: Why Global Cooperation Is Failing When We Need It Most*. Cambridge: Polity Press.
Hale, Thomas; Roger, Charles (2014). Orchestration and Transnational Climate Governance. *Review of International Organizations* 9 (1): 59–82.
Hall, Rodney Bruce; Biersteker, Thomas J., (eds). (2002a). *The Emergence of Private Authority in Global Governance*. Cambridge: Cambridge University Press.
Hall, Rodney Bruce; Biersteker, Thomas J. (2002b). The Emergence of Private Authority in the International System. In: Hall, Rodney Bruce; Biersteker, Thomas J. *The Emergence of Private Authority in Global Governance*. Cambridge: Cambridge University Press, 3–22.
Hasenclever, Andreas; Mayer, Peter; Rittberger, Volker (1997). *Theories of International Regimes*. Cambridge: Cambridge University Press.

Haufler, Virginia (1995). Crossing the Boundaries between Public and Private: International Regimes and Non-State Actors. In: Rittberger, Volker. *Regime Theory and International Relations*. Oxford: Clarendon Press, 94–111.

Held, David; Koenig-Archibugi, Mathias (2005). *Global Governance and Public Accountability*. Malden: Blackwell.

Hewson, Martin; Sinclair, Timothy J., (eds). (1999). *Approaches to Global Governance Theory*. Albany, NY: State University of New York Press.

Higgott, Richard A.; Underhill, Geoffrey R. D.; Bieler, Andreas, (eds). (2000). *Non-State Actors and Authority in the Global System*. London: Routledge.

Hoekman, Bernard M.; Kostecki, Michel M. (2001). *The Political Economy of the World Trading System: The WTO and Beyond*. Oxford: Oxford University Press.

Hoffmann, Matthew (2011). *Climate Governance at the Crossroads: Experimenting With a Global Response After Kyoto*. Oxford: Oxford University Press.

Jagers, Sverker C.; Stripple, Johannes (2003). Climate Governance Beyond the State. *Global Governance* 9 (3): 385–399.

Jönsson, Christer; Tallberg, Jonas, (eds). (2010). *Transnational Actors in Global Governance: Patterns, Explanations, and Implications*. Basingstoke: Palgrave.

Jordan, Andrew; Wurzel, Rüdiger; Zito, Anthony (2005). The Rise of 'New' Policy Instruments in Comparative Perspective: Has Governance Eclipsed Government? *Political Studies* 53 (3): 477–496.

Kahler, Miles; Lake, David A., (eds). (2003). *Governance in a Global Economy: Political Authority in Transition*. Princeton, NJ: Princeton University Press.

Keck, Margaret E.; Sikkink, Kathryn (1998). *Activists Beyond Borders: Advocacy Networks in International Politics*. Ithaca, NY: Cornell University Press.

Keohane, Robert O. (1984). *After Hegemony: Cooperation and Discord in the World Political Economy*. Princeton, NJ: Princeton University Press.

Keohane, Robert O. (2003). Global Governance and Democratic Accountability. In: Held, David; Koenig-Archibugi, Mathias. *Taming Globalization: Frontiers of Governance*. Cambridge: Polity Press, 130–159.

Keohane, Robert O.; Martin, Lisa L. (1995). The Promise of Institutionalist Theory. *International Security* 20 (1): 39–51.

Keohane, Robert O.; Victor, David G. (2011). The Regime Complex for Climate Change. *Perspectives on Politics* 9 (1): 7–23.

Kerwer, Dieter (2002). Standardising as Govenance: The Case of Credit-Rating Agencies. In: Héritier, Adrienne. *Common Goods: Reinventing European and International Governance*. Lanham, MD: Rowman & Littlefield, 293–315.

Koenig-Archibugi, Mathias (2003). Global Governance. In: Michie, Jonathan. *The Handbook of Globalization*. Cheltenham: Edward Elgar, 318–330.

Krasner, Stephen D. (1982). Structural Causes and Regime Consequences: Regimes as Intervening Variables. *International Organization* 36 (2): 185–205.

Kruck, Andreas (2011). *Private Ratings, Public Regulations: Credit Rating Agencies and Global Financial Governance*. New York: Palgrave Macmillan.

Leander, Anna (2005). The Power to Construct International Security: On the Significance of Private Military Companies. *Millennium: Journal of International Studies* 33 (3): 803–825.

Lederer, Markus; Müller, Philipp S., (eds). (2005). *Criticizing Global Governance*. New York: Palgrave Macmillan.

Levy, David L.; Newell, Peter, (eds). (2005). *The Business of Global Environmental Governance*. Cambridge, MA: MIT Press.

Levy, Marc A.; Young, Oran R.; Zürn, Michael (1995). The Study of International Regimes. *European Journal of International Relations* 1 (3): 267–330.

Liese, Andrea; Beisheim, Marianne (2011). Transnational Public-Private Partnerships and the Provision of Collective Goods in Developing Countries. In: Risse, Thomas. *Governance Without a State: Policies and Politics in Areas of Limited Statehood*. New York: Columbia University Press, 115–143.

Moran, Michael; Stevenson, Michael (2013). Illumination and Innovation: What Philanthropic Foundations Bring to Global Health Governance. *Global Society* 27 (2): 117–137.

Newell, Peter (2000). *Climate for Change: Non-State Actors and the Global Politics of the Greenhouse*. Cambridge: Cambridge University Press.

Newell, Peter; Pattberg, Philipp; Schroeder, Heike (2012). Multiactor Governance and the Environment. *Annual Review of Environment and Resources* 37: 365–387.

Nye, Joseph S. (1987). Nuclear Learning and US-Soviet Security Regimes. *International Organization* 41 (3): 371–402.

O'Neill, Kate (2009). *The Environment and International Relations*. Cambridge: Cambridge University Press.

Ougaard, Morten; Leander, Anna, (eds). (2010). *Business and Global Governance*. London: Routledge.

Pattberg, Philipp (2007). *Private Institutions and Global Governance: The New Politics of Environmental Sustainability*. Cheltenham: Edward Elgar.

Pattberg, Philipp (2012). The Role and Relevance of Networked Climate Governance. In: Biermann, Frank; Pattberg, Philipp; Zelli, Fariborz. *Global Climate Governance Beyond 2012: Architecture, Agency and Adaptation*. Cambridge: Cambridge University Press, 146–164.

Pattberg, Philipp; Stripple, Johannes (2008). Beyond the Public and Private Divide: Remapping Transnational Climate Governance in the 21st Century. *International Environmental Agreements* 8 (4): 367–388.

Pierre, Jon, (ed.). (2000). *Debating Governance*. Oxford: Oxford University Press.

Pierre, Jon; Peters, Guy B. (2000). *Governance, Politics and the State*. Basingstoke: Macmillan.

Raustiala, Kal (1997). States, NGOs and International Environmental Institutions. *International Studies Quartely* 41 (4): 719–740.

Reinicke, Wolfgang H.; Deng, Francis M., (eds). (2000). *Critical Choices: The United Nations, Networks, and the Future of Global Governance*. Ottawa, Canada: International Development Research Centre.

Risse, Thomas (2000). 'Let's Argue!': Communicative Action in World Politics. *International Organization* 54 (1): 1–39.

Risse, Thomas (2013). Transnational Actors and World Politics. In: Carlsnaes, Walter; Risse, Thomas; Simmons, Beth A. *Handbook of International Relations*. Los Angeles, CA: Sage, 426–452.

Risse, Thomas; Ropp, Stephen C.; Sikkink, Kathryn, (eds). (2013). *The Persistent Power of Human Rights: From Commitment to Compliance*. Cambridge: Cambridge University Press.

Rittberger, Volker; Nettesheim, Martin; Huckel, Carmen; Göbel, Thorsten (2008a). Conclusion: Authority Beside and Beyond the State. In: Rittberger, Volker; Nettesheim, Martin. *Authority in the Global Political Economy*. Basingstoke: Palgrave, 314–327.

Rittberger, Volker; Nettesheim, Martin; Huckel, Carmen; Göbel, Thorsten (2008b). Introduction: Changing Patterns of Authority. In: Rittberger, Volker; Nettesheim, Martin. *Authority in the Global Political Economy*. Basingstoke: Palgrave, 1–9.

Rosenau, James N. (1992). Governance, Order and Change in World Politics. In: Rosenau, James N.; Czempiel, Ernst Otto. *Governance Without Government: Order and Change in World Politics*. Cambridge: Cambridge University Press, 1–29.

Rosenau, James N. (1995). Governance in the Twenty-First Century. *Global Governance* 1 (1): 13–43.

Rosenau, James N. (1997). *Along the Domestic-Foreign Frontier: Exploring Governance in a Turbulent World.* Cambridge: Cambridge University Press.

Rosenau, James N. (2007). Governing the Ungovernable: The Challenge of a Global Disaggregation of Authority. *Regulation & Governance* 1 (1): 88–97.

Rosenau, James N.; Czempiel, Ernst Otto, (eds). (1992). *Governance Without Government: Order and Change in World Politics*. Cambridge: Cambridge University Press.

Ruggie, John G. (1975). International Responses to Technology. *International Organization* 29 (3): 557–583.

Sinclair, Timothy J. (2005). *The New Masters of Capital: American Bond Rating Agencies and the Politics of Creditworthiness*. Ithaca, NY: Cornell University Press.

Speth, James Gustave (2004). *Red Sky at Morning: America and the Crisis of the Global Environment.* New Haven, CT: Yale University Press.

Stein, Arthur (1993). Coordination and Collaboration: Regimes in an Anarchic World. In: Baldwin, David Allen. *Neorealism and Neoliberalism: The Contemporary Debate*. New York: Columbia University Press, 29–59.

Strange, Susan (1982). Cave! Hic Dragones: A Critique of Regime Analysis. *International Organization* 36 (2): 479–496.

Strange, Susan (1996). *The Retreat of the State: The Diffusion of Power in the World Economy*. Cambridge: Cambridge University Press.

United Nations Commission on Global Governance (1995). *Our Global Neighborhood: The Report of the Commission on Global Governance*. Oxford: Oxford University Press.

van Kersbergen, Kees; van Waarden, Frans (2004). 'Governance' as a Bridge Between Disciplines: Cross-Disciplinary Inspiration Regarding Shifts in Governance and Problems of Governability, Accountability and Legitimacy. *European Journal of Political Research* 43 (2): 143–171.

Victor, David G. (2011). *Global Warming Gridlock: Creating More Effective Strategies for Protecting the Planet*. Cambridge: Cambridge University Press.

Weiss, Thomas G. (2000). Governance, Good Governance and Global Governance: Conceptual and Actual Challenges. *Third World Quarterly* 21 (5): 795–814.

Weiss, Thomas G.; Gordenker, Leon, (eds). (1996). *NGOs, the UN, and Global Governance*. Boulder: Lynne Rienner.

Welch, Stephen; Kennedy-Pipe, Caroline (2004). Multi-Level Governance and International Relations. In: Bache, Ian; Flinders, Matthew V. *Multi-Level Governance*. Oxford: Oxford University Press, 127–145.

Wolf, Klaus Dieter (2006). Private Actors and the Legitimacy of Governance Beyond the State. In: Benz, Arthur; Papadopoulos, Yannis. *Governance and Democracy: Comparing National, European and International Experiences*. London: Routledge, 200–227.

Woods, Ngaire (1999). Good Governance in International Organizations. *Global Governance* 5 (1): 39–61.

Young, Oran R., (ed.). (1997). *Global Governance: Drawing Insights From the Environmental Experience*. Cambridge, MA: MIT Press.

Zürn, Michael (2013). Globalization and Global Governance. In: Carlsnaes, Walter; Risse, Thomas; Simmons, Beth A. *Handbook of International Relations*. Los Angeles, CA: Sage, 401–425.

Notes

1 In this book, the term 'sub- and non-state actors' refers to all actors who are not part of the central government. Hence, the term embraces a wide range of different actors, including sub-national governments, advocacy groups, non-profit organizations, business associations, and multinational corporations.
2 For a recent overview of the various roles and functions of sub- and non-state actors in global environmental politics, see Finger and Svarin (2012).
3 Initially, the term was used by John Ruggie (1975).
4 Different scholars have suggested other ways to distinguish the various uses of the term (e.g. Pierre 2000; van Kersbergen and van Waarden 2004; Biermann and Pattberg 2008). However, the distinction proposed by Dingwerth and Pattberg seems most appropriate for the purposes of this study.

2 The evolution of global climate governance

The growing importance of sub- and non-state actors

As already mentioned in the previous chapter, for many decades, nation-states have been considered by several analysts to be the only relevant actors in addressing cross-border issues. This also applies to the field of global environmental politics where transboundary problems often take the form of collective action dilemmas (Hardin 1968). From this view, global environmental problems are seen as 'stemming from a "tragedy of the commons", whereby individual actors (nation-states) pursuing their own self-interest will overuse open-access resources to the detriment of all, and/or "discrete trends", such as population growth, consumption, and industrialization, which force states to exploit nature' (Bulkeley and Betsill 2003: 12). Scholars in this tradition argue that global environmental problems can be solved through intergovernmental cooperation and the establishment of international institutions that constrain and regulate the use of global common pool resources (e.g. Keohane 1984).

In the past few years, however, this scholarly approach has been heavily criticized for its state-centric perspective and its failure to pay attention to the role played by actors other than nation-states and international institutions in world politics. In fact, numerous scholars have lately emphasized the growing importance of different types of sub- and non-state actors in global environmental policy-making (e.g. Biermann and Pattberg 2008; Dellas, Pattberg, and Betsill 2011; Newell, Pattberg, and Schroeder 2012). They have shown that sub- and non-state actors are directly involved in the formation and maintenance of international environmental regimes, as well as in the implementation of international environmental agreements (Conca 1995; Raustiala 1997; Keck and Sikkink 1998; Newell 2000; Betsill and Corell 2008). More recently, authors have also stressed that sub- and non-state actors have begun to adopt various policy-making functions in global environmental governance, which have traditionally been assigned to nation-states and international institutions, especially in the field of global environmental standard-setting (e.g. Pattberg 2007; Gulbrandsen 2010; Green 2014). While this trend is evident in various policy domains of global environmental politics, it seems to be particularly prevalent in the issue area of climate change. In this regard, numerous authors have analyzed the emergence of a wide variety of climate initiatives launched by different types of sub- and non-state actors, including cities, provinces, civil society groups, environmental organizations, and business associations (e.g. Bäckstrand 2008; Andonova, Betsill, and Bulkeley 2009; Hoffmann 2011).

Following this short overview of the growing importance of sub- and non-state actors in global environmental policy-making, in the next sections of this chapter, I first sketch the development of the political response to climate change from the late 1980s until today. Thereafter, I describe the institutional complexity in global climate governance that has emerged in recent years. And then, I point to a gap in the literature on global environmental governance, before I briefly summarize the research focus of this study.

The development of the political response to climate change

The 1972 *United Nations Conference on the Human Environment* held in Stockholm is often conceived as the event that put environmental issues onto the international policy agenda (e.g. Soroos 1994; Zürn 1998). In the years following this conference, the number of international environmental agreements increased considerably and the prescriptive character of many agreements has since then also been strengthened. However, the problem of climate change was not a prominent topic at this conference and did not receive much attention in the conference report (United Nations 1972). Only after scientific evidence grew in the 1980s showing that the earth was warming due to an increased concentration of GHG emissions in the atmosphere was the matter taken up as an international political concern. The *United Nations Environment Programme* and the *World Meteorological Organization* played an important role in fostering scientific consensus on the problem of climate change. In response to new findings on the problem of climate change, these two organizations convened a number of workshops and conferences and jointly established the *Intergovernmental Panel on Climate Change* (hereafter IPCC) in 1988 to conduct assessments of the current state of scientific knowledge on climate change.[1] Two years after its foundation, the IPCC released its *First Assessment Report* stating that human activity was leading to rising atmospheric GHG concentrations and an increase in the earth's global mean surface temperature by about 3° Celsius before the end of the next century (IPCC 1990). The report was endorsed by scientists and politicians at the *Second World Climate Conference* held in Geneva, at which nation-states agreed to adopt a *Ministerial Declaration* recommending that negotiations towards a framework convention on climate change should begin without delay (Jäger and Ferguson 1991).

Thereupon, the *United Nations General Assembly* formally started the negotiation process towards an international climate treaty by establishing the *Intergovernmental Negotiating Committee*, which met six times between February 1991 and May 1992. These negotiations led to the adoption of the UNFCCC, which was signed by over 150 nation-states at the *United Nations Conference on Environment and Development* in Rio de Janeiro in 1992. The UNFCCC constitutes the foundation of the international climate regime and marks the beginning of the international policy process to address the climate change problem. Today, the UNFCCC has near-universal membership with 195 nation-states that have ratified the agreement (UNFCCC 2014b). The ultimate objective of the UNFCCC is to achieve

> stabilization of greenhouse gas concentrations in the atmosphere at a level that would prevent dangerous anthropogenic interference with the climate system (...) within a time-frame sufficient to allow ecosystems to adapt naturally to climate change, to ensure that food production is not threatened, and to enable economic development to proceed in a sustainable manner.
> (United Nations 1992: Article 2)

In addition to this ultimate objective, the UNFCCC comprises several basic principles that aim to guide future climate policies. One of the most important of these principles, which influenced many debates and was incorporated in a number of later agreements, is the principle of 'common but differentiated responsibilities.' Basically, this principle stipulates that all Parties to the UNFCCC have an obligation to protect the climate, while taking into account their different national circumstances, especially each country's contribution to the problem and its ability to mitigate climate change. Other principles included in the UNFCCC urge nation-states to take precautionary measures in order to tackle the causes of climate change and its adverse effects, to reconcile climate policies with the right of each country to achieve sustainable development, and to cooperate with each other to promote a supportive and open international economic system that would lead to sustainable economic growth and development, particularly in developing countries (United Nations 1992: Article 3). Beyond that, the UNFCCC set a number of broadly defined commitments for nation-states to deal with climate change, established a secretariat providing support to all institutions involved in the international climate negotiations, and launched a financial mechanism managed by the *Global Environment Facility*. Above all, and most importantly, the UNFCCC paved the way for the ongoing international negotiation process to address the causes and impacts of the problem of climate change and laid the foundation for the negotiation of the *Kyoto Protocol*, which was adopted in 1997. For the first time, the Kyoto Protocol introduced legally binding obligations for a certain set of industrialized countries to reduce their GHG emissions by an average of 5.2 percent below 1990 emission levels until 2012 (UNFCCC 1997). The Kyoto Protocol also broadened the scope of the international climate regime by covering the emissions of six GHGs that are grouped together in a basket (i.e. *carbon dioxide*, *methane*, *nitrous oxide*, *hydrofluorocarbons*, *perfluorocarbons*, and *sulphur hexafluoride*). Furthermore, the Kyoto Protocol established three flexible instruments to lower the overall economic costs of achieving GHG emission reduction targets, such as *Emissions Trading*, the *Clean Development Mechanism*, and *Joint Implementation*.[2]

The years following the signing of the Protocol were marked by intense negotiations over the specific modalities for the flexible instruments and provisions for compliance with the Kyoto targets (Yamin and Depledge 2004). In 2001, nation-states settled many of the open questions with the *Marrakesh Accords* and provided concrete rules and procedures for the operation of the three flexible instruments (UNFCCC 2001). In particular, the agreement reached at the Conference of the Parties to the UNFCCC held in Marrakesh established the regulatory framework for the Clean Development Mechanism, the first global environmental investment and credit scheme. While the Clean Development Mechanism has been heavily criticized for various shortcomings (e.g. Green 2010a; Lund 2010; Hickmann 2013), it is undeniable that the market-based instrument has been conducive in generating low-carbon investments in developing countries and emerging economies (Fuhr and Lederer 2009; Lederer 2010). During the negotiation process for the flexible instruments, the United States announced that they would withdraw from the Protocol due to scientific uncertainties and the potential harmful effects to its economy. This meant that, without the United States, the Protocol could only enter into force if all other major industrialized countries joined the treaty, including reluctant Russia, because the Protocol required the ratification of 55 Parties to the Convention, accounting for at least 55 percent of the total 1990 GHG emissions of industrialized countries (UNFCCC 1997: Article 25). After a period of uncertainty concerning its intentions and major diplomatic efforts undertaken by the European Union, Russia eventually ratified the agreement, allowing the Protocol to enter into force in early 2005 (Dessler and Parson 2006: 16; Schreurs and Tiberghien 2007: 24–25).

After the Kyoto Protocol took effect, the international climate negotiations focused on specific issues concerning the implementation of the GHG emission reduction targets and the question of what might follow after the expiry of the Protocol's first commitment period in 2012. This process was characterized by various setbacks and difficult negotiations, with agreements based on the lowest common denominator. Accordingly, various observers of the international negotiations have expressed their disappointment about the modest accomplishments achieved at the international climate change conferences in the past few years (Depledge 2006; Falkner, Stephan, and Vogler 2010). The greatest frustration among environmentalists was probably caused by the outcome of the 2009 Conference of the Parties to the UNFCCC held in Copenhagen. Despite long and tedious preparations over several years and the participation of more than 120 heads of state or government, the meeting did not establish a legally binding replacement for the Kyoto Protocol as was expected, or at least hoped, by thousands of activists in and around the conference center. Instead of a breakthrough compromise, the attending national representatives could only agree upon the so-called *Copenhagen Accord* (UNFCCC 2009). This document has been described as 'a political agreement that fails to go significantly beyond the original UNFCCC and that is fearfully inadequate for meeting the challenge of climate change' (Hoffmann 2011: 16). Moreover, in the negotiations at the Copenhagen Climate Change Summit, developing countries and emerging economies repeatedly refused to enter into binding commitments to limit their GHG emissions until industrialized countries take stronger action to mitigate the problem and provide financial and technological assistance for the adaptation to climate change (Dimitrov 2010). As a result, various scholars have become increasingly concerned about the lack of progress in the international climate regime in recent years. They question whether the intergovernmental process can produce treaties and agreements that effectively address the climate change problem (e.g. Helm and Hepburn 2009; Bulkeley and Newell 2010; Rayner 2010; Hoffmann 2011; Victor 2011). Some of them have even questioned whether the long and slow negotiations and less ambitious international agreements are still necessary for the resolution of global environmental problems. Alternatively, these scholars highlight new modes of governance, such as transnational partnerships between sub- and non-state actors, and argue that these governance arrangements might be better suited than international alliances of nation-states to cope with the problem of climate change.

One important reason for the focus on the intergovernmental level to address the problem of climate change over the past two decades is the experience with the international ozone regime, which is widely regarded as one of the greatest success stories in international environmental politics (e.g. Parson 2003). As David Victor points out, the success of the international efforts to solve the problem of ozone depletion might have raised expectations too high regarding the problem-solving capacity of multilateral treaty-making (e.g. Victor 2011: 30). Through the success story of the *Montreal Protocol* agreed upon in 1987, scholars and policy-makers saw great potential for achieving a similar agreement to manage the problem of climate change. This also explains why the development of the international climate regime has initially followed a path very similar to the one of the international ozone regime. Several institutional arrangements established for addressing and managing the problem of ozone depletion have been used as a model or even a blueprint for the creation of the international climate regime (O'Neill 2009: 79). In both cases, a framework convention was adopted at first, which established basic principles and norms for addressing the respective environmental problem. Thereafter, concrete rules and procedures were negotiated and formulated in a more specific Protocol that also contained individual emission reduction targets for a number of nation-states (e.g. Betsill and Pielke 1998; Oberthür 2001; Thoms 2003). However, while the Montreal Protocol and its several amendments effectively scaled down the global production and consumption of *chlorofluorocarbons* and mitigated its adverse effects, the Kyoto Protocol has apparently made only a rather small impact on the limitation of global GHG emissions. In fact, the combined atmospheric concentration of the six GHGs targeted by the Kyoto Protocol continued to increase during the period from 2005 to 2011 (IPCC 2014a: chapter 2). This underlines the fact that the international ozone regime is very different from the international climate regime in a number of respects.

One of the main causes for the successful management of chlorofluorocarbons through the international ozone regime was the availability of alternative technologies and substitutes at low to virtually no cost (Keohane and Victor 2011: 18–19). Instead, low-carbon technologies have at least until now been only available at a much lower scale and at a relatively high cost compared with the price of fossil fuels. Moreover, while the bulk of the production and consumption of ozone-depleting substances was largely limited to a small number of industrialized countries (i.e. Germany, France, Italy, United Kingdom, United States), the regulation of GHG emissions is much more complex because GHG emission controls affect a wide range of industries due to the great number of different emission sources (e.g. Stern 2007). Another crucial factor that makes the issue of climate change distinct from the ozone case and other global environmental problems is that the least-developed countries are generally expected to suffer most from the adverse effects caused by climate change, such as sea-level rise, droughts, and declining agricultural productivity (IPCC 2014b: chapter 19). In addition, international GHG emission controls are perceived by many developing countries and emerging economies as a burden to their economic growth. These countries emphasize that they are highly vulnerable to climate change, while they have, in historical terms, only marginally contributed to the causes of the problem (O'Brien and Leichenko 2000; Adger 2006; Mendelsohn, Dinar, and Williams 2006). Hence, in comparison to the international ozone regime, it can be argued that the international climate regime is deadlocked at the level of *principles* and *norms*, while effective *rules* and *procedures* to reduce the global amount of GHG emissions could not yet be agreed upon by nation-states in the international climate negotiations. Many scholars therefore regard multilateral treaty-making in its present form as unable to trigger the societal and economic transformation necessary to cope with the potentially disastrous consequences associated with human-induced climate change (e.g. Hoffmann 2011; Victor 2011; Hale, Held, and Young 2013; Abbott 2014).

Furthermore, in the past few years, there has been a widespread perception that power has shifted in global affairs and that emerging economies are adopting a more prominent role in international environmental regimes (e.g. Hurrell and Sengupta 2012; Terhalle and Depledge 2013). This is also reflected in the international climate regime. While developing countries have traditionally been rather reactive in the international climate negotiations with industrialized countries (Najam, Huq, and Sokona 2003), emerging economies, most notably the BASIC group consisting of Brazil, South Africa, India, and China, have recently become major players in the international climate negotiations (Rong 2010; Qi 2011; Hallding *et al.* 2013). This became evident for the first time at the Copenhagen Climate Change Summit in 2009. At this event, the four major emerging economies sidelined the European Union in the final negotiations and played a key role in brokering the wording of the Copenhagen Accord (Bodansky 2010: 234). To what extent the increasing influence of these countries in the international climate regime renders the already difficult international negotiation process even more complex – or creates new opportunities for the adoption of a universal international climate treaty remains to be seen.

Nonetheless, despite all the difficulties in the international climate negotiations and the various setbacks in the UNFCCC process, it should be recognized that the international climate regime continues to evolve. After the disappointing outcome of the Conference of the Parties to the UNFCCC held in Copenhagen, nation-states kept the international climate negotiations alive by adopting the *Cancún Agreement* in 2010, 'which fleshed out the shorter and less concrete Copenhagen Accord' (van Asselt and Zelli 2014: 141). One year later, at the international climate change conference in Durban, the Parties to the UNFCCC launched a new negotiation platform to develop 'a protocol, another legal instrument or an agreed outcome with legal force under the Convention applicable to all Parties' (UNFCCC 2011: 2). The subsequent Conference of the Parties to the UNFCCC held in Doha in 2012 produced a package agreement called the *Doha Climate Gateway* that was important in two respects. First, the agreement comprised an amendment to the Kyoto Protocol that established the Protocol's second commitment period from 2013 until 2020 with new GHG emission reduction targets for a number of industrialized countries. Second, nation-states reaffirmed their commitment and set a timetable for an international climate agreement to be adopted in Paris by the end of 2015 (UNFCCC 2012). While the Conference of the Parties to the UNFCCC held in Warsaw in 2013 could settle some open questions on the way to a new international climate agreement, it also underscored the great deal of work still to be done on a number of critical issues, such as the legal character of the new agreement and the differentiation between the specific obligations of developing and industrialized countries (UNFCCC 2013). The Conference of the Parties to the UNFCCC held in Lima in December 2014 also had the overarching objective to pave the way for a new international climate treaty with GHG emission control targets for all major GHG emitters. It concluded with the *Lima Call for Climate Action* (UNFCCC 2014a) outlining some key aspects of a new global climate deal, but also largely sidestepped the critical question of how the issue of differentiation could be resolved in a post-2020 agreement.

Institutional complexity in global climate governance

Given the difficulties among national governments in agreeing on effective measures to cope with climate change, a variety of climate governance arrangements have been developed outside the auspices of the UNFCCC in the past few years (cf. Biermann *et al.* 2009: 21–24). In general, these initiatives can be divided into two categories: (i) *multilateral* governance arrangements and (ii) *transnational* governance arrangements. Multilateral arrangements are created at the intergovernmental level by nation-states and focus on the implementation of climate change mitigation and adaptation measures within domestic settings. Examples of such arrangements aimed at addressing the problem of climate change include the *Asia-Pacific Partnership on Clean Development and Climate*; the *Carbon Sequestration Leadership Forum*; the *Gleneagles-Dialogue on Climate Change, Clean Energy and Sustainable Development*; the *Global Methane Initiative* (formerly known as the *Methane to Markets Partnership*); the *International Carbon Action Partnership*; the *International Partnership for Hydrogen and Fuel Cells in the Economy*; and the *Major Economies Forum on Energy and Climate* (e.g. McGee and Taplin 2006; De Coninck *et al.* 2008; Karlsson-Vinkhuyzen and van Asselt 2009; Abbott 2012). Basically, these multilateral initiatives take the form of relatively loose dialogues between nation-states with joint interests and shared positions towards the problem of climate change. In contrast to the international climate negotiations under the UNFCCC, these governance arrangements bring together a limited number of countries and sometimes also involve corporations, environmental organizations, and sub-national governments (van Asselt and Zelli 2014: 142). They are principally concentrated on specific aspects, such as particular GHG emission abatement technologies and individual policies designed to respond to climate change. Although these initiatives are certainly of interest for studying the whole picture of global climate governance, the empirical analysis in this book is focused on transnational governance arrangements. As mentioned earlier, these arrangements have been launched by a variety of sub- and non-state actors, including cities, provinces, civil society groups, environmental organizations, and business corporations, which have different interests and intentions in dealing with the problem of climate change (e.g. Bulkeley and Betsill 2003; Pattberg and Stripple 2008; Bulkeley and Newell 2010; Hoffmann 2011; Green 2014). While it is beyond the scope of this study to exhaustively list the great number of transnational climate governance arrangements, in the following chapter, I discuss a number of illustrative examples and differentiate between three types of initiatives, such as transnational city networks, private certification schemes, and business self-regulation (see chapter 3). This categorization serves as the basis for the case selection and the empirical analysis undertaken in the present study.

The emergence of such a great variety of different climate governance arrangements beyond the international climate regime has led to a significant increase in the institutional complexity of global climate governance. In recent years, this phenomenon has attracted the attention of numerous scholars (e.g. Biermann *et al.* 2009; Keohane and Victor 2011; Zelli 2011). They have developed various concepts in order to capture the complex institutional landscape in the policy domain of climate change. Biermann *et al.*, for instance, introduced a typology to distinguish between different types and degrees of fragmentation across issue areas of world politics (Biermann *et al.* 2009). Based on this typology, they describe the issue area of climate change as a highly 'fragmented governance architecture' (Biermann *et al.* 2010: 15; see also Zelli 2011; Zelli and van Asselt 2013). In a similar vein, Keohane and Victor argue that the various institutional arrangements aimed at regulating climate change can be characterized as 'a regime complex rather than a comprehensive, integrated regime' (Keohane and Victor 2011: 7). Other scholars dealing with the same phenomenon have introduced related concepts, such as the 'polycentric system for coping with global climate change' (Ostrom 2010: 555), the 'multi-level and multi-arena nature of climate governance' (Bulkeley and Newell 2010: 13) and the 'experimental climate governance system' (Hoffmann 2011: 80). Although all these concepts have slightly varying connotations and are sometimes employed in different contexts, the multitude of terms underscores that institutional complexity is a commonly acknowledged phenomenon in contemporary global climate governance (Zelli 2011).

However, while scholars agree that global climate governance is characterized by a high degree of institutional complexity, they are divided on the question of whether multilateral or transnational initiatives are better suited to cope with the problem of climate change. In general, two different groups of scholars can be distinguished. The first group builds upon insights from classical regime analysis and focuses on climate diplomacy and top-down governance approaches to break the impasse in the multilateral response to climate change (e.g. Depledge and Yamin 2009; Falkner, Stephan, and Vogler 2010; Hare *et al.* 2010; Keohane and Victor 2011; Kjellén 2011; van Asselt and Zelli 2014). These scholars concede that the intergovernmental process has lost much of its spark over the past few years, but they seek to re-conceptualize the tools and strategies of traditional state-based forms of governance in order to render the international climate regime more effective. The second group of scholars calls attention to the emergence of new modes of governance that are characterized by multi-actor involvement and multilevel regulation with less hierarchical forms of steering (e.g. Jagers and Stripple 2003; Betsill and Bulkeley 2006; Pattberg 2007; Bäckstrand 2008; Andonova, Betsill, and Bulkeley 2009; Bulkeley and Newell 2010; Hoffmann 2011; Pattberg 2012; Green 2014). Building upon new concepts of authority in world politics, they emphasize the growing importance of sub- and non-state actors in global climate governance. Recently, they have started to explore the increasingly complex institutional interaction and interplay between different transnational climate governance arrangements (Bäckstrand 2008; Pattberg and Stripple 2008; Pattberg *et al.* 2012). This group of scholars is continuously increasing and has attained high visibility in research focused on climate policy-making and other policy domains of global environmental politics. In particular, these authors highlight four crucial characteristics of global climate governance, which are closely related to each other. These aspects reflect the broader discussion of the concept of global governance introduced in the first chapter of this book.

First of all, scholars argue that the initiatives to address the problem of climate change do not exclusively originate from national governments and international institutions, but are co-produced by different types of sub- and non-state actors (Dellas, Pattberg, and Betsill 2011). Scholars have conducted several case studies, in which they analyze the important role and function of sub- and non-state actors in global climate governance. In particular, two different research lines have emerged. On the one hand, scholars focus on the question of how sub- and non-state actors operate as agenda-setters and seek to influence individual nation-states or the outcome of international climate negotiations (e.g. Newell 2000; Gulbrandsen and Andresen 2004; Betsill and Corell 2008). The instruments employed by these actors include the provision of scientific knowledge, the development of particular policy solutions, and the application of different lobbying strategies (Betsill and Corell 2001). On the other hand, scholars conceive sub- and non-state actors as an integral part of global climate governance and argue that networks of local and regional governments, public-private partnerships, as well as private corporations are increasingly engaged in authoritative decision-making and problem-solving in the global response to climate change (e.g. Jagers and Stripple 2003; Betsill and Bulkeley 2004; Bäckstrand 2008; Hoffmann 2011).

Second, authors have shown that there are multiple levels of political decision-making involved in global climate governance (Bulkeley and Newell 2010). Initially, the term multilevel governance has been used by scholars focusing on the European Union to account for the vertical and horizontal interplay between sub-national, domestic, and European decision-making levels (e.g. Marks 1993; Hix 1994; Hooghe and Marks 2001). Other authors developed the concept of multilevel governance further to illuminate the wide distribution of decision-making capacities and policy-making responsibilities among a variety of actors in other issue areas of global affairs (Bache and Flinders 2004). Scholars concerned with global environmental politics have adopted the term and transferred it to the policy domain of climate change. They use the term to conceptualize the various linkages between international institutions, national governments, and sub- and non-state actors in global climate governance (e.g. Bulkeley and Betsill 2005; Gupta 2007; Bulkeley and Newell 2010). More precisely, they suggest that climate change should be conceived as 'a multi-level problem, in which different levels of decision-making – local, regional, national, and international – as well as new spheres and arenas of governance that cut across such boundaries – are involved in both creating and addressing climate change' (Bulkeley and Newell 2010: 3).

Third, authors have highlighted the wide range of governance arrangements with less hierarchical and less formal modes of steering in global climate governance. Karin Bäckstrand is one of the most important authors in this context. She conceptualized the various emerging partnerships among public and private actors dealing with the issue of climate change as transnational climate networks and defined them as a 'multi-sectoral collaboration between civil society, government and market actors' (Bäckstrand 2008: 74). Similarly, Liliana Andonova, Michele Betsill, and Harriet Bulkeley analyzed transnational climate networks as a distinct form of global climate governance and introduced a typology of public, private, and hybrid transnational governance networks that perform different governance functions (Andonova, Betsill, and Bulkeley 2009). The main argument put forward by these authors is that several new modes of governance have emerged to tackle the problem of climate change which are characterized by non-hierarchical regulation and a complex mix of public and private actors (Pattberg *et al.* 2012).

Fourth, and most relevant for this study, scholars focusing on global climate governance have identified the emergence of authority structures beyond central governments and the international climate regime. These authors argue that the shift from government to governance in the policy domain of climate change has led to a relocation of authority between nation-states, international institutions, and sub- and non-state actors across multiple levels of decision-making (e.g. Jagers and Stripple 2003; Betsill and Bulkeley 2006; Pattberg and Stripple 2008; Andonova, Betsill, and Bulkeley 2009; Bulkeley 2010; Bulkeley and Newell 2010; Hoffmann 2011; Green 2014). Basically, they contend that due to the multitude of actors and levels involved in decision-making, as well as the emergence of governance arrangements without clear hierarchical regulation, climate policy-making moves from and between national governments and the intergovernmental level to sub- and non-state actors. Importantly, this body of literature does not constrain the role of sub- and non-state actors to the agenda-setting phase or certain tasks in international environmental regimes, but recognizes the increasing importance of sub- and non-state actors at practically every stage of the policy cycle. Consequently, Philipp Pattberg and Johannes Stripple assert that the field of global climate politics 'cannot adequately be analysed from a purely international level, but has to take into account the multiple spheres of authority emerging in global climate governance today' (Pattberg and Stripple 2008: 380). Thus, these scholars challenge classical approaches to international relations and traditional concepts of authority in world politics.

Research gap

After reviewing the current state of research on global climate governance, this section points out two shortcomings in the literature that are addressed in this book. First, as shown above, many scholars focusing on global environmental politics increasingly pay attention to the growing significance of sub- and non-state actors in global climate policy-making. Indeed, they have provided important insights into the role and function of different types of sub- and non-state actors in the global response to climate change. Studies have, for example, examined the emergence of transnational city partnerships (e.g. Bulkeley and Betsill 2003; Betsill and Bulkeley 2006; Acuto 2013), climate-related public-private partnerships (e.g. Andonova 2010; Pattberg 2010), and private standard-setting initiatives for climate change mitigation projects and GHG accounting (Levin, Cashore, and Koppel 2009; Green 2010b). However, most of these studies have primarily been engaged in mapping exercises or the description of how particular transnational climate governance arrangements have emerged within the past few years.[3] Scholars have only recently started to study the implications associated with the development of transnational climate governance arrangements for global climate governance.

Second, in the last decade, a number of authors have considerably advanced both the conceptual and empirical research on institutional interplay in global environmental politics (e.g. Young 2002; Oberthür and Gehring 2006; Young, King, and Schroeder 2008; Biermann *et al.* 2009; Oberthür and Stokke 2011; Zelli 2011; Zelli and van Asselt 2013; van Asselt 2014). For instance, studies have examined the linkages between the international climate regime and other multilateral environmental agreements (Oberthür 2001; Kim 2004; Chambers 2008), the interaction of the international climate regime with economic institutions, especially the *World Trade Organization* (Chambers 2001; Charnovitz 2003; Zelli and van Asselt 2010), and the regulatory overlap of the international climate regime with the *International Civil Aviation Organization* and the *International Maritime Organization* (Oberthür 2003; 2006). Yet, while these scholars have devoted a great deal of effort to studying *horizontal* institutional interactions (i.e. interactions between institutions at the same level of governance), only a few attempts have been made to thoroughly analyze the *vertical* dimension of the institutional interplay (i.e. interactions between institutions at different levels of governance) in global climate governance.[4]

To be clear, the various case studies on newly emerging transnational climate initiatives have certainly consolidated our understanding of the role and function of transnational city networks, private certification schemes, and business self-regulation in the global response to climate change. But the interplay between transnational climate governance arrangements and the international climate regime has so far not been studied in much detail. Thus, what is lacking in the field of global environmental politics is a systematic analysis of how individual transnational governance arrangements relate to the existing institutions clustered around the UNFCCC dealing with the problem of climate change (Hoffmann 2011: 102). Therefore, this book addresses this research gap. It moves beyond the debate on the emergence of transnational governance arrangements and explores the consequences of this phenomenon for global climate governance.

Focus of the book

As stated in the previous section, this study focuses on the relationship between newly emerging transnational governance arrangements and the intergovernmental level in the issue area of climate change. More specifically, as laid out in more detail in the third chapter, the book examines to what extent transnational climate initiatives launched by different types of sub- and non-state actors *conflict*, *complement*, or *depend on* existing modes of inter-state cooperation and what this implies for the dispersion of authority in global climate governance. Hence, the study aims to contribute to the theoretical debate on the changing patterns of authority in world politics. Thereby, the book is not primarily interested in analyzing what the increasing involvement of sub- and non-state actors in global climate governance means for the authority of the nation-state and its role in the international system. Instead, this book assesses the theoretical and practical implications of the emergence of transnational climate governance arrangements for the international climate regime. To investigate these issues, the book builds upon different theoretical approaches to the concept of authority in world politics, which are discussed in the first part of the following chapter. This discussion constitutes the theoretical background of the book and links the analysis to the most important theories of international relations. In the concluding chapter of this book, I delineate the implications of the main findings of this study for the different theoretical approaches to the concept of authority in world politics.

To sum up, this book goes beyond many studies that simply assume that the authority of state-based forms of governance is eroding due to the growing involvement of sub- and non-state actors in global affairs. The book takes one step further and investigates the reconfiguration of authority in global climate governance resulting from the proliferation of transnational climate governance arrangements. In other words, the present study does not stop at the description of novel modes of governance beyond central governments and international institutions, but uses the concept of authority to analyze the broader significance of the development of transnational governance initiatives for contemporary global climate governance.

References

Abbott, Kenneth W. (2012). The Transnational Regime Complex for Climate Change. *Environment and Planning C: Government and Policy* 30 (4): 571–590.

Abbott, Kenneth W. (2014). Strengthening the Transnational Regime Complex for Climate Change. *Transnational Environmental Law* 3 (1): 57–88.

Acuto, Michele (2013). The New Climate Leaders. *Review of International Studies* 39 (4): 835–857.

Adger, W. Neil (2006). Vulnerability. *Global Environmental Change* 16 (3): 268–281.

Agrawala, Shardul (1998). Context and Early Origins of the Intergovernmental Panel on Climate Change. *Climatic Change* 39 (4): 605–620.

Andonova, Liliana B. (2010). Public-Private Partnerships for the Earth: Politics and Patterns of Hybrid Authority in the Multilateral System. *Global Environmental Politics* 10 (2): 25–53.

Andonova, Liliana B.; Betsill, Michele; Bulkeley, Harriet (2009). Transnational Climate Governance. *Global Environmental Politics* 9 (2): 52–73.

Bache, Ian; Flinders, Matthew V., (eds). (2004). *Multi-Level Governance*. Oxford: Oxford University Press.

Bäckstrand, Karin (2008). Accountability of Networked Climate Governance: The Rise of Transnational Climate Partnerships. *Global Environmental Politics* 8 (3): 74–102.

Betsill, Michele; Bulkeley, Harriet (2004). Transnational Networks and Global Environmental Governance: The Cities for Climate Protection Program. *International Studies Quarterly* 48 (2): 471–493.

Betsill, Michele; Bulkeley, Harriet (2006). Cities and the Multilevel Governance of Global Climate Change. *Global Governance* 12 (2): 141–159.

Betsill, Michele; Corell, Elisabeth (2001). NGO Influence in International Environmental Negotiations: A Framework for Analysis. *Global Environmental Politics* 1 (4): 65–85.

Betsill, Michele; Corell, Elisabeth (2008). *NGO Diplomacy: The Influence of Nongovernmental Organizations in International Environmental Negotiations*. Cambridge, MA: MIT Press.

Betsill, Michele; Pielke, Roger A. (1998). Blurring the Boundaries: Domestic and International Ozone Politics and Lessons for Climate Change. *International Environmental Affairs* 10 (3): 147–172.

Biermann, Frank; Pattberg, Philipp (2008). Global Environmental Governance: Taking Stock, Moving Forward. *Annual Review of Environment and Ressources* 33: 277–294.

Biermann, Frank; Pattberg, Philipp; van Asselt, Harro; Zelli, Fariborz (2009). The Fragmentation of Global Governance Architectures: A Framework for Analysis. *Global Environmental Politics* 9 (4): 14–40.

Biermann, Frank; Zelli, Fariborz; Pattberg, Philipp; van Asselt, Harro (2010). The Architecture of Global Climate Governance. In: Biermann, Frank; Pattberg, Philipp; Zelli, Fariborz. *Global Climate Governance Beyond 2012. Architecture, Agency and Adaptation*. Cambridge, UK: Cambridge University Press, 15–24.

Bodansky, Daniel (2010). Copenhagen Climate Change Conference: A Postmortem. *The American Journal of International Law* 104 (2): 230–240.

Bulkeley, Harriet (2010). Cities and the Governing of Climate Change. *Annual Review of Environment and Resources* 35: 229–253.
Bulkeley, Harriet; Betsill, Michele (2003). *Cities and Climate Change: Urban Sustainability and Global Environmental Governance*. London: Routledge.
Bulkeley, Harriet; Betsill, Michele (2005). Rethinking Sustainable Cities: Multilevel Governance and the 'Urban' Politics of Climate Change. *Environmental Politics* 14 (1): 42–63.
Bulkeley, Harriet; Newell, Peter (2010). *Governing Climate Change*. London: Routledge.
Chambers, W. Bradnee, (ed.). (2001). *Inter-Linkages: The Kyoto Protocol and the International Trade and Investment Regimes*. Tokyo, Japan: United Nations University Press.
Chambers, W. Bradnee (2008). *Interlinkages and the Effectiveness of International Environmental Agreements*. Tokyo, Japan: United Nations University Press.
Charnovitz, Steve (2003). *Trade and Climate: Potential Conflict and Synergies*. Washington, DC: Pew Center on Global Climate Change.
Conca, Ken (1995). Greening the United Nations: Environmental Organizations and the UN System. *Third World Quarterly* 16 (3): 441–457.
De Coninck, Heleen; Fischer, Carolyn; Newell, Richard G.; Ueno, Takahiro (2008). International Technology-Oriented Agreements to Address Climate Change. *Energy Policy* 36 (1): 335–356.
Dellas, Eleni; Pattberg, Philipp; Betsill, Michele (2011). Agency in Earth System Governance: Refining a Research Agenda. *International Environmental Agreements* 11 (1): 85–98.
Depledge, Joanna (2006). The Opposite of Learning: Ossification in the Climate Change Regime. *Global Environmental Politics* 6 (1): 1–22.
Depledge, Joanna; Yamin, Farhana (2009). The Global Climate-Change Regime: A Defence. In: Helm, Dieter; Hepburn, Cameron. *The Economics and Politics of Climate Change*. Oxford: Oxford University Press, 433–453.
Dessler, Andrew E.; Parson, Edward (2006). *The Science and Politics of Global Climate Change: A Guide to the Debate*. Cambridge, UK: Cambridge University Press.
Dimitrov, Radoslav S. (2010). Inside Copenhagen: The State of Climate Governance. *Global Environmental Politics* 10 (2): 18–24.
Falkner, Robert; Stephan, Hannes; Vogler, John (2010). International Climate Policy After Copenhagen: Towards a 'Building Blocks' Approach. *Global Policy* 1 (3): 252–262.
Fuhr, Harald; Lederer, Markus (2009). Varieties of Carbon Governance in Newly Industrializing Countries. *Journal of Environment & Development* 18 (4): 327–345.
Green, Jessica F. (2010a). Private Authority on the Rise: A Century of Delegation in Multilateral Environmental Agreements. In: Tallberg, Jonas; Jönsson, Christer. *Transnational Actors in Global Governance*. Basingstoke, UK: Palgrave, 155–176.
Green, Jessica F. (2010b). Private Standards in the Climate Regime: The Greenhouse Gas Protocol. *Business and Politics* 12 (3): Article 3.
Green, Jessica F. (2014). *Rethinking Private Authority: Agents and Entrepreneurs in Global Environmental Governance*. Princeton, NJ: Princeton University Press.
Grubb, Michael; Vrolijk, Christiaan; Brack, Duncan (1999). *The Kyoto Protocol: A Guide and Assessment*. London: Royal Institute of International Affairs.
Gulbrandsen, Lars H. (2010). *Transnational Environmental Governance: The Emergence and Effects of the Certification of Forests and Fisheries*. Cheltenham: Edward Elgar.
Gulbrandsen, Lars H.; Andresen, Steinar (2004). NGO Influence in the Implementation of the Kyoto Protocol: Compliance, Flexibility Mechanisms, and Sinks. *Global Environmental Politics* 4 (4): 54–75.
Gupta, Joyeeta (2007). The Multi-Level Governance Challenge of Climate Change. *Environmental Sciences* 4 (3): 131–137.

Hale, Thomas; Held, David; Young, Kevin (2013). *Gridlock: Why Global Cooperation Is Failing When We Need It Most*. Cambridge, UK: Polity Press.

Hallding, Karl; Jürisoo, Marie; Carson, Marcus; Atteridge, Aaron (2013). Rising Powers: The Evolving Role of BASIC Countries. *Climate Policy* 13 (5): 608–631.

Hardin, Garrett (1968). The Tragedy of the Commons. *Science* 162 (3859): 1243–1248.

Hare, William; Stockwell, Claire; Flachsland, Christian; Oberthür, Sebastian (2010). The Architecture of the Global Climate Regime: A Top-Down Perspective. *Climate Policy* 10 (6): 600–614.

Helm, Dieter; Hepburn, Cameron, (eds). (2009). *The Economics and Politics of Climate Change*. Oxford: Oxford University Press.

Hickmann, Thomas (2013). Private Authority in Global Climate Governance: The Case of the Clean Development Mechanism. *Climate and Development* 5 (1): 46–54.

Hix, Simon (1994). The Study of the European Community: The Challenge to Comparative Politics. *West European Politics* 17 (1): 1–30.

Hoffmann, Matthew (2011). *Climate Governance at the Crossroads: Experimenting With a Global Response After Kyoto*. Oxford: Oxford University Press.

Hooghe, Liesbet; Marks, Gary (2001). *Multi-Level Governance and European Integration*. Lanham: Rowman & Littlefield Publishers.

Hurrell, Andrew; Sengupta, Sandeep (2012). Emerging Powers, North-South Relations and Global Climate Politics. *International Affairs* 88 (3): 463–484.

IPCC (1990). *Climate Change: The IPCC Scientific Assessment*. Cambridge, UK: Cambridge University Press.

IPCC (2014a). *Climate Change 2013. The Physical Science Basis. Contribution of Working Group I to the Fifth Assessment Report of the Intergovernmental Panel on Climate Change*. Cambridge, UK: Cambridge University Press.

IPCC (2014b). *Climate Change 2014. Impacts, Adaptation, and Vulnerability. Contribution of Working Group II to the Fifth Assessment Report of the Intergovernmental Panel on Climate Change*. Cambridge, UK: Cambridge University Press.

Jäger, Jill; Ferguson, Howard L. (1991). *Climate Change: Science, Impacts and Policy: Proceedings of the Second World Climate Conference*. Cambridge, UK: Cambridge University Press.

Jagers, Sverker C.; Stripple, Johannes (2003). Climate Governance Beyond the State. *Global Governance* 9 (3): 385–399.

Karlsson-Vinkhuyzen, Sylvia I.; van Asselt, Harro (2009). Introduction: Exploring and Explaining the Asia-Pacific Partnership on Clean Development and Climate. *International Environmental Agreements* 9 (3): 195–211.

Keck, Margaret E.; Sikkink, Kathryn (1998). *Activists Beyond Borders: Advocacy Networks in International Politics*. Ithaca, NY: Cornell University Press.

Keohane, Robert O. (1984). *After Hegemony: Cooperation and Discord in the World Political Economy*. Princeton, NJ: Princeton University Press.

Keohane, Robert O.; Victor, David G. (2011). The Regime Complex for Climate Change. *Perspectives on Politics* 9 (1): 7–23.

Kim, Joy A. (2004). Regime Interplay: The Case of Biodiversity and Climate Change. *Global Environmental Change* 14 (4): 315–324.

Kjellén, Bo (2011). Climate Conondrum: Would a Transitional Agreement Offer a Way Out? *Global Policy* 2 (1): 112–114.

Lederer, Markus (2010). Evaluating Carbon Governance: The Clean Development Mechanism From an Emerging Economy Perspective. *Journal of Energy Markets* 3 (2): 3–25.

Levin, Kelly; Cashore, Benjamin; Koppel, Jonathan (2009). Can Non-State Certification

Systems Bolster State-Centered Efforts to Promote Sustainable Development Through the Clean Development Mechanism? *Wake Forest Law Review* 44 (3): 777–798.

Lund, Emma (2010). Dysfunctional Delegation: Why the Design of the Clean Development Mechanism's Supervisory System is Fundamentally Flawed. *Climate Policy* 10 (3): 277–288.

Marks, Gary (1993). Structural Policy and Multilevel Governance in the EC. In: Cafruny, Alan W.; Rosenthal, Glenda G. *The State of the European Community Vol. 2: The Maastricht Debate and beyond.* Boulder, CO: Lynne Riener Publishers, 391–411.

McGee, Jeffrey; Taplin, Ros (2006). The Asia-Pacific Partnership on Clean Development and Climate: A Competitor or Complement to the Kyoto Protocol. *Global Change, Peace and Security* 18 (3): 173–192.

Mendelsohn, Robert; Dinar, Ariel; Williams, Larry (2006). The Distributional Impact of Climate Change on Rich and Poor Countries. *Environment and Development Economics* 11 (2): 159–178.

Najam, Adil; Huq, Saleemul; Sokona, Youba (2003). Climate Negotiations Beyond Kyoto: Developing Countries Concerns and Interests. *Climate Policy* 3 (3): 221–231.

Newell, Peter (2000). *Climate for Change: Non-State Actors and the Global Politics of the Greenhouse*. Cambridge, UK: Cambridge University Press.

Newell, Peter; Pattberg, Philipp; Schroeder, Heike (2012). Multiactor Governance and the Environment. *Annual Review of Environment and Resources* 37: 365–387.

O'Brien, Karen L.; Leichenko, Robin M. (2000). Double Exposure: Assessing the Impacts of Climate Change Within the Context of Economic Globalization. *Global Environmental Change* 10 (3): 221–232.

O'Neill, Kate (2009). *The Environment and International Relations*. Cambridge, UK: Cambridge University Press.

Oberthür, Sebastian (2001). Linkages Between the Montreal and Kyoto Protocols: Enhancing Synergies Between Protecting the Ozone Layer and the Global Climate. *International Environmental Agreements* 1 (3): 357–377.

Oberthür, Sebastian (2003). Institutional Interaction to Address Greenhouse Gas Emissions From International Transport: ICAO, IMO and the Kyoto Protocol. *Climate Policy* 3 (3): 191–205.

Oberthür, Sebastian (2006). The Climate Change Regime: Interactions with ICAO, IMO, and the EU Burden-Sharing Agreement. In: Oberthür, Sebastian; Gehring, Thomas. *Institutional Interaction in Global Environmental Governance: Synergy and Conflict among International and EU Policies*. Cambridge, MA: MIT Press, 53–77.

Oberthür, Sebastian; Gehring, Thomas, (eds). (2006). *Institutional Interaction in Global Environmental Governance: Synergy and Conflict among International and EU Policies*. Cambridge, MA: MIT Press.

Oberthür, Sebastian; Stokke, Olav Schram, (eds). (2011). *Managing Institutional Complexity: Regime Interplay and Global Environmental Change*. Cambridge, MA: MIT Press.

Ostrom, Elinor (2010). Polycentric Systems for Coping with Collective Action and Global Environmental Change. *Global Environmental Change* 20 (4): 550–557.

Parson, Edward (2003). *Protecting the Ozone Layer: Science and Strategy*. Oxford: Oxford University Press.

Pattberg, Philipp (2007). *Private Institutions and Global Governance: The New Politics of Environmental Sustainability*. Cheltenham: Edward Elgar.

Pattberg, Philipp (2010). Public–Private Partnerships in Global Climate Governance. *Wiley Interdisciplinary Reviews: Climate Change* 1 (2): 279–287.

Pattberg, Philipp (2012). The Role and Relevance of Networked Climate Governance. In: Biermann, Frank; Pattberg, Philipp; Zelli, Fariborz. *Global Climate Governance Beyond*

2012: Architecture, Agency and Adaptation. Cambridge, UK: Cambridge University Press, 146–164.

Pattberg, Philipp; Biermann, Frank; Chan, Sander; Mert, Aysem, (eds). (2012). *Public-Private Partnerships for Sustainable Development: Emergence, Influence and Legitimacy*. Cheltenham: Edward Elgar.

Pattberg, Philipp; Stripple, Johannes (2008). Beyond the Public and Private Divide: Remapping Transnational Climate Governance in the 21st Century. *International Environmental Agreements* 8 (4): 367–388.

Qi, Xinran (2011). The Rise of BASIC in UN Climate Change Negotiations. *South African Journal of International Affairs* 18 (3): 295–318.

Raustiala, Kal (1997). States, NGOs and International Environmental Institutions. *International Studies Quartely* 41 (4): 719–740.

Rayner, Steve (2010). How to Eat an Elephant: A Bottom-Up Approach to Climate Policy. *Climate Policy* 10 (6): 615–621.

Rong, Fang (2010). Understanding Developing Country Stances on Post-2012 Climate Change Negotiations: Comparative Analysis of Brazil, China, India, Mexico, and South Africa. *Energy Policy* 38 (8): 4582–4591.

Schreurs, Miranda A.; Tiberghien, Yves (2007). Multi-Level Reinforcement: Explaining European Union Leadership in Climate Change Mitigation. *Global Environmental Politics* 7 (4): 19–46.

Soroos, Marvin S. (1994). From Stockholm to Rio: The Evolution of Global Environmental Governance. In: Vig, Norman J.; Kraft, Michael E. *Environmental Policy in the 1990s: Towards a New Agenda*. Washington, DC: Congressional Quarterly Books, 299–321.

Stern, Nicholas H. (2007). *The Economics of Climate Change: The Stern Review*. Cambridge, UK: Cambridge University Press.

Terhalle, Maximilian; Depledge, Joanna (2013). Great-Power Politics, Order Transition, and Climate Governance: Insights From International Relations Theory. *Climate Policy* 13 (5): 572–588.

Thoms, Laura (2003). A Comparative Analysis of International Regimes on Ozone and Climate Change With Implications for Regime Design. *Columbia Journal of Transnational Law* 41 (3): 795–859.

UNFCCC (1997). *Kyoto Protocol to the United Nations Framework Convention on Climate Change*. Bonn, Germany: UNFCCC Secretariat.

UNFCCC (2001). *Report of the Conference of the Parties on Its Seventh Session, held at Marrakesh from October 29 to November 10, 2001. Addendum: Part Two: Action Taken by the Conference of the Parties. Volume II: FCCC/CP/2001/13/Add.2*. Bonn, Germany: UNFCCC Secretariat.

UNFCCC (2009). *Copenhagen Accord. FCCC/CP/2009/L.7*. Bonn, Germany: UNFCCC Secretariat.

UNFCCC (2011). *Report of the Conference of the Parties on Its Seventeenth Session, held in Durban from November 28 to December 11, 2011: Addendum: Part Two: Action Taken by the Conference of the Parties at Its Seventeenth Session. FCCC/CP/2011/9/Add.2*. Bonn, Germany: UNFCCC Secretariat.

UNFCCC (2012). *Doha Amendment to the Kyoto Protocol: Adoption of Amendment to the Protocol. C.N.718.2012.TREATIES-XXVII.7.C.* Bonn, Germany: UNFCCC Secretariat.

UNFCCC (2013). *Report of the Conference of the Parties on Its Nineteenth Session, held in Warsaw from November 11 to 23, 2013: Addendum Part Two: Action Taken by the*

Conference of the Parties at Its Nineteenth Session. FCCC/CP/2013/10/Add.2. Bonn, Germany: UNFCCC Secretariat.

UNFCCC (2014a). *Report of the Conference of the Parties on Its Twentieth Session, held in Lima from December 1 to December 14, 2014: Addendum: Part Two: Action Taken by the Conference of the Parties at Its Twentieth Session*. FCCC/CP/2014/Add.2. Bonn, Germany: UNFCCC Secretariat.

UNFCCC (2014b). *Status of Ratification of the Convention*. Available at: http://unfccc.int/essential_background/convention/status_of_ratification/items/2631.php (accessed April 30, 2014).

United Nations (1972). *Report of the United Nations Conference on the Human Environment, held in Stockholm from June 5–16, 1972*. New York: United Nations Publications.

United Nations (1992). *United Nations Framework Convention on Climate Change*. New York: United Nations.

van Asselt, Harro (2014). *The Fragmentation of Global Climate Governance: Consequences and Management of Regime Interactions*. Cheltenham, UK: Edward Elgar.

van Asselt, Harro; Zelli, Fariborz (2014). Connect the Dots: Managing the Fragmentation of Global Climate Governance. *Environmental Economics and Policy Studies* 16 (2): 137–155.

Victor, David G. (2011). *Global Warming Gridlock: Creating More Effective Strategies for Protecting the Planet*. Cambridge, UK: Cambridge University Press.

Yamin, Farhana; Depledge, Joanna (2004). *The International Climate Change Regime: A Guide to Rules, Institutions and Procedures*. Cambridge, UK: Cambridge University Press.

Young, Oran R. (2002). *The Institutional Dimensions of Environmental Change: Fit, Interplay, and Scale*. Cambridge, MA: MIT Press.

Young, Oran R.; King, Leslie A.; Schroeder, Heike, (eds). (2008). *Institutions and Environmental Change: Principal Findings, Applications, and Research Frontiers*. Cambridge, MA: MIT Press.

Zelli, Fariborz (2011). The Fragmentation of the Global Climate Governance Architecture. *Wiley Interdisciplinary Reviews: Climate Change* 2 (2): 255–270.

Zelli, Fariborz; van Asselt, Harro (2010). The Overlap Between the UN Climate Regime and the World Trade Organization: Lessons for Post-2012 Climate Governance. In: Biermann, Frank; Pattberg, Philipp; Zelli, Fariborz. *Global Climate Governance Beyond 2012: Architecture, Agency and Adaptation*. Cambridge, UK: Cambridge University Press, 79–96.

Zelli, Fariborz; van Asselt, Harro (2013). Introduction: The Institutional Fragmentation of Global Environmental Governance: Causes, Consequences, and Responses. *Global Environmental Politics* 13 (3): 1–13.

Zürn, Michael (1998). Rise of International Environmental Politics: A Review of Current Research. *World Politics* 50 (4): 617–649.

Notes

1 For a detailed study on the origins of the IPCC, see Agrawala (1998).

2 For a concise overview of the Kyoto Protocol and its three flexible instruments, see Grubb, Vrolijk, and Brack (1999).

3 A notable exception is Green (2014).

4 For a comprehensive discussion of the concept of horizontal and vertical interplay, see Young (2002).

3 Setting the scene

Theoretical background and analytical framework

After the previous chapter outlined the current state of research on global climate governance and identified a substantial gap in the literature, this chapter describes the theoretical background and analytical framework of the book. I start with a general definition and conceptualization of the term 'authority' and continue with a thorough discussion of relevant theoretical approaches to the concept of authority. Next, I present the research design for the empirical analysis. In particular, I specify the project's primary research question and formulate three conceptual assumptions about the relationship between transnational climate initiatives and the international climate regime. And then, I introduce the case studies and briefly refer to the methods of data collection.

Defining authority

Authority is a central though very contested concept in the literature. Scholars from different academic disciplines and theoretical backgrounds have developed diverging understandings of the term 'authority.'[1] Despite the conceptual differences, however, a number of interrelated characteristics are widely recognized by many scholars as key features of authority. To begin with, most authors draw a distinction between authority and power (e.g. Weber 1968; Barnes 1986; Beetham 1991). While there are several similarities between these concepts, the decisive difference between authority and power is that authority does not rely on the exercise of coercion (e.g. Peters 1967: 92–94; Avant, Finnemore, and Sell 2010b: 10). In other words, 'authority involves a unique type of noncoercive command' (Lake 2003: 304). Moreover, and in consequence, authority depends on voluntary obedience. The concept of authority entails the voluntary compliance by an actor with certain decisions made by another (Blau 1963: 307; Sartorius 1981: 4). More precisely, the motive of an actor to conform to the rules and commands of another actor is his or her 'respect for certain attributes which the other actor possesses, such as knowledge, experience, or official position' (Day 1963: 259). Furthermore, and again related to the previous characteristics, most scholars share the view that authority is inextricably linked to the concept of legitimacy (e.g. Hurrelmann, Schneider, and Steffek 2007). According to these authors, authority must contain at least a certain measure of legitimacy and, most important, has to be viewed as legitimate by the people that are subject to it (Weber 1948; Hurd 1999; Kratochwil 2006). Put differently, 'authority represents the fusion of power with legitimate social purpose' (Ruggie 1982: 382). Thus, in general terms, authority can be understood as the *legitimate problem-solving and decision-making capacity of an actor that is voluntarily accepted and recognized by others*.

In recent years, the concept of authority has taken center stage in the scholarly debate within the field of international relations. Scholars concerned with global affairs have produced numerous accounts and provided many typologies of authority (e.g. Barnett and Finnemore 2004; Lake 2007; Avant, Finnemore, and Sell 2010a; Katsikas 2010; Lake 2010; Zürn, Binder, and Ecker-Ehrhardt 2012; Zürn 2013). For the purpose of this study, three matters are of particular relevance. First, many authors dealing with the concept of authority in world politics refer to Max Weber's famous distinction between three ideal types of legitimate rule, namely (i) *charismatic* authority that is based on specific personal characteristics of an actor, (ii) *traditional* authority that is based on the sanctity of tradition, which can, for instance, be found in monarchies, and (iii) *rational-legal* authority that is based on a consistent system of rules that have been intentionally established (Weber 1958). Thereby, the vast majority of scholars only elaborate and dwell on the latter form, which can be seen as one of the main features of modern societies.

Second, a crucial point that is often made in scholarly accounts on the concept of authority is the distinction between actors that are '*in* authority' and those that are '*an* authority' (e.g. Flathman 1980: 16–19; Connolly 1983: 110; Friedman 1990: 77–81; Kratochwil 2006: 306; Katsikas 2010: 117–118). On the one hand, actors that act '*in* authority' have the legitimacy to rule and the capacities to enforce the rules by virtue of their particular position. These actors possess authority by holding an office in a certain institution, such as a public agency, a private company, or a non-governmental organization. An example of this type of authority from the realm of global politics would be the *United Nations Secretary-General*. On the other hand, actors that are considered '*an* authority' exhibit certain qualities, such as specialized knowledge or moral expertise. They induce deference through their distinguished standing in a particular field. Winners of the *Nobel Prize* would be an example of this type of authority. Although these two forms of authority seem to be rather different, they are not mutually exclusive and may also coincide in reality. International organizations, especially United Nations agencies, are often considered being both '*in* authority' and '*an* authority' (Barnett and Finnemore 2004: 25).

Third, and most important for the focus of this study, numerous scholars of global affairs have developed new conceptualizations of authority in order to explore the various ways in which authority is exercised in world politics today. For instance, Michael Barnett and Martha Finnemore identify four different sources of authority from which international organizations derive their ability to act independently of control by national governments (Barnett and Finnemore 2004). In particular, the two authors contend that international organizations possess *rational-legal* authority, *delegated* authority, *expert* authority, and *moral* authority, where 'each contribute in different ways to making international organizations autonomous actors' (Barnett and Finnemore 2005: 174). Drawing on this conceptualization, Deborah Avant, Martha Finnemore, and Susan Sell distinguish between five, partially overlapping, forms of authority: *institutional* authority, *delegated* authority, *expert* authority, *principled* authority, and *capacity-based* authority (Avant, Finnemore, and Sell 2010a: 11–14). They maintain that the global policy arena is filled with a number of actors other than the nation-state, such as international organizations, corporations, professional associations, and advocacy groups that are central to global governance and can hence be regarded as 'global governors.' According to this group of scholars, the wide variety of 'global governors' that have emerged over the past few years exercise authority by creating issues and setting agendas, by establishing and implementing rules or programs, and by evaluating and adjudicating policy outcomes (Avant, Finnemore, and Sell 2010a: 14–16). Michael Zürn, Martin Binder, and Matthias Ecker-Ehrhardt provide a more general conceptualization and distinguish between only two types of authority: *political* authority and *epistemic* authority (Zürn, Binder, and Ecker-Ehrhardt 2012). They argue that *political* authority derives from a particular institutional role and is usually exercised by individuals who act on behalf of a certain institution. *Epistemic* authority, by contrast, derives solely from the status of an individual or an institution and can be acquired through special knowledge or moral expertise. These authors further point out that *epistemic* authority implies that the views expressed by the given actor are perceived as trustworthy, whereas *political* authority is based on the premise 'that someone should be entitled to make authoritative decisions in order to advance the common good and to avoid chaos' (Zürn, Binder, and Ecker-Ehrhardt 2012: 87). Hence, this conceptualization is closely related to the differentiation between '*in* authority' and '*an* authority' and can be understood as a conceptual refinement of this basic distinction.

Above all, while these conceptualizations of authority differ in a number of respects, they all build on the assumption that nation-states are not the only actors that exercise authority in the global arena. In fact, the different authors cited above all seek to capture the current phenomenon, namely that disparate actors have adopted various authoritative roles and functions in world politics. More specifically, they identify different types of authority in global governance that are not exclusively tied to national governments, and thereby broaden 'the concept of authority to include non-formal-legal foundations of legitimacy and non-violent means of enforcement' (Lake 2010: 596). Thus, in short, these scholars direct attention to the growing significance of sub- and non-state actors in world politics and emphasize the development of new 'structures of global authority' (Finnemore 2014: 221).

Theoretical approaches to the concept of authority

After having provided a general definition of authority and reviewed a number of recent conceptual accounts on authority in world politics, this chapter continues with a discussion of different theoretical approaches to the concept of authority in world politics. This depiction integrates the present study into the broader context of the field of international relations and lays the foundation for the key argument presented in the current study. Thereby, the book joins the series of current studies that investigate how different sub- and non-state actors have acquired authoritative roles and functions in global affairs, whether the nation-state has lost dominance in global affairs, and to what extent the authority of the nation-state and existing modes of inter-state cooperation is contested by the increasing importance of sub- and non-state actors in world politics. Scholars from different theoretical camps have formulated varying responses to these questions. First, two classical theoretical accounts are presented, i.e. the *neo-realist* and the *neo-liberal institutionalist* approach, which focus on nation-states as the primary units of analysis. Then, a number of alternative approaches to authority are presented that have been developed by various scholars over the past few years. This discussion of alternative approaches to the concept of authority focuses primarily on the literature on *private authority* that refers to processes in which a diverse set of actors develop rules and activities based on the principle of self-governance without being authorized by nation-states (cf. Zürn 2013: 410).

The neo-realist approach to the concept of authority

The realist school of thought is considered to be the oldest theory of international relations. Its origins date back to classical philosophers such as Thucydides, Machiavelli, or Thomas Hobbes. After the outbreak of the Second World War and the related demise of idealist thinking in the study of world politics, realist theory became the leading approach to international politics. In general, under realism, nation-states are the only source of authority in the international system, and no nation-state has authority over another. One of the most prominent representatives of classical realism is Hans Morgenthau. In his book *Politics Among Nations*, Morgenthau emphasizes the ubiquity of power in global politics and the competitive nature of international politics (Morgenthau 1948). He claims that the drive for power is a fundamental aspect of human nature. Hence, according to Morgenthau, it is the nature of man that explains why international politics is inevitably power politics (cf. Dunne and Schmidt 2011: 89). In the 1970s, the realist approach was challenged by the liberal institutionalist approach to international politics, which culminated in one of the most elaborate debates in the discipline of international relations theory (Baldwin 1993). In this debate about the role played by international institutions in world politics, scholars further developed classical realist thinking towards a structural theory of international politics. This approach, commonly termed *neo*-realist approach, is most often associated with the work entitled *Theory of International Politics* by Kenneth Waltz (Waltz 1979). Waltz and other authors in the neo-realist tradition agree with classical realists that international politics is primarily a struggle for power. However, they do not share the assumption that this can be attributed solely to human nature. Instead, neo-realists identify the lack of an overarching authority in the international realm as the main reason for inter-state conflict and security competition between nation-states (e.g. Milner 1991).

This perception of international politics is to a large extent derived from Max Weber's conception of the nation-state. According to Weber's classical definition, the nation-state can be understood as 'a human community that (successfully) claims the monopoly of the legitimate use of physical force within a given territory' (Weber 1948: 77–78). Endowed with this ability, the nation-state can rely on the habitual obedience of its citizens. Neo-realists have adopted this definition of the nation-state, and hold that due to the lack of a central authority in global politics, nation-states are the only legitimate actors and sole source of authority in the international system. Therefore, in the neo-realist approach to international politics, authority is associated exclusively with the public sphere (here synonymous with national government). In other words, the absence of a global government has led neo-realist scholars to deny the very existence of authority above the level of the nation-state. Based on the premise that the nation-state is the principal actor and sole source of authority in the international system, neo-realists contend that nation-states possess two kinds of sovereignty (e.g. Strayer 1970; Dyson 1980; Giddens 1985). Within its borders, the nation-state has the monopoly over the legitimate means of violence and holds the supreme authority to pass and enforce laws (i.e. internal sovereignty). Furthermore, in the international system, the nation-state is not subjected to any higher authority and can therefore act without interference from other nation-states (i.e. external sovereignty). Consequently, the international system is anarchic, meaning that the condition for long-term order is missing from the international realm. While hierarchy is the basis of domestic politics, anarchy (defined by neo-realists as the absence of an overarching authority above the level of the sovereign nation-state) constitutes the inevitable reality of international politics. Neo-realist scholars further claim that anarchy shapes the basic character of international politics. They contend that the anarchic structure of the international system leads to a logic of self-help that compels nation-states to maximize their security (Waltz 1979: 111). Nation-states can only provide for their own security by accumulating military capabilities. However, since the military preparations by one nation-state automatically pose a threat to others, nation-states are deadlocked in a situation known as a 'security dilemma' (Herz 1950). In such a system, all nation-states are concerned for their survival. Therefore, the international system is, according to neo-realist scholars, characterized by a permanent condition of insecurity, whereby the existence of a hegemon or the balance of power between two nation-states can temporarily reduce the threat of war (Kindleberger 1973; Waltz 1988; Mearsheimer 2001).

Hence, the neo-realist conception of international politics is essentially based on three theoretical assumptions. First, neo-realist scholars presume that nation-states are the primary actors in the global arena. Second, they claim that the fundamental structure of the international system is anarchic. And third, they contend that nation-states seek to maximize their security in order to ensure their survival. For many years, neo-realist scholars have been using these basic premises as starting points for their assessments of international politics, and they continue to emphasize the enduring validity of these assumptions for the analysis of global politics. Accordingly, in the latest debates in the field of international relations, neo-realists have been rather skeptical about the impacts of new developments on global affairs. In Guzzini's words, 'the bottom-line of realism is a particular form of skepticism' (Guzzini 1998: 203). While different events in global affairs have encouraged many scholars to develop alternative approaches to world politics, neo-realists stress the timeless wisdom of their school of thought. Neo-realist scholars, for instance, do not attach great importance to the role of international institutions in world politics. Furthermore, they question the influence of norms and moral principles on the behavior of nation-states and largely neglect the role played by sub- and non-state actors in global affairs. This does not mean that neo-realist scholars deny the various new developments that have occurred in world politics over the past decades. Indeed, they recognize that the international system has undergone profound changes, most notably associated with economic globalization and the increased role of private actors in world politics. Kenneth Waltz, for example, states that '[t]he importance of nonstate actors and the extent of transnational activities are obvious' (Waltz 1979: 94). However, scholars in the neo-realist tradition do not attribute the same significance to these developments as do scholars from other theoretical camps. According to Robert Jackson and Alan James, not one of the developments that have taken place in the past decades 'has reduced the significance of sovereign statehood as the fundamental way in which the world is politically organized' (James and Jackson 1993: 6). In fact, neo-realist scholars argue that nation-states have expanded their central position in the international system by transforming their authority to respond to new policy issues (Waltz 2000). Consequently, neo-realist scholars defend their state-centric view and insist that nation-states are the dominant actors in the international system (e.g. Gilpin 1981; Skolnikoff 1993; Drezner 2007).

The neo-liberal institutionalist approach to the concept of authority

The liberal tradition in political thinking is often referred to as the historic alternative to the (neo-)realist approach to international politics (cf. Dunne 2011: 102). This school of thought goes back to philosophers of the Enlightenment, such as John Locke and Immanuel Kant. Over the past decades, liberal ideas have inspired many scholars to formulate different approaches to world politics. After the First World War, a group of liberal scholars and policy-makers promoted the idea that inter-state conflict could be prevented by a strong role of international law and international organizations (e.g. Wilson 1918). However, with the collapse of the *League of Nations* and the outbreak of the Second World War, this approach fell into disrepute and has retrospectively been named the *idealist* or *utopian* variant of liberal thinking. After the horror of the Second World War, the language of liberal authors became more pragmatic. In the early post-1945 period, liberal scholars formulated a functional theory of regional integration (e.g. Haas 1958; Lindberg 1963; Mitrany 1965). This approach suggests that nation-states need to transfer some of their sovereignty to supranational organizations in order to attain economic growth or address transboundary problems, such as the proliferation of nuclear weapons, illicit trafficking, or increasing environmental degradation. A few years later, Robert Keohane and Joseph Nye published their book, *Power and Interdependence*, in which they developed the theoretical model of 'complex interdependence' (Keohane and Nye 1977). In this work, Keohane and Nye claim that nation-states have become highly dependent on one another due to an increasing amount of transnational activities. In such an interdependent world, nation-states have, according to the two authors, a strong incentive to cooperate with each other to achieve mutual gains. With this argument, Keohane and Nye laid the foundation for the neo-liberal institutionalist perspective on world politics. This approach represents one of the most prominent strands in contemporary liberal thinking and is considered by many authors to be a convincing challenge to the neo-realist theory of international politics.

Neo-liberal institutionalist scholars start with assumptions about world politics very similar to those of neo-realists. They adhere to the neo-realist premise that nation-states are the central actors in world politics, which seek to maximize their interests in an international system that lacks a central authority. But despite this common starting point, neo-liberal institutionalists have developed a very different assessment of the possibility of cooperation. According to neo-liberal institutionalist scholars, international institutions can assume important roles and functions in global politics. The main argument put forward by neo-liberal institutionalist scholars is that anarchy does not render durable patterns of inter-state cooperation unfeasible. This argument is most clearly elaborated by Robert Keohane. In his book, *After Hegemony*, he emphasizes the crucial role played by international institutions in world politics and develops a functional theory of international regimes (Keohane 1984). According to Keohane, the most important function of international regimes 'is to facilitate negotiations leading to mutually beneficial agreements among governments' (Keohane 1984: 107). Moreover, neo-liberal institutionalist scholars point out that international regimes support cooperative arrangements by providing information, reducing transaction costs, and making it easier for regime members to recognize defection from established rules and procedures (e.g. Axelrod 1984; Oye 1986; Keohane 1988). From this perspective, international regimes can be understood as a particular form of international institutions 'that consist of agreed upon principles, norms, rules, decision-making procedures, and programs that govern the interactions of actors in specific issue areas' (Young 1997b: 5–6).[2]

The focus of neo-liberal institutionalists on international regimes as a particular form of cooperation between nation-states has provoked neo-realist scholars to engage more deeply with international institutions. Neo-realists do not reject the existence of international institutions and recognize their role in the international system. However, they argue that adherents of the neo-liberal institutionalist approach ignore the importance of power in the establishment and maintenance of international institutions (Mearsheimer 1994/5). In particular, neo-realists claim that international institutions are first and foremost used by the most powerful nation-states as instruments with which to act out their dominant position in the international system (e.g. Grieco 1990; Gruber 2000; Drezner 2007). By contrast, neo-liberal institutionalists argue that international institutions considerably reduce uncertainty among actors and promote norms and rules that can mitigate the effects of anarchy in the international system (e.g. Keohane and Martin 1995). They further contend that international institutions may shape, or at least influence, the behavior of nation-states. In this view, international institutions can, under certain circumstances, restrain the foreign policies of individual national governments and outweigh the absence of a central authority in the international system.

While the focus of neo-liberal institutionalist scholars was initially on the international political economy, neo-liberal institutionalists have in the past few years increasingly paid attention to the field of global environmental politics (O'Neill 2009). In this policy domain, scholars have placed particular emphasis on the development, implementation, and effectiveness of multilateral environmental agreements (e.g. Young 1999; see also Andresen 2013). In particular, neo-liberal institutionalists have sought to explore how nation-states can prevent the over-exploitation of different common pool resources, such as international fishing stocks or the atmosphere (e.g. Ostrom 1990; Haas, Keohane, and Levy 1993; Young and Levy 1999). In this context, some international environmental agreements have proved to be very successful in alleviating global environmental problems, whereas others have been considered largely ineffective. One of the biggest obstacles for institutions to working effectively is that individual nation-states have an incentive to 'free-ride' on a particular agreement (Ostrom 1990). 'Free-riding' means that a certain actor takes advantage of the benefits of an agreement without bearing the costs of abatement. Neo-liberal institutionalist scholars argue that international institutions may solve the problem of 'free-riding' by providing means to monitor compliance and in certain cases also to impose sanctions (e.g. Greene 1993; Barrett 1994; Mitchell 1994). In this way, international institutions can, according to neo-liberal institutionalists, generate rule-governed behavior in the international system and constrain the behavior of nation-states in particular issue areas of world politics. Hence, neo-liberal institutionalist scholars contend that international institutions in certain respects constitute a substitute for a world government by ensuring that global common pool resources are not over-used (e.g. Young 1997a).

Alternative approaches to the concept of authority

In the past two decades, the two classical approaches to world politics described above have come under critical scrutiny. Different authors have questioned the appropriateness of these state-centric theories for understanding contemporary global politics. Many of these scholars argue that both the neo-realist and the neo-liberal institutionalist approach largely ignore the increasingly salient role played by sub- and non-state actors in world politics. This view has most prominently been formulated by James Rosenau. Analyzing the various changes associated with globalization that has occurred in past decades, Rosenau calls for a new way of thinking about world politics. In particular, he claims that the radical new developments in global affairs require an ontological shift in the discipline of international relations theory (Rosenau 1992). According to Rosenau, nation-states have 'lost some of their earlier dominance (…) as well as their ability to evoke compliance and to govern effectively' (Rosenau 1995: 39). While he acknowledges that nation-states are still important actors in world politics, Rosenau holds that 'states and governments should be posited not as first among equals, but simply as significant actors in a world marked by an increasing diffusion of authority and a corresponding diminution of hierarchy' (Rosenau 1999: 292). Consequently, he suggests that 'a fine line needs to be drawn between treating states as the only players on the global stage and as unimportant and aged players that have long since passed their prime' (Rosenau 1999: 292). Put differently, the new ontology Rosenau proposes is based on the premise that the nation-state constitutes only one of many 'spheres of authority' in world politics, which can be of a formal or an informal nature (Rosenau 1997; 1999; 2007). In line with Rosenau's main argument, several other scholars have provided alternative approaches to world politics that challenge classical state-centric perspectives on international politics. While these approaches differ in various ways, they are all based on the assumption that the nation-state is no longer the sole source of authority in world politics. Instead, they emphasize that a variety of sub- and non-state actors have taken on a number of authoritative roles and functions in global politics. In the following, I review some of the most prominent of these approaches and discuss their perception of authority in world politics.[3]

One of the most influential contributions to the debate on the role and function of sub- and non-state actors in global affairs was made by Claire Cutler, Virginia Haufler, and Tony Porter (Cutler, Haufler, and Porter 1999b). In their edited volume, the three scholars introduce the concept of private authority, which they define as decision-making power that is exercised by private actors and accepted as legitimate by all stakeholders (Cutler, Haufler, and Porter 1999c: 5). The individual chapters in their book focus on various arrangements between different corporate actors, such as multinational enterprises, bond-rating agencies, and business organizations. Adopting Stephen Krasner's classical definition of international regimes, they analyze how the *principles*, *norms*, *rules*, and *decision-making procedures* formulated by private actors become institutionalized and accepted by other actors. In particular, the three scholars show that nation-states not only recognize the norms and rules negotiated by private actors, but also incorporate them into domestic as well as international regulatory systems (e.g. Haufler 1995; Cutler, Haufler, and Porter 1999c; Cutler 2002). In the concluding chapter of their book, Cutler, Haufler, and Porter explore the causal explanations for the emergence of private authority in the global political economy. According to the three authors, institutionalized forms of cooperation among private corporations evolve because these actors expect to benefit from the cooperative arrangement through gains in efficiency or increased market dominance (Cutler, Haufler, and Porter 1999a: 336–338). Hence, the approach proposed by Cutler, Haufler, and

Porter does by no means contrast sharply with the neo-liberal institutional approach to world politics. Rather, it seems to complement this perspective with an analytical concept capturing the increasing importance of private actors in global policy-making.

A similar, though more encompassing concept of private authority in world politics was developed by Rodney Hall and Thomas Biersteker (Hall and Biersteker 2002a). These two authors adopt a more general approach to authority beyond the nation-state, and provide a comparative analysis of private authority in different domains of world politics. They distinguish between three types of private authority, which are *private market-based authority*, *private moral authority*, and *private illicit authority*. Hall and Biersteker suggest that these forms of authority are 'exercised by global market forces, by private market institutions engaged in the setting of international standards, by human rights and environmental non-governmental organizations, by transnational religious movements, and even by mafias or mercenary armies in some instances' (Hall and Biersteker 2002b: 4). Starting from this broad understanding of private actors, their chapters analyze the varying roles played by corporations, civil society groups, and organized criminal rings in global politics. Based on these empirical case studies, Biersteker and Hall contend that private forms of authority are a ubiquitous phenomenon in global affairs. More precisely, they maintain that '[a]uthoritative private actors are not only important players in the international political economy; they are increasingly beginning to play a critical role in the governance of other important spheres of social and political life' (Biersteker and Hall 2002: 203). The different contributions to the edited volume by Hall and Biersteker place particular emphasis on the question of how private actors establish norms and standards for themselves and other actors. According to the two scholars, the increasingly important role played by corporations and civil society groups in the promotion of norms and the setting of standards endows them with a heightened authority in global affairs (Hall and Biersteker 2002b: 3–5).

A third work dedicated to the changing nature of authority in world politics was edited by Volker Rittberger and Martin Nettesheim, who adopt a related analytical perspective (Rittberger and Nettesheim 2008). Together with Carmen Huckel and Thorsten Göbel, these two authors state in their introductory chapter 'that a broader conceptualization of authority is required to understand various phenomena that can be observed in interactions between states, international organizations, civil society actors and business actors' (Rittberger *et al.* 2008b: 2). Like the contributions in the two aforementioned books, the chapters in this volume analyze the various new roles and functions performed by sub- and non-state actors in global affairs. In addition, the group around Rittberger and Nettesheim also directs attention to the changing role of the nation-state in contemporary global politics. The scholars draw the conclusion that globalization and new transnational problems, such as increasing migration flows or environmental destruction, have considerably altered the roles played by both nation-states as well as sub- and non-state actors in global politics. More specifically, they claim that '[t]he authority of the state is increasingly challenged and has been shifting to new actors and institutions that are in a better position to deal with these issues' (Rittberger *et al.* 2008a: 318). In other words, they contend that sub- and non-state actors have taken on different authoritative functions in global politics that previously rested solely with nation-states. However, the authors also acknowledge that 'the state still emerges as a next to indispensable participant in the policy-making cycle' (Rittberger *et al.* 2008a: 326). Hence, while Rittberger and his colleagues consider sub- and non-state actors to be increasingly important providers of various public services in global affairs, they do not disregard the central role of nation-states in world politics. Nevertheless, like the scholars cited above, Rittberger and his colleagues aim to move beyond state-centric approaches to world politics and suggest a broader perspective on authority, one that takes account of the growing importance of sub- and non-state actors in global affairs.

In addition, most recently, Jessica Green addressed the matter of private authority in world politics (Green 2010b; 2010a; 2013; 2014). Building upon insights provided by many of the scholars mentioned above, she focuses on the role played by different types of private actors in the field of global environmental politics. Green also adopts a relatively broad understanding of private actors that includes 'non-governmental organizations (NGOs), private firms, multinational corporations, associations, foundations, transnational advocacy networks, and other nonstate actors' (Green 2014: 29). In a quantitative study of more than 150 multilateral environmental agreements, Green particularly examines to what extent nation-states have chosen to delegate authoritative functions to private actors, such as rule-making, adjudication, implementation, monitoring, and enforcement activities (Green 2010a). According to this study, the delegation of authority to private actors is still a rare phenomenon in global environmental policy-making, which has, however, occurred more frequently in the past few years (Green 2010a: 172). In another study that concentrates on private standards in global climate policy-making, Green explores how private actors have created rules for calculating and reporting corporate GHG emissions (Green 2010b). Hence, Green has analyzed both the delegation of policy-making functions by nation-states to private actors and the distinct role played by private actors as rule promoters and standard-setters in global environmental governance. In order to distinguish between these two types of private authority, she has introduced the terms *delegated private authority* and *entrepreneurial private authority* (Green 2014: 33–36). In particular, she points out that delegated private authority requires a transfer of authority by nation-states or international institutions to private actors, whereas entrepreneurial private authority emerges when stakeholders in a given issue area defer to rules or standards that have been formulated by private actors without the explicit delegation of authority (Green 2010b: 11–12; see also Green 2014).

Thus, according to alternative approaches to the concept of authority, the old paradigm in the field of international relations, which locates authority exclusively with sovereign states, can no longer be maintained in the study of contemporary global affairs. Adherents of these approaches point to the great diversity of problem-solving and decision-making capacities that sub- and non-state actors have developed and hold that authority structures beyond the realm of central governments and state-based international regimes have emerged. Some of these scholars even go one step further and convey the idea that the numerous transnational initiatives launched by public sub-national, private non-profit, and business actors have generated a shift of authority from nation-states and international institutions to sub- and non-state actors. However, as described in more detail in the previous chapter, scholars have only recently begun to investigate the interrelationship between the various newly emerging governance arrangements and existing modes of inter-state cooperation. Therefore, this study addresses this particular matter and analyzes the wider implications of the increasing importance of sub- and non-state actors for global climate governance. In the concluding chapter, I return to the discussion of the diverging understandings of authority and assess the theoretical implications that can be drawn from the empirical analysis undertaken in the present study for the concept of authority in world politics.

Research design

Against this theoretical background, I now depict the analytical framework for the empirical case studies. As already indicated above, this study focuses on the question of *how newly emerging transnational climate initiatives relate to the international climate regime*. This research question is addressed in three consecutive steps. First, I analyze how different transnational climate governance arrangements have emerged and acquired important problem-solving and decision-making capacities within the past few years. Second, I examine the specific relationship between these transnational climate initiatives and the intergovernmental level. And third, I compare across the cases and extract the most important insights that can be drawn from the analysis for the theoretical debate on the changing patterns of authority in global (climate) governance. While the first and second steps are dealt with in the empirical case studies that follow the description of the research design (see chapters 4 to 6), the third step is covered in the seventh and concluding chapter of this book.

Conceptual assumptions and theoretical expectations

To systematically address this study's primary research question, three conceptual assumptions are formulated that reflect different perspectives on the interrelationship between transnational climate governance arrangements and the international climate regime. These three conjectured relationships will guide the empirical analysis in this book. Several scholars have already developed different typologies to analyze actor constellations in global environmental politics (cf. Young 1996; 2002; Gehring and Oberthür 2006; Young, King, and Schroeder 2008; Biermann *et al.* 2009; Oberthür and Gehring 2011; Zelli and van Asselt 2013). Their analytical instruments inform the following conceptual considerations. The first conceptual assumption portrays a *conflictive relationship* between transnational governance arrangements and existing modes of inter-state cooperation in the policy domain of climate change. This perspective suggests that transnational climate initiatives *conflict* with the norms and rules set out in international climate agreements because their activities can be seen as contradictory to the international climate regime. Put differently, the emergence of transnational governance arrangements is assumed to generate an alternative set of norms and rules, which depart from the ultimate objective and basic principles laid down in the UNFCCC. In this scenario, the different transnational climate initiatives are thought to weaken the norms and rules negotiated by nation-states in international climate negotiations. Hence, the first assumption about the relationship between transnational climate governance arrangements and the intergovernmental level reads as follows:

Conceptual assumption 1 *Transnational governance arrangements conflict with existing modes of inter-state cooperation in the issue area of climate change and weaken the norms and rules of the international climate regime.*

The second conceptual assumption portrays a *complementary relationship* between transnational governance arrangements and existing modes of inter-state cooperation in the policy domain of climate change. This perspective implies that transnational climate initiatives *complement* the norms and rules anchored in international climate agreements because their activities have emerged in areas where international norms and rules do not exist or do not work effectively. In other words, the emergence of transnational climate governance arrangements is assumed to lead to a division of responsibilities between sub- and non-state actors and multilateral treaty-making under the UNFCCC. Within this framework, the different transnational climate initiatives are supposed to strengthen the norms and rules of the international climate regime. Therefore, the second assumption about the relationship between transnational climate governance arrangements and the intergovernmental level reads as follows:

Conceptual assumption 2 *Transnational governance arrangements complement existing modes of inter-state cooperation in the issue area of climate change and strengthen the norms and rules of the international climate regime.*

And the third conceptual assumption portrays a *dependency relationship* between transnational governance arrangements and existing modes of inter-state cooperation in the policy domain of climate change. This perspective supposes that transnational climate initiatives *depend on* the norms and rules established through international climate agreements because the issues dealt with at international climate change conferences largely drive their activities. Put another way, the emergence of transnational climate initiatives is assumed to be a side issue to the UNFCCC process. With regard to this scenario, the different transnational governance arrangements are conjectured to rely on the norms and rules established by nation-states in international climate negotiations. Accordingly, the third assumption about the relationship between transnational climate governance arrangements and the intergovernmental level reads as follows:

Conceptual assumption 3 *Transnational governance arrangements are dependent on existing modes of inter-state cooperation in the issue area of climate change and rely on the norms and rules of the international climate regime.*

For the operationalization of these conceptual assumptions, a number of general implications are derived that would be observable if the respective conjecture was correct (cf. King, Keohane, and Verba 1994: 28–29). If the first conceptual assumption of the *conflictive relationship* were valid, I would expect to observe in the empirical analysis that the different transnational climate initiatives would depart from key features of the international climate regime and propagate norms and rules that are opposed to those stipulated in international climate agreements. The transnational governance arrangements might moreover seek to establish their own rules and procedures as alternatives to the intergovernmental process and hence impair existing modes of inter-state cooperation. If the second conceptual assumption of the *complementary relationship* were true, I would expect to see in the empirical analysis that the different transnational climate initiatives would build on key features of the international climate regime and promote the norms and rules established through international climate agreements. The transnational governance arrangements might furthermore contribute to the implementation of the rules and procedures agreed upon at the intergovernmental level, and hence bolster existing modes of inter-state cooperation. And if the third conceptual assumption of the *dependency relationship* were right, I would expect to find in the empirical analysis that the effective operation of the different transnational climate initiatives would, to a large extent, rely on the nature and scope of the norms and rules of the international climate regime. More specifically, the transnational governance arrangements might blueprint certain rules and procedures set out in international climate agreements and depend on the regulatory framework established by nation-states at the intergovernmental level (see Table 3.1).

In the empirical analysis, the boundaries between the conjectured relationships are not easy to ascertain, because the three conceptual assumptions are not entirely mutually exclusive. In particular, it will be difficult to determine whether a certain observation supports the second or the third conceptual assumption. For that reason, the three conceptual assumptions and the different theoretical expectations should not be understood as accurate measuring instruments, but are rather meant as a conceptual tool to identify relevant empirical findings. Above all, the conceptual assumptions and theoretical expectations stated above will structure the empirical research undertaken in this book. In the following chapters, I link the individual case studies to the conceptual considerations made in the research

Table 3.1 General conceptual assumptions and theoretical expectations for the empirical analysis

Conceptual assumptions	*Theoretical expectations*
Conflictive relationship	Transnational governance arrangements propagate norms and rules opposed to those stipulated in international climate agreements and seek to establish their own rules and procedures as alternatives to the intergovernmental level
Complementary relationship	Transnational governance arrangements promote the norms and rules established through international climate agreements and contribute to the implementation of the rules and procedures agreed upon at the intergovernmental level
Dependency relationship	Transnational governance arrangements are dependent on an international regulatory framework and blueprint certain rules and procedures set out in international climate agreements

design. At the end of each case study, I briefly summarize the main findings of the analysis and assess the case studies within the analytical framework presented above.

Case studies

The cases examined in this book are selected on the basis of previous theoretical and empirical knowledge about the wide variety of transnational climate governance arrangements. In particular, the universe of cases in this study includes all *newly emerging transnational governance arrangements that aim to address the problem of climate change*. Due to the topicality and complexity of the subject matter, it is difficult (or rather impossible) to draw an accurate picture of all currently existing transnational climate initiatives. In recent years, a number of scholars have sought to enlist the various climate initiatives that have emerged outside the auspices of the UNFCCC. Matthew Hoffmann created a database that encompasses 58 climate governance experiments (Hoffmann 2011), Harriet Bulkeley and colleagues identified 60 different initiatives (Bulkeley *et al.* 2012), and Thomas Hale and Charles Roger, who build on these two projects, received a set of 75 transnational climate governance arrangements (Hale and Roger 2014). Overall, it is clear that the range of transnational governance arrangements, which have been developed to deal with the problem of climate change in the past few years, is very broad. For that reason, the following paragraph provides some examples of transnational climate initiatives and categorizes the various arrangements to identify criteria for a systematic case selection.

Although other options abound, in this study the various transnational climate governance arrangements are classified according to the type of actor that has initiated the particular arrangement.[4] Some transnational climate governance arrangements, as for instance the *Asian Cities Climate Change Resilience Network*; the C40 *Cities Climate Leadership Group*; the *Climate Alliance*; the *Energy Cities Association*; the *ICLEI Local Governments for Sustainability Network*; and the *Transition Towns Movement*, have been developed by groups of *public sub-national actors*. These networks can be conceived as transnational partnerships between different municipalities with joint interests, which aim to invent, evaluate, and disseminate best (or good) practices to cope with the problem of climate change in urban areas (e.g. Betsill and Bulkeley 2006; Toly 2008; Bulkeley 2010; Acuto 2013). *Private non-profit actors* have primarily launched other transnational climate governance arrangements, such as *private certification schemes*. Examples include the *Carbon Disclosure Project*; the *Climate, Community and Biodiversity Alliance*; the *Gold Standard for Carbon Offsets*; *Plan Vivo*; *Social Carbon*; and the *Verified Carbon Standard*. Basically, these private certification schemes call for responsible business behavior and seek to prevent environmentally harmful business practices (e.g. Capoor and Ambrosi 2008; Bernstein *et al*. 2010). The vast majority of these initiatives provide standards to quantify and verify climate change mitigation projects in carbon offset markets (Green 2013: 10–11). Still other transnational climate governance arrangements, as, for example, the *2Degrees Network*; the *Business Environmental Leadership Council*; the *Combat Climate Change Initiative*; the *e8 Group*; the *Global GHG Register*; the *Greenhouse Gas Protocol*; and the *International Climate Change Partnership* have been mainly propelled by *business actors*. These arrangements can be regarded as instances of private self-regulation that essentially intend to introduce norms and rules for certain industry sectors and promote the measurement, reporting, and mitigation of GHG emissions (e.g. Levy and Newell 2005; Pinkse and Kolk 2009).

This threefold classification is not totally clear-cut since hybrid forms of transnational governance arrangements also exist. A prominent example of a hybrid transnational climate governance arrangement is the *SlimCity Initiative*, in which local governments and private corporations collaborate and formulate climate change mitigation policies at the local level (World Economic Forum 2009). Nevertheless, the distinction between arrangements that have been created by (i) *public sub-national actors*, (ii) *private non-profit actors*, and (iii) *business actors* serves as the basis for the case selection in this book. In fact, one transnational climate governance arrangement is analyzed from each category. The logic behind this first step of the case selection procedure is to cover the wide spectrum of transnational climate governance arrangements and to study three cases that can be conceived as typical cases of the broader population of newly emerging transnational climate initiatives (Gerring 2004; Seawright and Gerring 2008; Rohlfing 2012). Hence, the aim of the case selection strategy is to examine cases that are representative of several other cases with similar characteristics. This strategy shall increase the confidence level of the empirical analysis and ensure that the observed empirical phenomena are not idiosyncratic to one specific case (Hall 2008: 315). In a second step, particular transnational climate initiatives have to be selected from each category. This choice is essentially based on the criteria of data richness, which specifically means that the respective transnational climate governance arrangement needs to have existed for a certain time period, i.e. in the present study for at least ten years. The availability of appropriate data in form of primary and secondary sources and expert opinions is particularly important for the case studies conducted in this book, because the empirical analysis builds upon the *method of structured, focused comparison* (George 1979; George and Bennett 2005: 67–72). The benefits of this method can only be exploited adequately if the data basis of the individual cases is equally solid.

Based on these considerations, the following three transnational climate governance arrangements were selected for the empirical analysis in this study (see Table 3.2). First, a *transnational city network* is analyzed as an instance of a transnational climate governance arrangement that has been developed by a group of *public sub-national actors*. Within this category, the *ICLEI Local Governments for Sustainability Network* best fulfills the criterion of data richness. This particular network was established in the early 1990s and consists today of more than 1,000 cities and municipalities from both developing and industrialized countries concerned with measures for addressing the problem of climate change at the local level (ICLEI 2013). While the role of transnational city networks in global climate governance has only recently aroused wider scholarly interest (e.g. Betsill and Bulkeley 2004; 2006; Bulkeley 2010; Bulkeley and Betsill 2013), the data basis on the *ICLEI Local Governments for Sustainability Network* appears to be sound enough for an in-depth investigation.

Second, a *private certification scheme* is examined as an instance of a transnational climate governance arrangement that has been launched by *private non-profit actors*. Among the different private certification initiatives addressing climate change, the *Gold Standard for Carbon Offsets* best meets the criterion of data richness. This initiative was introduced by the *World Wide Fund for Nature* in 2003 to ensure that carbon offset projects demonstrate real and permanent GHG emission reductions and contribute to sustainable development in emerging economies and developing countries (Gold Standard Foundation 2013). In the past decade, the *Gold Standard for Carbon Offsets* has evolved into one of the most prominent private certification schemes for carbon credits and increasingly attracted the attention of practitioners and scholars concerned with climate policy-making (e.g. Schlup 2005; Bayon, Hawn, and Hamilton 2007; Headon 2009).

Table 3.2 Case selection for the empirical analysis

Transnational climate initiatives		
Public sub-national arrangement	**Private non-profit arrangement**	**Business arrangement**
The ICLEI Local Governments for Sustainability Network	The Gold Standard for Carbon Offsets	The Greenhouse Gas Protocol

Third, a *business self-regulation* initiative is studied as an instance of a transnational climate governance arrangement that has been mainly propelled by *business actors*. Although business self-regulation in the issue area of climate change is still a relatively new phenomenon, an arrangement that nonetheless satisfies the criterion of data richness is the *Greenhouse Gas Protocol*. This arrangement was launched in the late 1990s and can be conceived as an instrument used by different private corporations to hold themselves accountable for their practices with regard to climate change (Greenhouse Gas Protocol 2013). Scholarly interest in business self-regulation initiatives dealing with the problem of climate change has increased considerably in the past few years, and the *Greenhouse Gas Protocol* is considered by various authors as a prime example of voluntary business responses to climate change (e.g. Sundin and Ranganathan 2002; Green 2010b; Andrew and Cortese 2011).

Methods of data collection

According to Cameron Thies, '[t]he selection of source materials for a research project *always* incurs the potential for claims of unwarranted selectivity and investigator bias. This is an unavoidable part of qualitative research' (Thies 2002: 355, emphasis in original). In order to minimize the potential adverse effects of selectivity and bias, multiple independent sources are used in the empirical case studies to cross-validate the findings (King, Keohane, and Verba 1994; Gerring 2007; Rohlfing 2012). In particular, three different methods of data collection are employed in this project (Mayring 2004; Rothbauer 2008; Bogner, Littig, and Menz 2009; Berg and Lune 2014): (i) an extensive literature review of existing scholarly work on the three transnational governance arrangements, (ii) a systematic content analysis of official documents and 'gray literature' published by the respective transnational governance arrangement, and (iii) a series of 20 semi-structured expert interviews, most of them with representatives of the different transnational climate initiatives conducted at the 18th Conference of the Parties to the UNFCCC held in Doha from 26 November to 8 December 2012 (see Appendix I for a list of interviews conducted). At this occasion, I also had numerous in-depth discussions with relevant stakeholders at related formal and informal social events taking place in conjunction with the international climate negotiations (see Appendix II for a list of attended meetings). In all these conversations, I took potential biases through stakeholder interests and narrow questions into account. Through an open conversational situation, many statements given in the interviews considerably deviated from the standard phrases often reproduced at formal events as well as in official publications and online material of transnational climate initiatives.

After having presented the underlying theoretical background and analytical framework, the book now proceeds with the actual case studies. In the first case study, I analyze the relationship between the *ICLEI Local Governments for Sustainability Network* and the international climate regime. In the second case study, I examine the relationship between the *Gold Standard for Carbon Offsets* and the international climate regime. And in the third case study, I explore the relationship between the *Greenhouse Gas Protocol* and the international climate regime. In the final chapter that follows the three empirical case studies, I then evaluate the findings of the empirical analysis in a comparative manner, before drawing general conclusions from the analysis for the theoretical debate on the concept of authority in global (climate) governance.

References

Acuto, Michele (2013). The New Climate Leaders. *Review of International Studies* 39 (4): 835–857.

Andonova, Liliana B. (2010). Public-Private Partnerships for the Earth: Politics and Patterns of Hybrid Authority in the Multilateral System. *Global Environmental Politics* 10 (2): 25–53.

Andonova, Liliana B.; Betsill, Michele; Bulkeley, Harriet (2009). Transnational Climate Governance. *Global Environmental Politics* 9 (2): 52–73.

Andresen, Steinar (2013). International Regime Effectiveness. In: Falkner, Robert. *The Handbook of Global Climate and Environment Policy*. Chichester: Wiley-Blackwell, 304–319.

Andrew, Jane; Cortese, Corinne (2011). Carbon Disclosures: Comparability, the Carbon Disclosure Project and the Greenhouse Gas Protocol. *Australasian Accounting, Business and Finance Journal* 5 (4): 5–18.

Avant, Deborah D.; Finnemore, Martha; Sell, Susan K. (2010a). Who Governs the Globe? In: Avant, Deborah D.; Finnemore, Martha; Sell, Susan K. *Who Governs the Globe?* Cambridge: Cambridge University Press, 1–31.

Avant, Deborah D.; Finnemore, Martha; Sell, Susan K., (eds). (2010b). *Who Governs the Globe?* Cambridge: Cambridge University Press.

Axelrod, Robert (1984). *The Evolution of Cooperation*. New York: Basic Books.

Baldwin, David A. (1993). *Neorealism and Neoliberalism: The Contemporary Debate*. New York: Columbia University Press.

Barnes, Barry (1986). On Authority and Its Relationship to Power. In: Law, John. *Power, Action and Belief. A New Sociology of Knowledge?* London: Routledge & Paul, 180–195.

Barnett, Michael N.; Finnemore, Martha (2004). *Rules for the World: International Organizations in Global Politics*. Ithaca, NY: Cornell University Press.

Barnett, Michael N.; Finnemore, Martha (2005). The Power of Liberal International Organizations. In: Barnett, Michael N.; Duvall, Raymond. *Power in Global Governance*. Cambridge: Cambridge University Press, 161–184.

Barrett, Scott (1994). Self-Enforcing International Environmental Agreements. *Oxford Economic Papers* 46: 878–894.

Bayon, Ricardo; Hawn, Amanda; Hamilton, Katherine (2007). *Voluntary Carbon Markets: An International Business Guide to What They Are and How They Work*. London: Earthscan.

Beetham, David (1991). *The Legitimation of Power*. New York: Macmillan.

Berg, Bruce L.; Lune, Howard (2014). *Qualitative Research Methods for the Social Sciences*. Boston: Pearson Education.

Bernstein, Steven; Betsill, Michele; Hoffmann, Matthew; Paterson, Matthew (2010). A Tale of Two Copenhagens: Carbon Markets and Climate Governance. *Millennium: Journal of International Studies* 39 (1): 161–173.

Bernstein, Steven; Cashore, Benjamin (2004). Non-State Global Governance: Is Forest Certification a Legitimate Alternative to a Global Forest Convention? In: Kirton, John; Trebilcock, Michael. *Hard Choices, Soft Law: Combining Trade, Environment, and Social Cohesion in Global Governance*. Aldershot: Ashgate, 33–64.

Betsill, Michele; Bulkeley, Harriet (2004). Transnational Networks and Global Environmental Governance: The Cities for Climate Protection Program. *International Studies Quarterly* 48 (2): 471–493.

Betsill, Michele; Bulkeley, Harriet (2006). Cities and the Multilevel Governance of Global Climate Change. *Global Governance* 12 (2): 141–159.

Biermann, Frank; Pattberg, Philipp; van Asselt, Harro; Zelli, Fariborz (2009). The Fragmentation of Global Governance Architectures: A Framework for Analysis. *Global Environmental Politics* 9 (4): 14–40.

Biersteker, Thomas J.; Hall, Rodney Bruce (2002). Private Authority as Global Governance. In: Hall, Rodney Bruce; Biersteker, Thomas J. *The Emergence of Private Authority in Global Governance*. Cambridge: Cambridge University Press, 203–222.

Blau, Peter M. (1963). Critical Remarks on Weber's Theory of Authority. *The American Political Science Review* 57 (2): 305–316.

Bogner, Alexander; Littig, Beate; Menz, Wolfgang, (eds). (2009). *Interviewing Experts*. London: Palgrave Macmillan.

Bulkeley, Harriet (2010). Cities and the Governing of Climate Change. *Annual Review of Environment and Resources* 35: 229–253.

Bulkeley, Harriet; Andonova, Liliana; Bäckstrand, Karin; Betsill, Michele; Compagnon, Daniel; Duffy, Rosaleen; Kolk, Ans; Hoffmann, Matthew; Levy, David; Newell, Peter; Milledge, Tori; Paterson, Matthew; Pattberg, Philipp; VanDeveer, Stacy D. (2012). Governing Climate Change Transnationally: Assessing the Evidence From a Database of Sixty Initiatives. *Environment and Planning C-Government and Policy* 30 (4): 591–612.

Bulkeley, Harriet; Betsill, Michele (2013). Revisiting the Urban Politics of Climate Change. *Environmental Politics* 22 (1): 136–154.

Capoor, Karan; Ambrosi, Philippe (2008). *State and Trends of the Carbon Market 2008*. Washington, DC: The World Bank.

Cashore, Benjamin (2002). Legitimacy and the Privatization of Environmental Governance: How Non-State Market-Driven (NSMD) Governance Systems Gain Rule-Making Authority. *Governance* 15 (4): 503–529.

Connolly, William E. (1983). *The Terms of Political Discourse*. Oxford: Robertson.

Cutler, A. Claire (2002). Private International Regimes and Interfirm Cooperation. In: Hall, Rodney Bruce; Biersteker, Thomas J. *The Emergence of Private Authority in Global Governance*. Cambridge: Cambridge University Press, 23–40.

Cutler, A. Claire; Haufler, Virginia; Porter, Tony (1999a). The Contours and Significance of Private Authority in International Affairs. In: Cutler, A. Claire; Haufler, Virginia; Porter, Tony. *Private Authority in International Affairs*. Albany, NY: State University of New York Press, 333–376.

Cutler, A. Claire; Haufler, Virginia; Porter, Tony, (eds). (1999b). *Private Authority and International Affairs*. Albany, NY: State University of New York Press.

Cutler, A. Claire; Haufler, Virginia; Porter, Tony (1999c). Private Authority and International Affairs. In: Cutler, A. Claire; Haufler, Virginia; Porter, Tony. *Private Authority and International Affairs*. Albany, NY: State University of New York Press, 3–28.

Day, John (1963). Authority. *Political Studies* 11 (3): 257–271.

Dellas, Eleni; Pattberg, Philipp; Betsill, Michele (2011). Agency in Earth System Governance: Refining a Research Agenda. *International Environmental Agreements* 11 (1): 85–98.

Drezner, Daniel W. (2007). *All Politics Is Global: Explaining International Regulatory Regimes*. Princeton, NJ: Princeton University Press.

Dunne, Tim (2011). Liberalism. In: Baylis, John; Smith, Steve; Owens, Patricia. *The Globalization of World Politics: An Introduction to International Relations*. New York: Oxford University Press, 100–113.

Dunne, Tim; Schmidt, Brian C. (2011). Realism. In: Baylis, John; Smith, Steve; Owens, Patricia. *The Globalization of World Politics: An Introduction to International Relations*. New York: Oxford University Press, 84–99.

Dyson, Kenneth H. F. (1980). *The State Tradition in Western Europe: A Study of an Idea and Institution*. New York: Oxford University Press.

Finnemore, Martha (2014). Dynamics of Global Governance: Building on What We Know. *International Studies Quarterly* 58 (1): 221–224.

Flathman, Richard E. (1980). *The Practice of Political Authority: Authority and the Authoritative*. Chicago, IL: University of Chicago Press.

Friedman, Richard B. (1990). On the Concept of Authority in Political Philosophy. In: Raz, Joseph. *Authority*. Oxford: Basil Blackwell, 56–91.

Gehring, Thomas; Oberthür, Sebastian (2006). Empirical Analysis and Ideal Types of Institutional Interaction. In: Oberthür, Sebastian; Gehring, Thomas. *Institutional Interaction in Global Environmental Governance: Synergy and Conflict Among International and EU Policies*. Cambridge, MA: MIT Press, 307–371.

George, Alexander L. (1979). Case Studies and Theory Development: The Method of Structured, Focused Comparison. In: Lauren, Paul Gordon. *Diplomacy: New Approaches in History, Theory, and Policy*. New York: Free Press, 43–68.

George, Alexander L.; Bennett, Andrew (2005). *Case Studies and Theory Development in the Social Sciences*. Cambridge, MA: MIT Press.

Gerring, John (2004). What Is a Case Study and What Is It Good For? *American Political Science Review* 98 (2): 341–354.

Gerring, John (2007). *Case Study Research: Principles and Practices*. New York: Cambridge University Press.

Giddens, Anthony (1985). *The Nation-State and Violence*. Cambridge, MA: Polity Press.

Gilpin, Robert (1981). *War and Change in World Politics*. Cambridge: Cambridge University Press.

Gold Standard Foundation (2013). *Who We Are*. Available at: www.cdmgoldstandard.org/about-us/who-we-are (accessed May 21, 2013).

Green, Jessica F. (2010a). Private Authority on the Rise: A Century of Delegation in Multilateral Environmental Agreements. In: Tallberg, Jonas; Jönsson, Christer. *Transnational Actors in Global Governance*. Basingstoke: Palgrave, 155–176.

Green, Jessica F. (2010b). Private Standards in the Climate Regime: The Greenhouse Gas Protocol. *Business and Politics* 12 (3): Article 3.

Green, Jessica F. (2013). Order out of Chaos: Public and Private Rules for Managing Carbon. *Global Environmental Politics* 13 (2): 1–25.

Green, Jessica F. (2014). *Rethinking Private Authority: Agents and Entrepreneurs in Global Environmental Governance*. Princeton, NJ: Princeton University Press.

Greene, Owen (1993). International Environmental Regimes: Verification and Implementation Review. *Environmental Politics* 2 (4): 156–173.

Greenhouse Gas Protocol (2013). *About the GHG Protocol*. Available at: www.ghgprotocol.org/about-ghgp (accessed August 19, 2013).

Grieco, Joseph M. (1990). *Cooperation Among Nations: Europe, America, and Non-Tariff Barriers to Trade*. Ithaca, NY: Cornell University Press.

Gruber, Lloyd (2000). *Ruling the World: Power Politics and the Rise of Supranational Institutions*. Princeton, NJ: Princeton University Press.

Guzzini, Stefano (1998). *Realism in International Relations and International Political Economy: The Continuing Story of a Death Foretold*. London: Routledge.

Haas, Ernst B. (1958). *The Uniting of Europe: Political, Social, and Economic Forces 1950–1957*. Stanford: Stanford University Press.

Haas, Peter M.; Keohane, Robert O.; Levy, Marc A. (1993). *Institutions for the Earth: Sources of Effective International Environmental Protection*. Cambridge, MA: MIT Press.

Hale, Thomas; Roger, Charles (2014). Orchestration and Transnational Climate Governance. *Review of International Organizations* 9 (1): 59–82.

Hall, Peter A. (2008). Systematic Process Analysis: When and How to Use It. *European Political Science* 7 (3): 304–317.

Hall, Rodney Bruce; Biersteker, Thomas J., (eds). (2002a). *The Emergence of Private Authority in Global Governance*. Cambridge: Cambridge University Press.

Hall, Rodney Bruce; Biersteker, Thomas J. (2002b). The Emergence of Private Authority in the International System. In: Hall, Rodney Bruce; Biersteker, Thomas J. *The Emergence of Private Authority in Global Governance*. Cambridge: Cambridge University Press, 3–22.

Haufler, Virginia (1995). Crossing the Boundaries between Public and Private: International Regimes and Non-State Actors. In: Rittberger, Volker. *Regime Theory and International Relations*. Oxford: Clarendon Press, 94–111.

Headon, Sam (2009). Whose Sustainable Development? Sustainable Development under the Kyoto Protocol, the 'Coldplay Effect', and the CDM Gold Standard. *Colorado Journal of International Environmental Law and Policy* 20 (2): 127–156.

Herz, John H. (1950). Idealist Internationalism and the Security Dilemma. *World Politics* 2 (2): 171–201.

Hoffmann, Matthew (2011). *Climate Governance at the Crossroads: Experimenting With a Global Response After Kyoto*. Oxford: Oxford University Press.

Hurd, Ian (1999). Legitimacy and Authority in International Politics. *International Organization* 53 (2): 379–408.

Hurrelmann, Achim; Schneider, Steffen; Steffek, Jens, (eds). (2007). *Legitimacy in an Age of Global Politics*. Basingstoke: Palgrave.

ICLEI (2013). *ICLEI Global: Who We Are*. Available at: www.iclei.org/iclei-global/who-is-iclei.html (accessed March 14, 2013).

James, Alan; Jackson, Robert H. (1993). The Character of Independent Statehood. In: James, Alan; Jackson, Robert H. *States in a Changing World: A Contemporary Analysis*. Oxford: Clarendon Press, 3–25.

Katsikas, Dimitros (2010). Non-State Authority and Global Governance. *Review of International Studies* 36: 113–135.

Keohane, Robert O. (1984). *After Hegemony: Cooperation and Discord in the World Political Economy*. Princeton, NJ: Princeton University Press.

Keohane, Robert O. (1988). International Institutions: Two Approaches. *International Studies Quarterly* 32 (4): 379–396.

Keohane, Robert O.; Martin, Lisa L. (1995). The Promise of Institutionalist Theory. *International Security* 20 (1): 39–51.

Keohane, Robert O.; Nye, Joseph S. (1977). *Power and Interdependence: World Politics in Transition*. Boston, MA: Little & Brown.

Kindleberger, Charles P. (1973). *The World in Depression: 1929–1939*. Berkeley, CA: University of California Press.

King, Gary; Keohane, Robert O.; Verba, Sidney (1994). *Designing Social Inquiry: Scientific Inference in Qualitative Research*. Princeton, NJ: Princeton University Press.

Krasner, Stephen D. (1982). Structural Causes and Regime Consequences: Regimes as

Intervening Variables. *International Organization* 36 (2): 185–205.
Kratochwil, Friedrich (2006). On Legitimacy. *International Relations* 20 (3): 302–308.
Lake, David A. (2003). The New Sovereignty in International Relations. *International Studies Review* 5 (3): 303–323.
Lake, David A. (2007). Escape From the State of Nature: Authority and Hierarchy in World Politics. *International Security* 32 (1): 47–79.
Lake, David A. (2010). Rightful Rules: Authority, Order, and the Foundations of Global Governance. *International Studies Quarterly* 54 (3): 587–613.
Levy, David L.; Newell, Peter, (eds). (2005). *The Business of Global Environmental Governance*. Cambridge, MA: MIT Press.
Lindberg, Leon N. (1963). *The Political Dynamics of European Economic Integration*. Stanford, CA: Stanford University Press.
Mayring, Philipp (2004). Qualitative Content Analysis. In: Flick, Uwe; von Kardorff, Ernst; Steinke, Ines. *A Companion to Qualitative Research*. London: Sage, 266–269.
Mearsheimer, John J. (1994/5). The False Promise of International Institutions. *International Security* 19 (3): 5–49.
Mearsheimer, John J. (2001). *The Tragedy of Great Power Politics*. New York: Norton.
Milner, Helen (1991). The Assumption of Anarchy in International Relations Theory: A Critique. *Review of International Studies* 17: 67–85.
Mitchell, Ronald B. (1994). *Intentional Oil Pollution at Sea: Environmental Policy and Treaty Compliance*. Cambridge, MA: MIT Press.
Mitrany, David (1965). The Prospects of Integration: Federal or Functional? *Journal of Common Market Studies* 4 (2): 119–149.
Morgenthau, Hans J. (1948). *Politics Among Nations: The Struggle for Power and Peace*. New York: Alfred A. Knopf.
O'Neill, Kate (2009). *The Environment and International Relations*. Cambridge: Cambridge University Press.
Oberthür, Sebastian; Gehring, Thomas (2011). Institutional Interaction: Ten Years of Scholarly Development. In: Oberthür, Sebastian; Stokke, Olav Schram. *Managing Instiutional Complexity: Regime Interplay and Global Environmental Change*. Cambridge, MA: MIT Press, 25–58.
Ostrom, Elinor (1990). *Governing the Commons: The Evolution of Institutions for Collective Action*. Cambridge: Cambridge University Press.
Oye, Kenneth A. (1986). *Cooperation Under Anarchy*. Princeton, NJ: Princeton University Press.
Pattberg, Philipp (2007). *Private Institutions and Global Governance: The New Politics of Environmental Sustainability*. Cheltenham: Edward Elgar.
Pattberg, Philipp; Biermann, Frank; Chan, Sander; Mert, Aysem, (eds). (2012). *Public-Private Partnerships for Sustainable Development: Emergence, Influence and Legitimacy*. Cheltenham: Edward Elgar.
Pattberg, Philipp; Stripple, Johannes (2008). Beyond the Public and Private Divide: Remapping Transnational Climate Governance in the 21st Century. *International Environmental Agreements* 8 (4): 367–388.
Peters, Richard S. (1967). Authority. In: Quinton, Anthony. *Political Philosophy*. New York: Oxford University Press, 83–96.
Pinkse, Jonatan; Kolk, Ans (2009). *International Business and Global Climate Change*. London: Routledge.
Rittberger, Volker; Nettesheim, Martin, (eds). (2008). *Authority in the Global Political Economy*. Basingstoke: Palgrave.

Rittberger, Volker; Nettesheim, Martin; Huckel, Carmen; Göbel, Thorsten (2008a). Conclusion: Authority Beside and Beyond the State. In: Rittberger, Volker; Nettesheim, Martin. *Authority in the Global Political Economy*. Basingstoke: Palgrave, 314–327.

Rittberger, Volker; Nettesheim, Martin; Huckel, Carmen; Göbel, Thorsten (2008b). Introduction: Changing Patterns of Authority. In: Rittberger, Volker; Nettesheim, Martin. *Authority in the Global Political Economy*. Basingstoke: Palgrave, 1–9.

Rohlfing, Ingo (2012). *Case Studies and Causal Inference: An Integrative Framework*. Basingstoke: Palgrave.

Rosenau, James N. (1992). Governance, Order and Change in World Politics. In: Rosenau, James N.; Czempiel, Ernst Otto. *Governance Without Government: Order and Change in World Politics*. Cambridge: Cambridge University Press, 1–29.

Rosenau, James N. (1995). Governance in the Twenty-First Century. *Global Governance* 1 (1): 13–43.

Rosenau, James N. (1997). *Along the Domestic-Foreign Frontier: Exploring Governance in a Turbulent World*. Cambridge: Cambridge University Press.

Rosenau, James N. (1999). Toward an Ontology for Global Governance. In: Hewson, Martin; Sinclair, Timothy J. *Approaches to Global Governance Theory*. Albany: State University of New York Press, 287–301.

Rosenau, James N. (2007). Governing the Ungovernable: The Challenge of a Global Disaggregation of Authority. *Regulation & Governance* 1 (1): 88–97.

Rothbauer, Paulette (2008). Triangulation. In: Given, Lisa M. *The SAGE Encyclopedia of Qualitative Research Methods*. Los Angeles, CA: Sage, 892–894.

Ruggie, John G. (1982). International Regimes, Transactions, and Change: Embedded Liberalism in the Post-War Economic Order. *International Organization* 36 (2): 379–415.

Sartorius, Rolf (1981). Political Authority and Political Obligation. *Virginia Law Review* 67 (1): 3–17.

Schlup, Michael (2005). One Goal Is Not Enough. *Carbon Finance* 2 (21): 14–15.

Seawright, Jason; Gerring, John (2008). Case Selection Techniques in Case Study Research: A Menu of Qualitative and Quantitative Options. *Political Research Quarterly* 61 (2): 294–308.

Simmons, John A. (2002). Political Obligation and Authority. In: Simon, Robert L. *The Blackwell Guide to Social and Political Philosophy*. Malden: Blackwell, 17–37.

Skolnikoff, Eugene B. (1993). *The Elusive Transformation: Science, Technology, and the Evolution of International Politics*. Princeton, NJ: Princeton University Press.

Strayer, Joseph R. (1970). *On the Medieval Origins of the Modern State*. Princeton, NJ: Princeton University Press.

Sundin, Heidi; Ranganathan, Janet (2002). Managing Business Greenhouse Gas Emissions: The Greenhouse Gas Protocol – A Strategic and Operational Tool. *Corporate Environmental Strategy* 9 (2): 137–144.

Thies, Cameron G. (2002). A Pragmatic Guide to Qualitative Historical Analysis in the Study of International Relations. *International Studies Perspectives* 3 (4): 351–372.

Toly, Noah J. (2008). Transnational Municipal Networks in Climate Politics: From Global Governance to Global Politics. *Globalizations* 5 (3): 341–356.

Waltz, Kenneth N. (1979). *Theory of International Politics*. Boston, MA: McGraw-Hill.

Waltz, Kenneth N. (1988). The Origins of War in Neorealist Theory. *Journal of Interdisciplinary History* 18 (4): 615–628.

Waltz, Kenneth N. (2000). Globalization and American Power. *National Interest* 59 (Spring): 46–56.

Weber, Max (1948). Politics as a Vocation. In: Gerth, Hans Heinrich; Mills, C. Wright. *From Max Weber: Essays in Sociology*. London: Routledge, 77–128.

Weber, Max (1958). The Three Types of Legitimate Rule. *Berkeley Publications in Society and Institutions* 4 (1): 1–11.

Weber, Max (1968). *Economy and Society: An Outline of Interpretive Sociology*. New York: Bedminster Press.

Wilson, Woodrow (1918). *U.S. President Woodrow Wilson's Fourteen Points: A Speech Delivered in a Joint Session of the U.S. Congress, January* 8. Washington, DC.

World Economic Forum (2009). *SlimCity: A Cross-Industry Public Private Initiative on Urban Sustainability*. Geneva: World Economic Forum.

Young, Oran R. (1996). Institutional Linkages in International Society: Polar Perspectives. *Global Governance* 2 (1): 1–24.

Young, Oran R. (1997a). Global Governance: Toward a Theory of Decentralized World Order. In: Young, Oran R. *Global Governance: Drawing Insights From the Environmental Experience*. Cambridge, MA: MIT Press, 273–299.

Young, Oran R. (1997b). Rights, Rules, and Resources in World Affairs. In: Young, Oran R. *Global Governance: Drawing Insights From the Environmental Experience*. Cambridge, MA: MIT-Press, 1–23.

Young, Oran R., (ed.). (1999). *The Effectiveness of International Environmental Regimes: Causal Connections and Behavioral Mechanisms*. Cambridge, MA: MIT Press.

Young, Oran R. (2002). *The Institutional Dimensions of Environmental Change: Fit, Interplay, and Scale*. Cambridge, MA: MIT Press.

Young, Oran R.; King, Leslie A.; Schroeder, Heike, (eds). (2008). *Institutions and Environmental Change: Principal Findings, Applications, and Research Frontiers*. Cambridge, MA: MIT Press.

Young, Oran R.; Levy, Marc A. (1999). The Effectiveness of International Environmental Regimes. In: Young, Oran R. *The Effectiveness of International Environmental Regimes: Causal Connections and Behavioral Mechanisms*. Cambridge, MA: MIT Press, 1–32.

Zelli, Fariborz; van Asselt, Harro (2013). Introduction: The Institutional Fragmentation of Global Environmental Governance: Causes, Consequences, and Responses. *Global Environmental Politics* 13 (3): 1–13.

Zürn, Michael (2013). Globalization and Global Governance. In: Carlsnaes, Walter; Risse, Thomas; Simmons, Beth A. *Handbook of International Relations*. Los Angeles, CA: Sage, 401–425.

Zürn, Michael; Binder, Martin; Ecker-Ehrhardt, Matthias (2012). International Authority and Its Politicization. *International Theory* 4 (1): 69–106.

Notes

1 For a comprehensive overview of different academic accounts on authority, see Simmons (2002).

2 This definition of international regimes is a slight alteration of Krasner's classical definition of international regimes (Krasner 1982: 186), which was introduced in the first chapter of this book.

3 The list of authors dealing with authority structures beyond the nation-state is very long. Recent examples of studies concerned with global environmental politics include Cashore (2002), Bernstein and Cashore (2004), Pattberg (2007), Pattberg and Stripple (2008), Andonova, Betsill, and Bulkeley (2009), Bulkeley (2010), Dellas, Pattberg, and Betsill (2011), Hoffmann (2011), Pattberg *et al.* (2012), Green (2014).

4 Other scholars have proposed different options for categorizing the broad range of transnational governance arrangements operating in the issue area of climate change (e.g. Pattberg and Stripple 2008; Andonova, Betsill, and Bulkeley 2009; Andonova 2010). Because of the book's particular interest in the locus of authority of the various transnational climate initiatives, the actor-centered classification adopted here seems most useful for the present study.

4 Transnational city networks

The ICLEI network

Overview

The beginnings of the modern form of city networking across national boundaries can be traced back to the early twentieth century. Two early examples of city networks are the *International Union of Local Authorities* (hereafter IULA) and the *International City/County Management Association* (hereafter ICMA). These organizations were founded in 1913 and 1914, respectively, to promote democratic self-government at the local level and to advance professional local governments worldwide. While the ICMA still exists today and continues to provide technical and management assistance to local governments throughout the world, in 2004, IULA merged with other organizations to form the *United Cities and Local Governments* (hereafter UCLG), the world's largest local government organization (UCLG 2013). For most part of the last century, the number of partnerships and networks of urban actors from different countries has slowly but steadily increased. Yet, since the 1990s, city networks have experienced tremendous growth (e.g. Friedmann 2001; Sassen 2002; Keiner and Kim 2007). One of the key drivers behind this development was Agenda 21, launched at the United Nations Conference on Environment and Development held in Rio de Janeiro in 1992. Agenda 21 is a voluntary action plan agreed upon by the members of the United Nations to promote sustainable development at the global, national, and local level (United Nations 1992). It stipulates that local governments should enter into a dialogue with their citizens, community organizations, and private companies, and adopt a Local Agenda 21 to steer their development in a more sustainable direction. In addition, Agenda 21 explicitly encourages all cities in the signatory countries to 'participate in international "sustainable city networks" to exchange experiences and mobilize national and international technical and financial support' (United Nations 1992: chapter 7). To facilitate the efforts of local governments, several United Nations initiatives were considerably strengthened in the 1990s, such as the *Sustainable Cities Program*, a joint initiative between United Nations Habitat and the United Nations Environment Programme, and the *Healthy Cities Project* of the *World Health Organization* (Keiner and Kim 2007: 1372). These developments have led to the emergence of numerous city networks concerned with sustainable development over the past few years.

Classical approaches to international politics have largely neglected the role of city networks in world politics. As stated earlier in this book, these approaches focus primarily on the relations between nation-states. In recent years, however, a number of scholars have placed particular emphasis on the cross-border interactions between urban actors, and explore how local governments establish transnational networks in order to pursue common interests (e.g. Taylor 2004; Kübler and Piliutyte 2007; Campbell 2012). Many of these scholars build upon the analytical concept developed by Robert Keohane and Joseph Nye in the early 1970s. In the introduction to a Special Issue of *International Organization* edited by the two scholars, Nye and Keohane stress the rapid growth of transnational relations, which they define as 'contacts, coalitions, and interactions across state boundaries that are not controlled by the central foreign policy organs of governments' (Nye and Keohane 1971: 331). The main concern of this Special Issue was to shed light on the influence exerted by different transnational actors, including multinational corporations, non-profit organizations, and the Catholic Church, on the behavior of nation-states in various domains of world politics. In the 1990s, different scholars revived and broadened the study of transnational relations. In 1992, Peter Haas, for instance, emphasized the impact of *epistemic communities* on international politics and put forward the argument that scientists and other 'knowledge-based' experts can, under certain circumstances, influence the outcome of international negotiations (Haas 1992). A few years later, Thomas Risse-Kappen edited a book analyzing a wide array of transnational actors and their relation to domestic politics and international institutions (Risse-Kappen 1995). The contributors to this volume concentrated their analyses on the relationship between nation-states and different kinds of transnational actors in particular fields of global affairs. And in the late 1990s, Margaret Keck and Kathryn Sikkink explored how transnational advocacy networks, such as *Amnesty International* and *Greenpeace*, affect human rights and environmental politics (Keck and Sikkink 1998). This list is not exhaustive and could be further expanded.[1] While all these approaches differ in certain aspects, they share the view that transnational networks have become an important feature of world politics.

Drawing on this body of literature, a number of scholars have recently also begun to study the role of transnational city networks in global climate governance (e.g. Betsill and Bulkeley 2004; Kern and Alber 2008; Toly 2008; Kern and Bulkeley 2009; Bulkeley and Newell 2010; Acuto 2013; Lee 2013). These scholars focus on networks of local governments and other urban actors, which undertake joint efforts to address the problem of climate change. Philipp Pattberg and Johannes Stripple define these networks as 'cooperative arrangements to exchange information, learn from best practices and consequently mitigate carbon dioxide emissions independently from national government decisions' (Pattberg and Stripple 2008: 379). One of the most comprehensive reviews of the broad range of transnational city networks operating in the issue area of climate change was provided by Harriet Bulkeley (Bulkeley 2010). In her review article, she points to the great variety of newly emerging networks, ranging from partnerships between large cities to associations of small urban communities, and notes that the overall number of transnational city networks dealing with climate change has increased considerably since the early 1990s (Bulkeley 2010: 232). According to Karin Bäckstrand, these developments 'challenge the idea that climate change should primarily be dealt with at the global level' (Bäckstrand 2008: 94).

Thus, in sum, numerous city networks have emerged in the past decades that are concerned with a wide range of different issues. While these networks have long been disregarded in the literature of world politics, they have attracted growing attention among scholars in the past few years. Recently, networks of local governments have also become increasingly prominent in climate policy-making. In the following sections, I first depict the emergence of transnational city networks in the policy domain of climate change. Then, I examine how these networks operate, summarize why they are conceived as important actors in global climate governance, and link the discussion to the theoretical background presented in the third chapter of this book. Thereafter, I focus on one transnational city network and explore its interplay with the intergovernmental level. Using the analytical framework outlined above, I particularly analyze how the *ICLEI Local Governments for Sustainability Network's* different fields of activity relate to the international climate regime. Finally, I summarize the main findings from the empirical analysis and draw conclusions for the theoretical debate about the concept of authority in global climate governance.

The emergence of transnational city networks in global climate governance

The idea to address transboundary environmental problems at the local level was first raised by the *Brundtland Report* published in 1987. One of the report's chapters focuses especially on the environmental challenges of urban areas and calls attention to the importance of cities in attaining sustainable development in the twenty-first century (World Commission on Environment and Development 1987: chapter 9). As noted earlier, the 1992 United Nations Conference on Environment and Development in Rio reinforced the role played by cities in the global response to environmental problems. Since then, various initiatives have been launched by local governments world-wide to implement the concepts of sustainable cities and urban sustainability (Bulkeley and Betsill 2005). These different programs and projects range from improved waste management and low-carbon transportation systems to sustainable land-use planning.

Around the time of the conference in Rio, transnational city networks also began to actively engage in global climate governance. In the early 1990s, shortly before the start of the conference, three different transnational city networks were established (cf. Bulkeley 2010: 232). One of the earliest networks of local governments operating in the issue area of climate change was the *International Council for Local Environmental Initiatives* that was established in 1990 and later renamed the *ICLEI Local Governments for Sustainability* (hereafter ICLEI). From 1991 to 1993, this organization conducted the *Urban* CO_2 *Reduction Project* involving 14 cities and counties from various countries with the purpose of encouraging the development of local action plans to reduce GHG emissions (ICLEI 1993a). Based on the experience from this initial project, ICLEI announced the establishment of the *Cities for Climate Protection Program* at the first *Municipal Leaders' Summit on Climate Change* held in New York at the United Nations headquarters in 1993 (ICLEI 1993b). This program grew rapidly in the past two decades and today consists of more than 1,000 cities and municipalities from around the world (van Staden and Klas 2010: 103). A second network of local governments formed in the early 1990s is the *Climate Alliance*. This network is a partnership between European cities and indigenous peoples living in rainforest areas in the Amazon Basin. Since its foundation, more than 1,600 cities, municipalities, and districts from 20 European countries have joined this network. Basically, the *Climate Alliance* pursues two targets. On the one hand, it intends to halve the per capita GHG emissions of its members by 2030 compared with 1990 emission levels by pursuing local climate strategies, particularly in the energy and transport sectors. On the other hand, it aims to protect the tropical rainforests by implementing different projects and building partnerships with certain indigenous groups (Climate Alliance 2013c). And a third network of local governments created in the early 1990s is the *Energy Cities Partnership*, formerly known as *Energie-Cité Partnership*. This network was founded as a relatively loose collaboration between six European cities involved in a particular program initiated by the European Union. In the mid-1990s, the network was constituted as a European association of municipalities with a focus on the development of sustainable and low-carbon energy strategies. Today, it represents about 1,000 European municipalities (Energy Cities 2013).

In the past two decades, numerous other transnational city networks have been established with the goal of tackling the challenges associated with climate change. An outstanding example is the *C40 Cities Climate Leadership Group* (hereafter C40 Group). This network, originally known as the C20, has received widespread attention among both scholars and policy-makers concerned with climate change (e.g. Román 2010; Lee and van de Meene 2012; Acuto 2013). The C40 Group was created by representatives from 18 cities at the *World Cities Leadership Climate Change Summit* organized by the Mayor of London in 2005. Since its foundation, the C40 Group has increased in both size and substance and currently comprises around 60 member cities on six continents (C40 Group 2013). Two factors distinguish the C40 Group from other city networks (Hoffmann 2011: 93). First, shortly after its creation, the network entered into a partnership with the *Clinton Climate Initiative*. This initiative has become the implementing actor of the C40 Group and conducts different projects aimed at improving energy efficiency and reducing GHG emissions in member cities by actively engaging the private sector. Second, the C40 Group only consists of large cities. While most other networks of local governments are characterized by a highly diverse membership, the C40 Group is composed of a relatively small number of prominent members, including most (if not all) of the ten most populous cities in the world.

Three further recent developments are worth mentioning with regard to transnational city networks concerned with the problem of climate change. First, a growing number of cities from emerging economies and developing countries are participating in transnational city networks. While most early transnational city networks aimed at tackling climate change primarily consisted of cities from Europe, North America, and Australia, the members of today's networks also include cities, municipalities, and other urban actors from less-developed regions (Betsill and Bulkeley 2007: 453). Second, the range of concerns addressed by transnational city networks has broadened considerably. While climate change mitigation was initially the sole focus of the activities, issues of vulnerability and adaptation can now also be found on the agenda of many networks (Kern and Alber 2008: 171). Third, and most important, the activities of transnational city networks are receiving growing recognition by national policy-makers concerned with the matter of climate change. While, at first, national governments showed only little interest in the programs and projects launched by transnational city networks to cope with climate change, they now carefully observe these local activities (Bulkeley *et al.* 2011: 125).

Underlining the increasing importance of transnational city networks in global climate governance, Harriet Bulkeley states that 'urban networks have taken a more overtly political stance toward the issue, seeking to position cities as critical sites for addressing the issue of climate change or even opposing national governments' (Bulkeley 2010: 233). This has become particularly evident at the UNFCCC conferences. At the 2007 Conference of the Parties to the UNFCCC held in Bali, representatives of local governments formed the second largest delegation participating in the conference and signed the *World Mayors and Local Governments Climate Protection Agreement* (ICLEI *et al.* 2007). This document, which calls for an ambitious legally binding international climate treaty, has been considered one of the first collaborative efforts undertaken by transnational city networks to address the climate change problem (Bulkeley and Newell 2010: 60). In the following sections of this chapter, I return to this point and thoroughly discuss the involvement of one transnational city network (i.e. the ICLEI network) in the international climate change conferences.

Transnational city networks and climate change

One of the most basic features of transnational city networks dealing with climate change and other issues is their voluntary character. The members of transnational city networks are free to join and leave the network and voluntarily participate in the different network activities (e.g. Kern and Bulkeley 2009: 309). Consequently, transnational city networks lack the capacity to coerce their members to adopt or implement specific policies and to sanction certain members in cases of non-compliance. In contrast to traditional forms of governance that are based on binding agreements and similar policy instruments, such as economic incentives or sanctions, transnational city networks rely on softer forms of governance to encourage their members to achieve the overall network goals (e.g. Bäckstrand 2008: 77; Kern and

Bulkeley 2009: 319; Bulkeley and Newell 2010: 56). Drawing on Kristine Kern and Harriet Bulkeley, the different strategies deployed by transnational city networks to steer their constituents can be grouped into three broad categories: (i) *information sharing*, (ii) *capacity building and implementation*, and (iii) *self-regulation* (cf. Kern and Bulkeley 2009: 319–323). To gain a better understanding of the role and function of transnational city networks in global climate governance, these strategies are described in more detail in the following paragraphs.

Information sharing

First and foremost, transnational city networks use the strategy of information sharing to achieve their goals. According to Kern and Bulkeley, '[n]etworks are frequently established for the explicit purpose of creating and sharing "best" or "good" practice, and municipalities indicate that the opportunity to learn about "what works" from other places is a key motivation for their participation in networks' (Kern and Bulkeley 2009: 319). Many transnational city networks have created good-practice databases or brochures containing information about particularly innovative local climate projects (e.g. C40 Group 2013; Climate Alliance 2013a; ICLEI 2013b). The fundamental idea behind this instrument is to foster learning processes among member cities and municipalities in order to propagate the application of innovative techniques to reduce GHG emissions at the local level. Most recently, this instrument has also been used to provide knowledge about climate change adaptation measures (Andonova, Betsill, and Bulkeley 2009: 64). Moreover, based on the good-practice examples, transnational city networks have begun to develop general methodologies and comprehensive toolkits for the implementation of climate change mitigation and adaptation strategies (e.g. ICLEI 2008b). These guidelines shall increase the transferability of projects and prepare local governments for their first steps in tackling climate change in their communities (Kern and Bulkeley 2009: 320–321). Hence, the exchange of information and knowledge can be regarded as a main strategy used by transnational city networks to achieve their goals. For the purpose of this book, this kind of internal information and communication strategy has to be distinguished from the use of information as a lobbying or advocacy instrument discussed further below. While the instruments described above are all oriented to the members of the network, transnational city networks also employ information and other means of communication as political pressure targeting actors outside of the network, such as national governments or international institutions (Andonova, Betsill, and Bulkeley 2009: 64–65).

Capacity building and implementation

A second strategy used by transnational city networks to steer their constituents can be grouped under the term 'capacity building and implementation.' This strategy includes the provision of financial, managerial, and technological resources, and is regarded as a 'more direct approach to internal governing used by the networks' (Kern and Bulkeley 2009: 321). By providing access to funding, expertise, and technologies, transnational city networks aim to enhance the capacities of their members to implement certain projects or programs that help them cope with climate change (Bulkeley and Newell 2010: 57). For instance, the C40 Group, in collaboration with the Clinton Climate Initiative and the private sector, has released funds for a number of low-carbon projects in different cities, particularly in the energy efficiency sector (Clinton Climate Initiative 2013). According to Kern and Bulkeley, these instruments not only increase the network's cohesion by binding the members more closely to the network, but also enable the transnational city network to actively pursue its stated goals (Kern and Bulkeley 2009: 321). Because of their limited budgets, transnational city networks can only use this strategy to support a certain sub-group of their members. Hence, capacity and implementation strategies deployed by transnational city networks can be conceived as a project-based instrument, which benefits the most committed members of the network and strengthens the network's core.

Self-regulation

The third strategy available to transnational city networks for internal governing comprises different mechanisms of self-regulation. This strategy includes standard-setting and benchmarks for GHG emission reductions as well as other means of performance measuring, and is designed to promote members' compliance with the network goals by creating 'peer pressure' (Kern and Bulkeley 2009: 322). At first sight, these instruments closely resemble traditional forms of governance, as they establish concrete norms and rules to guide constituents. However, since networks cannot force their members to conform to a standard, follow a benchmark, or undertake performance-measuring programs, these instruments provide no more and no less than a specific incentive for cities and municipalities to tackle the problem of climate change (Andonova, Betsill, and Bulkeley 2009: 65). In contrast to the other two strategies, which are widely employed by transnational city networks operating in the issue area of climate change, the different mechanisms of self-regulation have thus far only been used to a limited extent. Two examples in this regard are ICLEI's *Five-Milestone Methodology* that member cities may apply in order to improve their GHG emission reduction performance and adaptation measures (ICLEI 2012b), and the *Climate Cities Benchmark* developed by the Climate Alliance (Climate Alliance 2013b). According to Bulkeley and Newell, the fact that transnational city networks use these self-regulatory mechanisms suggests 'that networks are able to exert a degree of power over their members' (Bulkeley and Newell 2010: 58).

Strategies of external governing

As already indicated above, in addition to these strategies of internal governing, transnational city networks use information and communication campaigns as well as other lobbying instruments in order to influence governmental organizations at different levels. One of the most widespread external governing strategies employed by transnational city networks to pursue their goals is their involvement in the UNFCCC process. As Kern and Bulkeley acknowledge, '[w]ithin the international climate change regime, climate change networks have been granted observer status and hold side-events to publicize the achievements of their members and the possibilities for taking action at the annual Conference of the Parties' (Kern and Bulkeley 2009: 323). While in the 1990s, the number of transnational city networks participating in the UNFCCC conferences was still limited, it has steadily increased since then. In early 2013, 17 local government organizations were accredited under the UNFCCC, which coordinate their activities and interact with the UNFCCC Secretariat through the *Local Governments and Municipal Authorities* (hereafter LGMA) constituency (UNFCCC 2013). At side-events, local government organizations regularly call attention to local policies designed to mitigate climate change and emphasize the importance of the local level in dealing with the problem of climate change. These events are usually held in the form of panel discussions, and can be conceived as an open forum for interactions among representatives of national governments, international institutions, observer organizations, and the media (Schroeder and Lovell 2012). In the past few years, local government organizations have also organized so-called parallel events, such as the *Municipal Leaders' Summits on Climate Change*. These events bring together local government representatives from around the world to facilitate the involvement of the LGMA constituency in the UNFCCC process (Zimmermann, Van Begin, and Vergara Cristobál 2010: 84–85). Moreover, networks of local governments maintain exhibition booths, deliver statements in high-level plenary sessions, and hold informal discussions at social events and in the corridors of the conference center. In general, through these activities, local government organizations highlight their efforts to address climate change at the local level and seek to convince national delegations to adopt a more ambitious stance towards tackling climate change.

Besides these advocacy activities at the UNFCCC conferences, transnational city networks also aim to obtain third-party funding for their projects from national governments, international institutions, and the private sector (Kern and Bulkeley 2009: 324). Since membership fees account for only a small portion of their total budget, transnational city networks are heavily dependent on funding from outside actors. National governments are generally the largest source of external funds for transnational city networks. Other funding sources include the European Commission, international institutions, such as United Nations Habitat, the United Nations Environment Programme, and the World Bank, as well as the private sector. Without this external financial support, cities would not be able to implement large-scale projects alleviating the problem of climate change (Kern and Alber 2008: 189). This is crucial for the present case study and will be discussed in more detail in the following sections. Since national and international funding schemes for local climate projects are limited, transnational city networks compete with each other for external funds to conduct projects at the local level (Hoffmann 2011: 113–114). However, despite their naturally competitive relationship, transnational city networks have undertaken a number of joint projects in the past few years. The C40 Group and the ICLEI network, in collaboration with the *World Resources Institute* and different international institutions, for instance, have recently launched the pilot version of the *Global Protocol for Community-Scale Greenhouse Gas Emissions* (C40 Group, ICLEI, and World Resources Institute 2012a). This initiative seeks to establish a common standard for the measurement and reporting of GHG emissions in urban areas.

In sum, transnational city networks employ a wide range of internal and external governing strategies to steer their constituents and influence governmental actors at different levels in order to pursue their goals. While the specific objectives might vary from network to network because of different regional scopes and available capacities, the general aims and actions of transnational city networks are very similar (Kern and Bulkeley 2009: 317). In particular, the networks seek voluntary GHG emission reduction commitments from their members, aim at enhancing local capacities to cope with climate change, foster the exchange of good practices, and represent the interests of their members at higher levels of decision-making.

The relevance of transnational city networks

Over the past two decades, different scholars have emphasized the increasing importance of cities in world politics (e.g. Sassen 1994; Brenner 1998; Scott 2001; Campbell and Fuhr 2004b; Amen *et al.* 2011; Curtis 2011; Barber 2013). These scholars point to global trends towards decentralized decision-making, refer to the changing relationship between local governments and the nation-state, and highlight statistics showing that, at the beginning of the twenty-first century, more than half of the world's population lives in urban areas (United Nations Population Fund 2007). As indicated above, the particular role played by cities in the policy domain of climate change has recently also received widespread scholarly recognition. Authors perceive cities both as part of the climate change problem and as a key part of the solution (e.g. Kamal-Chaoui and Robert 2009). On the one hand, recent reports suggest that cities account for about 60 to 80 percent of the global amount of GHG emissions (Stern 2007; International Energy Agency 2008; United Nations Habitat 2011). Accordingly, cities can be conceived as a main driver of the problem of climate change. As the trend towards growing urbanization is projected to continue in the years to come, the share of global GHG emissions produced in cities will likely further increase throughout the twenty-first century (United Nations Department of Economic and Social Affairs 2012). On the other hand, cities have adopted several programs to introduce innovative technologies and management systems for mitigating climate change (e.g. Corfee-Morlot *et al.* 2009). Cities can thus also be regarded as 'engines of change' in the global response to climate change. Measures adopted by cities, municipalities, and other urban actors to reduce their GHG emissions include solid waste management, low-carbon public transportation systems, and energy-efficient building plans (Hoornweg, Sugar, and Gómez 2011).

Moreover, climate change adaptation issues have become increasingly important for cities in recent years. According to the IPCC, cities are highly affected by the potential negative effects associated with climate change because of the high concentration of people living in cities combined with their reliance on complex systems, such as water and energy distribution, sewage, and waste removal (IPCC 2014a: chapter 8). Two types of cities are particularly vulnerable to climate change: (i) cities located in coastal areas, since they are exposed to water-related climate hazards, such as sea-level rise, hurricanes, or floods, and (ii) cities in developing countries, because in these regions climate change exacerbates already existing grievances. In response, many projects have recently been launched to enhance the capacities of cities and municipalities located in hazardous areas to adapt to climate change. For instance, in 2010, a consortium of different organizations, including the German Environment Ministry, set up the *Asian Cities Adapt* program to develop local climate change adaptation strategies in four Indian cities and four cities in the Philippines (German Environment Ministry 2010). In the same year, ICLEI started the first climate change adaptation program for cities, counties, and communities in the United States (ICLEI 2010a). And in 2012, the European Commission established the *EU Cities Adapt* project to support European cities in their efforts to cope with the adverse effects associated with climate change (European Commission 2012).

Furthermore, a few years ago, a group of scholars put forward the argument that cities are particularly suited to address the problem of climate change. These scholars argue that cities have considerable experience in addressing environmental impacts and are well-positioned to produce co-benefits from sustainable climate policies, such as economic savings, better air quality, or improved liveability of communities (Kousky and Schneider 2003; Campbell and Fuhr 2004a; Campbell-Lendrum and Corvalán 2007; Lebel *et al.* 2007; Barber 2013). They contend that cities have very good chances of agreeing on cooperative solutions because city networks often involve face-to-face communication promoting the development of trust and reciprocity among stakeholders (Ostrom 2010). In addition, they highlight the fact that transnational city networks act more and more as policy entrepreneurs and agenda setters that seek to overcome the constraints imposed by national and international administrative decision-making, party politics, and political timetables (Bulkeley and Betsill 2005; Bäckstrand 2008; Pattberg and Stripple 2008). These authors point out that the efforts undertaken by local governments across the world considerably contribute to achieving national emission reduction targets and reporting obligations agreed upon by nation-states in international climate negotiations.

Link to the theoretical background

The above discussion has underlined the fact that many scholars perceive transnational city networks as crucial governance arrangements for dealing with the problem of climate change. Some of these scholars argue that networks of local governments operating in the issue area of climate change have acquired authoritative functions in global climate governance that were previously only performed by national governments and international institutions (e.g. Betsill and Bulkeley 2006; Bäckstrand 2008; Pattberg and Stripple 2008; Bulkeley 2010; Hoffmann 2011). According to these authors, the emergence of transnational city networks leads to a shift of authority in the policy domain of climate change from state-centric intergovernmental decision-making towards transnational governance arrangements. These scholars claim that cooperation between nation-states is by no means the only way to cope with the climate change problem and point to the different activities undertaken by transnational city networks concerned with climate change. In particular, they convey the idea that transnational city networks contribute to solving the problem of climate change independently from the policies formulated by nation-states and international institutions. Hence, these scholars assert that the centrality of the international climate regime is increasingly called into question through the emergence of transnational climate governance arrangements. Nevertheless, I argue that the relationship between transnational city networks and the intergovernmental level has not been studied in enough detail. While the various case studies on individual networks of local governments have yielded important insights into the role played by cities in the global response to climate change, only little systematic research has been carried out to analyze the interplay between transnational city networks and the international climate regime. Thus, the present chapter does not simply delineate the rise of transnational city networks concerned with the issue of climate change, but explores the wider implications associated with this development for global climate governance. Drawing on the theoretical background and analytical framework outlined in the third chapter of this book, this chapter particularly examines the interrelationship between the ICLEI network and the international climate regime. Thereby, ICLEI is conceived as an illustrative example of a *sub-national* climate governance arrangement. I begin with an overview of the ICLEI network and briefly describe the network's main initiatives, organizational structure, and perception in the literature. Thereafter, I recall the three conceptual assumptions about the interrelationship between transnational governance arrangements and the international climate regime, before I examine how ICLEI's central fields of activity relate to the intergovernmental level.

The ICLEI network and the international climate regime

Overview of the ICLEI network

The ICLEI network was founded in 1990 with the aim of enhancing local capacities to cope with environmental problems and representing the environmental concerns of local governments at the global level (Betsill and Bulkeley 2004: 477). On its website, ICLEI asserts itself as 'a powerful movement of 12 mega-cities, 100 super-cities and urban regions, 450 large cities as well as 450 small and medium-sized cities and towns in 84 countries' (ICLEI 2013c). While ICLEI's agenda comprises a number of topics ranging from biodiversity and eco-mobility to resource-efficiency, the vast majority of its initiatives deal with the problem of climate change or have at least a close connection to climate change mitigation and adaptation measures (ICLEI 2013e).

Main initiatives

Shortly after its foundation, ICLEI began working on the matter of climate change and launched the Urban CO_2 Reduction Project, which ran from 1991 to 1993. The project included 14 members from North America, Europe, and the Middle East that developed local action plans for the reduction of GHG emissions and energy management. On the basis of the success of the Urban CO_2 Reduction Project, ICLEI launched the Cities for Climate Protection Program in early 1993. This program has grown rapidly in the past two decades. According to Yunus Arikan, ICLEI's *Cities Climate Center Manager*, it comprises today 'more than 1,000 local governments worldwide (…) covering around 10 percent of the world's urban population and including approximately 20 percent of global anthropogenic greenhouse gas emissions' (Arikan 2011: 101). The Cities for Climate Protection Program is designed around a program of five milestones aimed at guiding local governments when they address climate change in their communities (van Staden and Klas 2010: 104). While the initial goal of the Cities for Climate Protection Program was to stipulate a certain reduction target for all member cities and municipalities, ICLEI dropped this goal shortly after the program's foundation. In the past few years, ICLEI has taken a more proactive stance towards the problem of climate change. On different occasions, it highlighted the role played by local governments in global climate governance and called for a new binding international regulatory framework for managing climate change to be negotiated and adopted by nation-states at the intergovernmental level. As part of this strategy, the ICLEI network, together with other local government organizations, launched the *Local Government Climate Roadmap* in 2007 to advocate 'for a strong, global, comprehensive post-2012 climate agreement, where the crucial role of cities and local governments in climate protection is emphasized' (ICLEI 2010b: 70).

Organizational structure

ICLEI's organizational structure is relatively complex. While the network is a membership organization, which means that the member cities and municipalities govern themselves on the basis of democratic principles and decisions, several bodies have been established to take and implement decisions on behalf of the organization (ICLEI 2012c: 8). The supreme body of the ICLEI network is the *Council* that represents the network's overall membership. The Council is composed of several *Regional Executive Committees* representing different world regions. Each Regional Executive Committee appoints one member to the *Global Executive Committee*, which is the governing body of the network. The members of the Global Executive Committee appoint the *Management Committee* responsible for the network's technical affairs, and the *Secretary General* who serves as

ICLEI's *Chief Executive Officer*. The Secretary General is supported in his duties by ICLEI's *World Secretariat* consisting of 30 to 35 staff members (ICLEI 2012c: 12). In particular, the Secretary General represents the network at the intergovernmental level, including the UNFCCC conferences. Moreover, the Secretary General oversees the work of the network's different regional and national branches and takes care of ICLEI's strategic direction.

In the past two decades, ICLEI's organizational structure has been considerably expanded. While ICLEI started its operations with only two offices in 1990, today it comprises in addition to the World Secretariat eight regional secretariats in all continents of the world and four country offices in Canada, Japan, South Korea, and the United States (ICLEI 2013a). These branches cooperate closely with the World Secretariat and adjust the different projects of the network to the specific regional circumstances. Beyond that, in several countries, national campaigns for ICLEI's Cities for Climate Protection Program have been established to coordinate the various local activities undertaken by the network. Most interesting for the focus of this book is the close partnership between the national campaigns and their hosting national governments. The different national campaigns receive significant financial support from national governmental bodies (Bulkeley and Betsill 2003: 51). As recognized by various scholars, without these financial flows from the central government to the local level, many ICLEI members were not able to develop and implement climate projects in their communities (e.g. Betsill and Bulkeley 2007). This point is of great importance for the analysis in this chapter and will be taken up and discussed in more detail in the following sections.

Perception in the literature

Scholars have come to different conclusions about ICLEI's role in global climate governance. On the one hand, authors highlight the achievements of the various initiatives launched by the ICLEI network. For instance, Gard Lindseth considers ICLEI's Cities for Climate Protection Program 'a success because the network managed to extend itself and cities have taken up the idea of climate change protection work' (Lindseth 2004: 330). In a similar vein, a number of scholars emphasize that the member cities and municipalities of the ICLEI network have undergone a learning process, which enables them to produce significant co-benefits from climate change policies (e.g. Bulkeley and Betsill 2003; Campbell 2009; Nakamura, Elder, and Mori 2010). Moreover, authors acknowledge that the different projects undertaken by ICLEI members have, at least in some countries including Australia and the United States, led to modest reductions of GHG emissions (e.g. Kousky and Schneider 2003; Betsill and Bulkeley 2007; Bulkeley *et al.* 2011).

On the other hand, authors point to the limitations of the activities undertaken by the ICLEI network. Several scholars argue that cities and municipalities have only limited responsibilities in key sectors that are relevant for climate change mitigation and adaptation policies (e.g. Collier 1997; DeAngelo and Harvey 1998; Schreurs 2008). These authors state that the GHG emission reductions achieved by ICLEI members are often only a by-product of measures that were actually implemented to serve more urgent local needs. More specifically, they criticize that local governments merely redefine already existing policies as climate-related initiatives and do not go beyond the 'business-as-usual' scenario (e.g. Betsill 2001; Bulkeley and Betsill 2003; Lindseth 2004). Furthermore, different studies indicate that the ICLEI network faces considerable budgetary constraints and lacks the necessary capacities to launch effective programs and projects to address the problem of climate change (e.g. Betsill and Bulkeley 2007; Kern and Alber 2008; Kern and Bulkeley 2009). These studies suggest that transnational city networks operating in the policy domain of climate change strongly rely on external funding, especially from national governments and international institutions. While these scholarly assessments are taken as an important starting point, this book puts forward the argument that ICLEI's role in global climate governance cannot adequately be evaluated in isolation from the international climate regime. Therefore, the remainder of the present case study examines the interrelationship between the ICLEI network and the intergovernmental level.

Conceptual assumptions and theoretical expectations

After this overview of ICLEI's main initiatives, organizational structure, and perception in the literature, the following sections connect the case study to the analytical framework of this book. In the research design, I formulated three conceptual assumptions regarding the interrelationship between transnational governance arrangements and existing modes of inter-state cooperation. These perspectives will now be applied to the case of ICLEI's interplay with the intergovernmental level. The first conceptual assumption portrays a *conflictive relationship* between transnational climate initiatives and the international climate regime. It suggests that transnational governance arrangements depart from the ultimate objective and basic principles of the UNFCCC and weaken the norms and rules stipulated in international climate agreements. Hence, in the particular case analyzed here, I would expect that the ICLEI network pursues its own agenda and aims to position transnational city networks concerned with the problem of climate change as alternative governance arrangements to multilateral treaty-making. The second conceptual assumption portrays a *complementary relationship* between transnational climate initiatives and the international climate regime. It implies that the emergence of transnational governance arrangements leads to a division of responsibilities between sub- and non-state actors and the UNFCCC, thereby strengthening the norms and rules set out in international climate agreements. Accordingly, in the present case study, I would expect that the ICLEI network helps implement the rules and procedures agreed upon at the intergovernmental level and strives for a close collaboration with existing modes of inter-state cooperation. And the third conceptual assumption portrays a *dependency relationship* between transnational climate initiatives and the international climate regime. It supposes that transnational governance arrangements are a side issue to the UNFCCC process and rely on the norms and rules anchored in international climate agreements. Consequently, in the case study in this chapter, I would expect that the ICLEI network remains largely dependent on the international regulatory framework to address the problem of climate change at the local level. As stated above, these conceptual assumptions and theoretical expectations guide the following analysis and help identify relevant empirical findings (see Table 4.1). At the end of the case study, I revert to this analytical framework and derive conclusions for the theoretical debate on the concept of authority in global climate governance.

ICLEI's central fields of activity

The examination of ICLEI's interplay with the international climate regime is structured around three central fields of activity through which the ICLEI network aims to achieve its goals. At first, I examine the different initiatives that the ICLEI network has undertaken in the past few years to encourage local governments to tackle climate change. Then, I study the different strategies employed by the ICLEI network to direct its constituents towards the overall network goals. Finally, I focus the analysis on the involvement of the ICLEI network in the UNFCCC conferences.

ICLEI's initiatives in the issue area of climate change

In the past two decades, the ICLEI network has launched various initiatives aimed at addressing climate change at the local level. The first project carried out by ICLEI was the Urban CO_2 Reduction Project. Based on the experience gained from this project, ICLEI started the Cities for Climate Protection Program,

Table 4.1 Conceptual assumptions and theoretical expectations for the empirical analysis of the relationship between the ICLEI network and the international climate regime

Conceptual assumptions	*The ICLEI network: Theoretical expectations*
Conflictive relationship	The ICLEI network pursues its own agenda and aims to position transnational city networks concerned with the problem of climate change as alternative governance arrangements to multilateral treaty-making
Complementary relationship	The ICLEI network helps implement the rules and procedures agreed upon at the intergovernmental level and strives for a close collaboration with existing modes of inter-state cooperation
Dependency relationship	The ICLEI network remains to a large extent dependent on the international regulatory framework to address the problem of climate change at the local level

conceived as one of the most prominent initiatives undertaken by a transnational city network to mitigate climate change. More recent global initiatives started by the ICLEI network include the *Global Protocol for Community-Scale* GHG *Emissions* and the *Carbonn* [sic] *Cities Climate Registry*. These two projects are illustrative of ICLEI's current approach towards the introduction of self-regulatory instruments for local governments. The following sections analyze the relationship between these different initiatives and the intergovernmental level.

THE URBAN CO_2 REDUCTION PROJECT

Shortly after its foundation, ICLEI launched the Urban CO_2 Reduction Project in 1991, which brought together seven cities and counties from the United States and Canada, six cities from Western Europe, and one city from Turkey.[2] This project, which ran until 1993, was designed to 'develop comprehensive local strategies to reduce greenhouse gas emissions and quantification methods to support such strategies' (ICLEI 1997). The project was funded by the United States Environmental Protection Agency, the City of Toronto, as well as different private foundations, and comprised a relatively small budget of about US$ 300,000 per year (Lambright, Changnon, and Harvey 1996: 465). The key player in the Urban CO_2 Reduction Project was the City of Toronto, which had already passed a resolution in 1990 committing itself to reduce its GHG emissions by 20 percent compared to 1988 levels by 2005 (Harvey 1993). The City of Toronto, which hosted ICLEI's World Secretariat from 1991 to 2009, also took the lead role in defining the aims of the project.

The Urban CO_2 Reduction Project was based on the idea to exchange information and discuss mutual problems and solutions for reducing GHG emissions through a series of six workshops (ICLEI 1993a: 16). Moreover, the project urged the 14 members to adopt individual action plans with concrete GHG reduction targets. In particular, the participating local governments were expected to commit to reducing their CO_2 emissions from energy use within their area of influence by 10 to 20 percent (Lambright, Changnon, and Harvey 1996: 465). Despite its relatively small scope, the project was considered a very successful pilot initiative for tackling climate change at the local level (Betsill 2001). Most interesting for the focus of this book is the fact that nation-states had at that time not yet agreed on binding targets for GHG emission reductions. Hence, the different local governments that participated in the Urban CO_2 Reduction Project adopted the climate change mitigation measures in the absence of an international agreement that required national governments to reduce GHG emissions.

THE CITIES FOR CLIMATE PROTECTION PROGRAM

In early 1993, discussions among local government representatives involved in the Urban CO_2 Reduction Project raised the concern that ICLEI should launch a follow-up project to broaden the efforts undertaken by urban actors to mitigate climate change (ICLEI 1993a: 17). As a result, ICLEI established the Cities for

Climate Protection Program 'to strengthen local governments' ability to develop and implement municipal energy policies that reduce local emissions of greenhouse gases' (ICLEI 1993b: 2). At the beginning, the goal of this program was to set a certain reduction target for all member cities. Soon after the program had been established, however, it became clear that this goal could not be realized because many members did not receive sufficient support from their central governments to undertake local climate actions. The program's approach was therefore altered and concrete GHG emission reduction requirements were abandoned 'in favor of locally legitimated targets for the purpose of attracting broader membership' (Toly 2008: 350). This explains the rapid growth of the Cities for Climate Protection Program in the past two decades.

Instead of demanding intensive commitments from its members, the ICLEI network provided a support framework for cities, municipalities, and other urban actors around the world to cope with the problem of climate change. In particular, ICLEI developed a Five-Milestone Methodology meant to guide local governments when dealing with climate-related issues in their communities (van Staden and Klas 2010: 101–102). Using these five milestones, various local governments throughout the world have taken various measures to reduce their GHG emissions, mainly by decreasing energy consumption, introducing low-carbon technologies, and converting waste to energy (ICLEI 2006). Different scholars have shown that the Cities for Climate Protection Program has been influential in the development of local climate change mitigation policies in several countries (e.g. Holgate 2007; Parker and Rowlands 2007; Romero Lankao 2007). For instance, according to the Oceania Regional Secretariat of the ICLEI network, the Cities for Climate Protection Program has resulted in the reduction of about 18 million tons of GHG emissions in Australia from 1998 to 2008 (ICLEI 2008a: 5). The United States is also often cited as a prominent example of a country in which ICLEI's Cities for Climate Protection Program has encouraged numerous local governments to adopt climate change mitigation and adaptation measures, despite the lack of national leadership (e.g. Gore and Robinson 2009: 41). In recent years, the ICLEI network has moreover sought to integrate local climate efforts into *Nationally Appropriate Mitigation Actions*[3] undertaken by emerging economies and developing countries to reduce GHG emissions (ICLEI 2009c). This underscores that the member cities and municipalities of the ICLEI network have implemented climate policies leading to quantifiable GHG emission reductions. These GHG emission reductions were partly realized before the Kyoto Protocol came into force and have also been achieved in countries without binding emission reduction targets (ICLEI 2010b).

Despite these successes, different scholars contend that the GHG emission reductions attained at the local level are in fact at best fairly modest (e.g. Betsill 2001; Kousky and Schneider 2003; Kern and Bulkeley 2009). Concrete figures are rarely published and it is therefore difficult to ascertain the exact amount of GHG emissions reduced or avoided through the measures supported by the ICLEI network. According to ICLEI's Global Progress Report published in 2006, the total annual GHG emission reductions achieved by local governments participating in the Cities for Climate Protection Program add up to around 60 million tons of

GHG emissions (ICLEI 2006). This amount is only a small fraction of the approximately 49.5 billion tons of GHGs that are emitted globally each year (IPCC 2014b). Moreover and most relevant for the analysis in this book, it is clear that local climate projects largely depend on governmental funding (Bulkeley and Betsill 2003: 184; Kern and Bulkeley 2009: 324; van Staden and Klas 2010: 104). Cities and municipalities often lack the financial resources, technical capacity, and staff to develop and implement local climate policies. This is reflected in statements given in personal conversations with local government representatives from Belo Horizonte in Brazil, Buenos Aires in Argentina, Kaohsiung City in Taiwan, Nane in India, and Tokyo in Japan (who are all members of ICLEI's Cities for Climate Protection Program). They stated that they are highly dependent on funding from their national governments to undertake climate projects at the local level in key sectors, such as energy management, public transportation, and land use planning.[4] In particular, and most importantly, the local government representatives noticed that due to the lack of an international regulatory framework that obligates national governments to significantly reduce their GHG emissions, they do not receive sufficient funds from the central government or international institutions to carry out large-scale climate projects in their communities.

SELF-REGULATORY INSTRUMENTS FOR LOCAL GOVERNMENTS

In recent years, the ICLEI network has started a number of projects to record and publicize the GHG emission reductions achieved by local governments around the world. A first initiative of global reach in this regard is the Global Protocol for Community-Scale Greenhouse Gas Emissions. This initiative grew out of an earlier initiative launched by ICLEI in 2008 and was informed by a number of other accounting standards for measuring GHG emissions, including the *IPCC 2006 Guidelines for National Greenhouse Gas Inventories* (van Staden and Klas 2010: 105–106). In May 2012, the ICLEI network, together with the C40 Group and in collaboration with the World Resources Institute, launched the Protocol at a side-event during the Bonn climate change conference organized by the UNFCCC Secretariat (C40 Group, ICLEI, and World Resources Institute 2012b). The Protocol is designed to assist cities, municipalities, and other urban actors in quantifying their GHG emissions. In particular, it seeks to 'help local governments (…) accelerate their emission reduction activities whilst meeting the needs of climate financing, national monitoring and reporting requirements' (ICLEI 2011b). A second initiative of global reach in this regard is the Carbonn Cities Climate Registry established by the ICLEI network in 2011. The Registry aims to facilitate local GHG emissions accounting and encourage local governments to regularly report on their GHG reduction measures (ICLEI 2011a). This initiative supports local governments throughout the world to deliver information about their GHG emission reduction commitments, the performance of their GHG emissions and their climate change mitigation and adaptation actions (Lefèvre 2012). The different local climate measures are registered and published by the *Bonn Center for Local Climate Action and Reporting* that works closely with the

UNFCCC Secretariat in order to establish a credible worldwide database of the different actions undertaken by local governments to address climate change (ICLEI 2010b: 78).

These two initiatives, which are still in their initial stages, supplement each other and should enhance the quality of information about local climate actions. While the Global Protocol for Community-Scale Greenhouse Gas Emissions provides a standard for local GHG inventories, the Carbonn Cities Climate Registry collects and promulgates the efforts undertaken by urban actors. Interestingly, both initiatives were explicitly developed and designed to scale up the financial support for local climate actions (ICLEI 2012a). The idea is that if local governments demonstrate their ability to undertake measurable, reportable, and verifiable climate change mitigation measures, national governments will be more inclined to finance local climate actions because they can integrate these actions into their national climate programs. Moreover, when the GHG emission reductions achieved by local governments become officially recognized, local climate projects can more easily be incorporated into a global market-based instrument. Hence, these measures undertaken by the ICLEI network seek to enhance the ability of its member cities and municipalities to access the sources of international carbon financing (ICLEI 2011b). However, this strategy will only succeed if a wide-ranging international regulatory framework is adopted, which compels national governments and incentivizes private companies to reduce GHG emissions. In a personal interview, ICLEI's Secretary General, Gino Van Begin, highlighted the importance of a more ambitious international climate agreement to unlock the financial support needed for local climate actions:

> It is not easy to overcome the financial gap when undertaking projects at the local level to mitigate emissions. (...) In fact, it is not possible without the support of the central government. This is why we need a future climate regime that integrates all major economies of the world to generate financial flows from the central government to the ground where the action is taking place.[5]

This underscores the fact that the recent projects undertaken by the ICLEI network are clearly oriented towards the intergovernmental level and aim at increasing the abilities of local governments to access funding from national governments and private companies for their local climate actions.

ICLEI's strategies of internal governing

As indicated above, the ICLEI network has used different internal governing strategies to direct its members towards achieving the overall network goals. These strategies include information sharing, capacity building and implementation, as well as different modes of self-regulation, such as standard-setting and benchmarking. The following sections examine the relation of these strategies to the intergovernmental level.

INFORMATION SHARING

Since its foundation, information sharing has been a key element of ICLEI's activities with regard to the issue of climate change (Collier 1997; Betsill and Bulkeley 2004; Kern and Bulkeley 2009). The ICLEI network has used different means to provide information about local climate actions and to facilitate the exchange of experiences among local governments dealing with the problem of climate change. In particular, ICLEI has organized numerous networking events, disseminated case studies of different local climate measures through publications, and compiled a sample of 'best' or 'good' practices on its website (ICLEI 2013d). Among these information-sharing activities, the various workshops and conferences convened by the ICLEI network are conceived as particularly important components. At these events, ICLEI has highlighted especially successful local climate actions and repeatedly emphasized the co-benefits associated with local climate change mitigation efforts, such as economic savings, better air quality, and improved liveability of communities. In the past few years, these events have often taken place in parallel to the UNFCCC conferences (ICLEI 2010c). The ICLEI network uses these events as a forum to present its different climate-related activities to a large audience, including representatives from national delegations, international institutions, other local government organizations, and the media. In this way, ICLEI also seeks to attract new members and, more generally, highlights the role played by local governments in global climate governance.

CAPACITY BUILDING AND IMPLEMENTATION

To support the different local climate actions, the ICLEI network provides several services to its members. These services range from training courses on specific issues related to climate change mitigation and adaptation, to technical assistance through expert teams, and small grants that are occasionally awarded to certain member cities and municipalities for specific climate projects (Kousky and Schneider 2003: 363; Betsill and Bulkeley 2004: 478; Kern and Bulkeley 2009: 321). Because of the limited financial capacities of many local governments to develop and implement climate projects at the local level, resource provision constitutes a critical means through which transnational city networks can steer their constituents towards the overall network goals (Andonova, Betsill, and Bulkeley 2009: 64). The ICLEI network usually does not directly finance climate projects in member cities and municipalities due to its limited budget. Rather, ICLEI has assisted its members when they applied for funds from external sources, such as the European Commission, various international institutions, and national governments (Kern and Bulkeley 2009: 321; Bulkeley and Newell 2010: 61–62). However, the application procedure for receiving funds from external donors is relatively complicated and resource-intensive. Accordingly, this service provided by the ICLEI network benefits essentially only those local governments that already possess strong expertise, management skills, and financial capacities (Kern and Bulkeley 2009: 321). In addition, and most important for the focus of this case study, in the absence of an international regulatory framework that stipulates national governments to meet a certain GHG emission reduction target, national and international funding for local climate projects will arguably remain uncertain and scarce.

SELF-REGULATION

Until recently, the ICLEI network has made only limited use of regulative functions to steer its members towards the overall network goals. Basically, ICLEI's regulatory strategy was constrained to the establishment of the Five-Milestone Methodology. As already mentioned above, ICLEI's Cities for Climate Protection Program is based around five milestones of progress that will guide local governments in undertaking measures to mitigate climate change. The methodology comprises the following steps: (i) conducting a GHG emissions inventory, (ii) adopting a GHG emission reduction target, (iii) developing a local action plan, (iv) implementing policies and measures, and (v) monitoring and verifying the results (ICLEI 2012b). Local governments participating in the Cities for Climate Protection Program throughout the world have employed these guidelines for climate change mitigation actions. In 2006, ICLEI's European Secretariat further developed the methodology and also applied the five milestones to the issue of climate change adaptation (van Staden and Klas 2010: 101–102). In general, rather than constituting hard rules for its members, the Five-Milestone Methodology is conceived as a tool to assist its members in their efforts to address climate change at the local level. In particular, the milestones help local governments 'to understand how municipal decisions affect energy use and how these decisions can be used to mitigate global climate change while improving community quality of life' (van Staden and Klas 2010: 101). Hence, members of ICLEI's Cities for Climate Protection Program that do not comply with certain steps of the Five-Milestone Methodology do not have to fear exclusion from the network. While the methodology has been used by many local governments across the world, it has generally been considered rather ineffective in encouraging cities and municipalities to plan and conduct ambitious climate actions (Bulkeley and Betsill 2003; Allman, Fleming, and Wallace 2004; Lindseth 2004).

In response, the ICLEI network has strengthened its instruments for the self-regulation of local governments in the past few years. The most prominent examples have already been described above, namely the Global Protocol for Community-Scale Greenhouse Gas Emissions and the Carbonn Cities Climate Registry. As indicated in the previous section, however, these instruments were not primarily established by the ICLEI network to induce local governments to undertake more ambitious policies that reduce GHG emissions or to increase the compliance of local governments with their commitments. Instead, these instruments aimed at raising the global level of ambition to reduce GHG emissions (ICLEI 2012a). In a personal interview, ICLEI's *Cities Climate Center Manager* Yunus Arikan stated that these instruments were developed in the first place to push the intergovernmental level towards a far-reaching international climate agreement and to enhance the ability of local governments to access funding from national governments and private companies for their climate actions. More specifically, he noticed: 'We hope that national governments become inspired by our activities and to some extent encouraged to undertake measures and agree on more stringent regulations at the multilateral level.'[6] Without an international regulatory framework, he continued, not enough funds are delivered from national governments and international institutions to local actors enabling them to develop and implement projects that avert the problem of climate change.

The ICLEI network at the UNFCCC conferences

The ICLEI network has been constantly involved in the annual Conferences of the Parties to the UNFCCC and the various related events, which have been open for non-governmental organizations since the mid-1990s. Moreover, it serves as the focal point of the LGMA constituency and is one of the most active observer organizations registered with the UNFCCC Secretariat. In the following sections, I examine key elements of ICLEI's involvement in the UNFCCC process.

ICLEI AS OBSERVER AND FOCAL POINT IN THE UNFCCC PROCESS

The ICLEI network was officially accredited as an observer organization under the UNFCCC in the early 1990s and already attended the first Conference of the Parties to the UNFCCC held in Berlin in 1995. In subsequent years, ICLEI participated in basically all annual Conferences of the Parties to the UNFCCC as well as in numerous workshops and meetings organized by the UNFCCC Secretariat. As the official focal point of the LGMA constituency, the ICLEI network currently represents 17 local government organizations, which hold observer status under the UNFCCC (UNFCCC 2013). Over the past few years, the ICLEI network has actively lobbied for the official recognition of the role played by cities, municipalities, and other urban actors in global climate governance. For a long time, these efforts were not very successful. In fact, the local level has largely been neglected in the UNFCCC conferences. As stated by Bulkeley and Betsill, '[d]espite ICLEI's regular attendance and participation, neither the UNFCCC nor the *Kyoto Protocol* makes reference to the role of local authorities in mitigating climate change' (Bulkeley and Betsill 2003: 192, emphasis in original).

In recent years, the ICLEI network has further intensified its efforts towards the formal recognition of local governments in the UNFCCC process. For instance, the ICLEI network has made several interventions in plenary sessions of the Conferences of the Parties to the UNFCCC, in which it pointed to the unique position of local governments to address climate change (e.g. ICLEI 2008c; 2009d; 2010c). In addition, ICLEI has convened various informal meetings with influential individuals from the UNFCCC negotiation process and communicated its particular concerns to almost every national delegation (Lefèvre 2012: 578). As a result, at the 2010 Conference of the Parties to the UNFCCC held in Cancún, the UNFCCC Secretariat officially recognized for the first time the crucial role of local governments in addressing climate change and referred to cities as 'governmental stakeholders' (UNFCCC 2010). This was celebrated by the ICLEI network in an immediate press release as 'an important step in enabling cities to keep delivering real climate change action' (ICLEI 2010d).

ICLEI EVENTS

In parallel with the international climate negotiations under the UNFCCC, the ICLEI network has organized several events to bring together local government representatives from around the world. For instance, in 1995, 1997, and 2005, ICLEI hosted the so-called *Municipal Leaders' Summits on Climate Change*, which coincided with the Conferences of the Parties held in Berlin, Kyoto, and Montreal (ICLEI 2010b). On these occasions, cities, municipalities, and other urban actors produced declarations and statements, in which they laid out their positions and perspectives on the problem of climate change. Back-to-back with the 2007 and 2008 Conferences of the Parties held in Bali and Poznan, ICLEI convened the more informal *Local Government Climate Sessions* to contribute to the debate on a post-2012 international climate agreement (Zimmermann, Van Begin, and Vergara Cristobál 2010). And in 2009, ICLEI and the C40 Group jointly endorsed the *Copenhagen Climate Summit for Mayors*, which took place during the Conference of the Parties to the UNFCCC held in Copenhagen. At this event, ICLEI established a *Local Government Climate Lounge* that was designed as an advocacy base during the international climate negotiations to present successful local climate actions and to get in touch with representatives from national governments (ICLEI 2009a). According to ICLEI, '[t]hroughout these processes, ICLEI attracted thousands of local government delegations to the COP [Conference of the Parties] sessions, contributed to negotiations through submissions and interventions and facilitated effective involvement of the LGMA Constituency' (ICLEI 2010c). In addition to these parallel events taking place sometimes outside of the official remit of the UNFCCC, the ICLEI network organized numerous official side-events at UNFCCC conferences. In basically all these events, ICLEI highlighted the efforts undertaken by its members to mitigate and adapt to climate change and called for the adoption of more ambitious targets for nation-states to reduce their GHG emissions.

THE LOCAL GOVERNMENT CLIMATE ROADMAP

In 2007, ICLEI began to situate its activities at the UNFCCC conferences in a wider framework and joined a consortium of transnational city networks to set up the *Local Government Climate Roadmap* (ICLEI 2010b: 70).[7] This initiative was launched at the Conference of the Parties to the UNFCCC held in Bali and paralleled the international climate negotiations culminating in the adoption of the *Bali Action Plan* (UNFCCC 2007). The ICLEI network acted as a facilitator of the Roadmap, which was 'designed to be an accompanying process to the international negotiations leading up to COP [Conference of the Parties] 15 in Copenhagen, Denmark in December 2009, where the post-2012 (post-Kyoto) climate agreement shall be negotiated and hopefully adopted' (Zimmermann, Van Begin, and Vergara Cristobál 2010: 81). The *Local Government Climate Roadmap* comprises various elements of advocacy work undertaken by ICLEI and partner organizations (ICLEI 2010b: 70–71). One of the first steps taken by the consortium was the development of the *World Mayors and Local Governments Climate Protection Agreement*. This document calls for far-reaching GHG reduction commitments to be adopted by industrialized and developing countries (ICLEI *et al.* 2007). Another important step of the Roadmap was the *City Climate Catalogue* that was jointly launched by ICLEI and the City of Copenhagen in the run-up to the 2009 Conference of the Parties to the UNFCCC held in Copenhagen (ICLEI 2009b). This initiative was based on the collection of individual commitments from cities and municipalities around the world to reduce GHG emissions, mainly in the energy sector. ICLEI used these voluntary pledges by local governments to 'send a strong message to the United Nations, national governments and other important actors around the globe, showing the ambitious climate work of the world's communities' (van Staden and Klas 2010: 104–105).

In addition, as mentioned earlier, the ICLEI network prepared different contributions to the international climate negotiations, in which it urged the international community to raise the global ambition to mitigate climate change and stressed the need to involve cities more actively in the UNFCCC process (e.g. ICLEI 2010c; 2010b; 2011a). In an official submission to the international climate change conference in Copenhagen, the ICLEI network stated that 'despite the willingness, necessity and urgency of local mitigation and adaptation actions, cities and local authorities can not fulfil these tasks without the access to Best Available Technology and adequate financing opportunities' (ICLEI 2009d). Hence, while transnational city networks often position themselves as being capable of effectively dealing with the problem of climate change independently from the intergovernmental level, this statement aptly illustrates the fact that local governments very much rely on an international regulatory framework, which binds national governments to commit to a certain reduction target.

Summary

This chapter focused on the interrelationship between a transnational city network and the intergovernmental level in the policy domain of climate change. In this section, I return to the theoretical background and analytical framework of this book and summarize the main findings from the case study conducted in this chapter. Firstly, it can be stated that there is no indication that the activities undertaken by the ICLEI network conflict with the intergovernmental level. The ICLEI network neither pursues its own agenda separately from the UNFCCC process, nor does it aim to position transnational city networks as alternative governance arrangements to multilateral treaty-making. By contrast, the analysis indicates that the ICLEI network directs its activities very much to the UNFCCC process.

Secondly, a number of findings could be identified that suggest that the activities of the ICLEI network complement existing modes of inter-state cooperation. The case study in this chapter shows that the ICLEI network contributes to the implementation of the norms and rules stipulated in international climate agreements by developing local climate policies, which have led to quantifiable reductions of GHG emissions. Thereby, it is apparent that the ICLEI network helps achieve the national GHG emission reduction targets laid out in the Kyoto Protocol and the ultimate objectives of the UNFCCC. What is most interesting in this context is that the GHG emission reductions were partly realized before an international regulatory framework came into force and were also attained in countries without binding emission reduction obligations. Despite the fact that ICLEI members have accomplished only minor GHG emission reductions, local governments can accordingly be perceived as pioneers in the global response to climate change. In particular, local climate actions could make international climate agreements more attractive and feasible for national governments because they might integrate the GHG emission reductions attained at the local level into their national climate programs. However, the individual success stories of cities and municipalities in addressing climate change should not disguise the limited ability of most local governments to obtain tangible GHG emission reductions.

Thirdly, the case study also demonstrates that the climate-related activities undertaken by the ICLEI network are first and foremost oriented towards the intergovernmental level. The main reason for this is that the ICLEI members strongly depend on funds from their national governments and international institutions to implement climate projects in their communities. In the absence of an ambitious international climate agreement, national governments are not bound to climate change mitigation measures. Accordingly, national as well as international funding for local climate actions remains uncertain and scarce. As a result, in the past few years, the ICLEI network has focused its activities increasingly on raising the global level of ambition to reduce GHG emissions and pushed for a wide-ranging international climate agreement. Moreover, the ICLEI network has recently sought to enhance the ability of its constituents to access funds from global market-based instruments. These findings imply that the efforts undertaken by ICLEI members to address the problem of climate change at the local level are largely dependent on the existence of an international regulatory framework that obligates national governments and incentivizes private companies to reduce their GHG emissions. Thus, it can be argued that transnational city networks have only few opportunities to cope with the problem of climate change at the local level without the further evolution of the international climate regime (see Table 4.2).

Conclusions

The analysis in this chapter has underlined the fact that the ICLEI network plays an important role in global climate governance. It has been shown that the different activities undertaken by the ICLEI network have contributed to the implementation of the norms and rules stipulated in international climate agreements. The

Table 4.2 Main findings from the analysis of the relationship between the ICLEI network and the international climate regime

Conceptual assumptions	*The ICLEI network: Main findings*
Conflictive relationship	No indication
Complementary relationship	The ICLEI network contributes to the implementation of the norms and rules of the international climate regime by developing local climate policies, which have led to quantifiable GHG emission reductions
	These GHG emission reductions were partly realized before an international regulatory framework came into force and have also been achieved in countries without binding emission reduction obligations
Dependency relationship	The ICLEI members largely rely on external funding from their national governments and international institutions to implement climate projects in their communities
	In the absence of an ambitious international climate agreement, the financial support for local climate actions will remain uncertain and scarce
	The activities of the ICLEI network are hence first and foremost oriented towards the intergovernmental level in order to raise the global level of ambition

ICLEI network can hence be conceived as complementary to the international climate regime. Indeed, it is clear that to achieve significant GHG emission reductions, the involvement of all levels of government are required. In particular, the present case study suggests that the various climate actions undertaken by local governments might increase the confidence of national governments to adopt more ambitious GHG emission reduction commitments.

However, the investigation has also demonstrated that the effective operation of ICLEI's activities to tackle the problem of climate change relies heavily on the existence of an international regulatory framework created by nation-states at international climate change conferences. Most importantly, the members of the ICLEI network remain highly dependent on funding from their national governments and international institutions when they develop and implement projects to reduce GHG emissions at the local level. Without an adequate international regulatory framework, which compels nation-states to take action on climate change, local climate projects are not sufficiently funded. Hence, unless a wide-ranging international climate treaty is established by nation-states at the intergovernmental level, the ICLEI network has only a limited scope of action to address the problem of climate change. Based on this finding, transnational city networks can be regarded as important climate governance arrangements. Yet, their activities need to be underpinned by a far-reaching international climate agreement with GHG emission reduction obligations for nation-states that would trigger financial flows from national governments and international institutions to the local level.

Put in theoretical terms, it can be concluded that the ICLEI network performs various authoritative functions in global climate governance that formerly rested solely with national governments and international institutions. The ICLEI network has established concrete GHG emission reduction targets for local governments, developed standards for local GHG inventories, and introduced programs for the actual reporting of local climate actions. This implies that the ICLEI network exercises a certain degree of authority over its members. Nevertheless, the analysis in this chapter suggests that the growing role and function of transnational city networks in the policy domain of climate change does not generate a shift of authority in global climate governance away from multilateral treaty-making towards local governments. While transnational networks of cities and municipalities can indeed be regarded as increasingly important actors in climate politics, their emergence does on no account imply a weakening of existing modes of inter-state cooperation. In fact, the present case study has shown that the development of the ICLEI network does not challenge the authority of state-based forms of governance. Rather, the analysis has pointed out that the principles, norms, rules, and decision-making procedures agreed upon by nation-states in international climate negotiations have a substantial influence on local climate policies. Thus, this case study underscores the centrality of the international climate regime in the global response to climate change.

References

Acuto, Michele (2013). The New Climate Leaders. *Review of International Studies* 39 (4): 835–857.

Allman, Lee; Fleming, Paul; Wallace, Andrew (2004). The Progress of English and Welsh Local Authorities in Addressing Climate Change. *Local Environment* 9 (3): 271–283.

Amen, Mark; Toly, Noah J.; McCarney, Patricia L.; Segbers, Klaus, (eds). (2011). *Cities and Global Governance: New Sites for International Relations*. Farnham: Ashgate.

Andonova, Liliana B.; Betsill, Michele; Bulkeley, Harriet (2009). Transnational Climate Governance. *Global Environmental Politics* 9 (2): 52–73.

Arikan, Yunus (2011). Cities for Climate Protection (CCP) Campaign of ICLEI-Local Governments for Sustainability. In: Rosenzweig, Cynthia; Solecki, William D.; Hammer, Stephen A.; Mehrotra, Shagun. *Climate Change and Cities: First Assessment Report of the Urban Climate Change Research Network*. Cambridge, UK: Cambridge University Press, 101–102.

Bäckstrand, Karin (2008). Accountability of Networked Climate Governance: The Rise of Transnational Climate Partnerships. *Global Environmental Politics* 8 (3): 74–102.

Barber, Benjamin R. (2013). *If Mayors Ruled the World: Dysfunctional Nations, Rising Cities*. New Haven, CT: Yale University Press.

Betsill, Michele (2001). Mitigating Climate Change in US Cities: Opportunities and Obstacles. *Local Environment* 6 (4): 393–406.

Betsill, Michele; Bulkeley, Harriet (2004). Transnational Networks and Global Environmental Governance: The Cities for Climate Protection Program. *International Studies Quarterly* 48 (2): 471–493.

Betsill, Michele; Bulkeley, Harriet (2006). Cities and the Multilevel Governance of Global Climate Change. *Global Governance* 12 (2): 141–159.

Betsill, Michele; Bulkeley, Harriet (2007). Looking Back and Thinking Ahead: A Decade of Cities and Climate Change Research. *Local Environment* 12 (5): 447–456.

Brenner, Neil (1998). Global Cities, Glocal States: Global City Formation and State Territorial Restructuring in Contemporary Europe. *Review of International Political Economy* 5 (1): 1–37.

Bulkeley, Harriet (2010). Cities and the Governing of Climate Change. *Annual Review of Environment and Resources* 35: 229–253.

Bulkeley, Harriet; Betsill, Michele (2003). *Cities and Climate Change: Urban Sustainability and Global Environmental Governance*. London: Routledge.

Bulkeley, Harriet; Betsill, Michele (2005). Rethinking Sustainable Cities: Multilevel Governance and the 'Urban' Politics of Climate Change. *Environmental Politics* 14 (1): 42–63.

Bulkeley, Harriet; Newell, Peter (2010). *Governing Climate Change*. London: Routledge.

Bulkeley, Harriet; Schroeder, Heike; Janda, Katy; Zhao, Jimin; Armstrong, Andrea; Chu, Shu Yi; Ghosh, Shibani (2011). The Role of Institutions, Governance, and Urban Planning for Mitigation and Adaptation. In: Hoornweg, Daniel; Freire, Mila; Lee, Marcus J.; Bhada-Tata, Perinaz; Yuen, Belinda. *Cities and Climate Change: Responding to an Urgent Agenda*. Washington, DC: The World Bank, 125–159.

C40 Group (2013). *C40 Cities*. Available at: www.c40cities.org/c40cities (accessed January 4, 2013).

C40 Group; ICLEI; World Resources Institute (2012a). *Global Protocol for Community-Scale Greenhouse Gas Emissions (GPC): Pilot Version 1.0*.

C40 Group; ICLEI; World Resources Institute (2012b). *International Partners Relase Pilot Global Protocol for Community-Scale Greenhouse Gas Emissions. Press Release, May 14*. Bonn: ICLEI World Secretariat.

Campbell-Lendrum, Diarmid; Corvalán, Carlos (2007). Climate Change and Developing Country Cities: Implications for Environmental Health and Equity. *Journal of Urban Health* 84 (1): 109–117.

Campbell, Tim (2009). Learning Cities: Knowledge, Capacity and Competitiveness. *Habitat International* 33 (2): 195–201.

Campbell, Tim (2012). *Beyond Smart Cities: How Cities Network, Learn and Innovate*. Abingdon: Earthscan.

Campbell, Tim; Fuhr, Harald (2004a). Conclusions and Policy Lessons. In: Cambell, Tim; Fuhr, Harald. *Leadership and Innovation in Subnational Government: Case Studies from Latin America*. Washington, DC: World Bank, 433–450.

Campbell, Tim; Fuhr, Harald, (eds). (2004b). *Leadership and Innovation in Subnational Government: Case Studies from Latin America*. Washington, DC: The World Bank.

Climate Alliance (2013a). *Best Practice*. Available at: www.klimabuendnis.org/best-practice0.html (accessed January 4, 2013).

Climate Alliance (2013b). *Climate Cities Benchmark*. Available at: www.klimabuendnis.org/benchmark1.html?&L=2 (accessed January 23, 2013).

Climate Alliance (2013c). *Our Profile*. Available at: www.klimabuendnis.org/our_profile0.html?&L=0 (accessed January 3, 2013).

Clinton Climate Initiative (2013). *CCI in Partnership with the C40 Cities Climate Leadership Group*. Available at: www.clintonfoundation.org/main/our-work/by-initiative/clinton-climate-initiative/programs/c40-cci-cities.html (accessed January 17, 2013).

Collier, Ute (1997). Local Authorities and Climate Protection in the European Union: Putting Subsidiarity into Practice? *Local Environment* 2 (1): 39–57.

Corfee-Morlot, Jan; Kamal-Chaoui, Lamia; Donovan, Michael G.; Cochran, Ian; Robert, Alexis; Teasdale, Pierre-Jonathan (2009). *Cities, Climate Change and Multilevel Governance*. Paris: OECD Publishing.

Curtis, Simon (2011). Global Cities and the Transformation of the International System. *Review of International Studies* 37 (4): 1923–1947.

DeAngelo, Benjamin J.; Harvey, L. D. Danny (1998). The Jurisdictional Framework for Municipal Action to Reduce Greenhouse Gas Emissions: Case Studies from Canada, the USA and Germany. *Local Environment* 3 (2): 111–136.

Energy Cities (2013). *About: Association*. Available at: www.energy-cities.eu/ (accessed January 2, 2013).

European Commission (2012). *Mainstreaming Adaptation and Low Carbon Technology: DG CLIMA/C3/AW/J1 Ares (2012)*. Brussels: Directorate-General Climate Action.

Friedmann, John (2001). Intercity Networks in a Globalizing Era. In: Scott, Allen J. *Global City Regions: Trends, Theorym Policy*. Oxford: Oxford University Press, 119–136.

German Environment Ministry (2010). *Cities in Asia Develope Climate Sensitive Adaptation Plans*. Berlin: German Environment Ministry's International Climate Initiative.

Gore, Christopher; Robinson, Pamela (2009). Local Government Response to Climate Change: Our Last, Best Hope? In: Selin, Henrik; VanDeveer, Stacy D. *Changing Climates in North American Politics*. Cambridge, MA: MIT Press, 137–158.

Haas, Peter M. (1992). Introduction: Epistemic Communities and International Policy Coordination. *International Organization* 46 (1): 1–35.

Harvey, L. D. Danny (1993). Tackling Urban CO_2 Emissions in Toronto. *Environment* 35 (7): 16–44.

Hoffmann, Matthew (2011). *Climate Governance at the Crossroads: Experimenting With a Global Response After Kyoto*. Oxford: Oxford University Press.

Holgate, Claudia (2007). Factors and Actors in Climate Change Mitigation: A Tale of Two South African Cities. *Local Environment* 12 (5): 471–484.

Hoornweg, Daniel; Sugar, Lorraine; Gómez, Claudia Lorena Trejos (2011). Cities and Greenhouse Gas Emissions: Moving Forward. *Environment and Urbanization* 23 (1): 207–227.

ICLEI (1993a). *Biennial Report: 1991–1993*. Toronto: ICLEI World Secretariat.

ICLEI (1993b). *Cities for Climate Protection: An International Campaign to Reduce Urban Emissions of Greenhouse Gases*. Toronto: ICLEI World Secretariat.

ICLEI (1993c). *Findings and Implications From the Urban CO_2 Reduction Project*. Toronto: ICLEI World Secretariat.

ICLEI (1997). *Local Government Implementation of Climate Protection: Report to the United Nations*. Toronto: ICLEI World Secretariat.

ICLEI (2006). *ICLEI International Progress Report: Cities for Climate Protection*. Oakland, CA: ICLEI USA.

ICLEI (2008a). *Local Government Action on Climate Change: CCP Australia Measures Evaluation Report*. Melbourne: ICLEI Oceania.

ICLEI (2008b). *Local Government Climate Change Adaptation Toolkit*. Melbourne: ICLEI Oceania.

ICLEI (2008c). *Submission From ICLEI for Ideas and Proposals on Paragraph 1 of the Bali Action Plan Item 3 (a-e) of the Provisional Agenda, as Elements for a UNFCCC COP Decision*. Toronto, Canada: ICLEI World Secretariat.
ICLEI (2009a). *Base Camp at COP15: Local Government Climate Lounge. Press Release, November 3*. Toronto, Canada: ICLEI World Secretariat.
ICLEI (2009b). *City Climate Catalogue to Influence International Climate Negotiations. Press Release, February 3*. Toronto, Canada: ICLEI World Secretariat.
ICLEI (2009c). *Local Government Climate Roadmap. The Local Government Responses: Input to International Climate Negotiations for a Strong, Comprehensive and Global Agreement*. Toronto, Canada: ICLEI World Secretariat.
ICLEI (2009d). *Submission of ICLEI for Inclusion in the Negotiating Text of the Long-Term Cooperative Action under the Convention, April 24*. Toronto, Canada: ICLEI World Secretariat.
ICLEI (2010a). *8 Leading Cities and Counties Commit to Prepare for Climate Change Impacts by Participating in Nation's First Adaptation Program*. Oakland, CA: ICLEI USA.
ICLEI (2010b). *Cities in a Post-2012 Climate Policy Framework*. Bonn: ICLEI World Secretariat.
ICLEI (2010c). *Submission of ICLEI – Local Governments for Sustainability on Ways to Enhance the Engagement of Observer Organizations as Discussed in SBI32 Agenda Item 16.d with Respect to Para.19 Contained in Document FCCC/SBI/2010/L.21*. Bonn: ICLEI World Secretariat.
ICLEI (2010d). *UN Refers to Cities as Key Governmental Stakeholders Supporting Global Climate Action. Press Release, December 10*. Bonn: ICLEI World Secretariat.
ICLEI (2011a). *Cities Say: Urbanize the Climate Agenda. Press Release, December 5*. Bonn: ICLEI World Secretariat.
ICLEI (2011b). *Future Cities Need to be Resilient. Press Release, June 1*. Bonn: ICLEI World Secretariat.
ICLEI (2012a). *Carbonn Cities Climate Registry: Raising the Global Level of Ambition through Local Climate Action*. Bonn: Bonn Center for Local Climate Action and Reporting.
ICLEI (2012b). *Cities for Climate Protection Milestone Guide*. Oakland, CA: ICLEI USA.
ICLEI (2012c). *ICLEI: Corporate Report 2011/12*. Bonn: ICLEI World Secretariat.
ICLEI (2013a). *ICLEI Around the World*. Available at: www.iclei.org/iclei-global/iclei-around-the-world.html (accessed March 14, 2013).
ICLEI (2013b). *ICLEI Case Studies*. Available at: http://iclei.org/index.php?id=11546 (accessed January 4, 2013).
ICLEI (2013c). *ICLEI Global: Who We Are*. Available at: www.iclei.org/iclei-global/who-is-iclei.html (accessed March 14, 2013).
ICLEI (2013d). *Local Action Moves the World*. Available at: www.iclei.org/en/local-action.html (accessed March 12, 2013).
ICLEI (2013e). *Our Themes*. Available at: www.iclei.org/index.php?id=global-themes (accessed February 28, 2013).
ICLEI; World Mayors Council on Climate Change; UCLG; C40 Group (2007). *The World Mayors and Local Governments Climate Protection Agreement*. Toronto, Canada: ICLEI World Secretariat.
International Energy Agency (2008). *World Energy Outlook*. Paris: International Energy Agency.
IPCC (2014a). *Climate Change 2014. Impacts, Adaptation, and Vulnerability. Contribution of Working Group II to the Fifth Assessment Report of the Intergovernmental Panel on Climate Change*. Cambridge, UK: Cambridge University Press.

IPCC (2014b). *Climate Change 2014. Mitigation of Climate Change. Contribution of Working Group III to the Fifth Assessment Report of the Intergovernmental Panel on Climate Change.* Cambridge, UK: Cambridge University Press.

Kamal-Chaoui, Lamia; Robert, Alexis (2009). *Competitive Cities and Climate Change.* Paris: OECD Publishing.

Keck, Margaret E.; Sikkink, Kathryn (1998). *Activists Beyond Borders: Advocacy Networks in International Politics.* Ithaca, NY: Cornell University Press.

Keiner, Marco; Kim, Arley (2007). Transnational City Networks for Sustainability. *European Planning Studies* 15 (10): 1369–1395.

Kern, Kristine; Alber, Götelind (2008). Governing Climate Change in Cities: Modes of Urban Climate Governance in Multi-Level Systems. In: Organisation for Economic Co-operation and Development (OECD). *Competitive Cities and Climate Change: Proceedings of the OECD Conference, held in Milan from October 9–10.* Paris: OECD Publishing, 171–196.

Kern, Kristine; Bulkeley, Harriet (2009). Cities, Europeanization and Multi-level Governance: Governing Climate Change through Transnational Municipal Networks. *Journal of Common Market Studies* 47 (2): 309–332.

Kousky, Carlolyn; Schneider, Stephen H. (2003). Global Climate Policy: Will Cities Lead the Way? *Climate Policy* 3 (4): 359–372.

Kübler, Daniel; Piliutyte, Jolita (2007). Intergovernmental Relations and International Urban Strategies: Constraints and Opportunities in Multilevel Polities. *Environment and Planning* C 25 (3): 357–373.

Lambright, W. Henry; Changnon, Stanley A.; Harvey, L. D. Danny (1996). Urban Reactions to the Global Warming Issue: Agenda Setting in Toronto and Chicago. *Climatic Change* 34 (3–4): 463–478.

Lebel, Louis; Garden, Po; Banaticla, Ma. Regina N.; Lasco, Rodel D.; Contreras, Antonio; Mitra, A. P.; Sharma, Chhemendra; Nguyen, Hoang Tri; Ooi, Giok Ling; Sari, Agus (2007). Integrating Carbon Management into the Development Strategies of Urbanizing Regions in Asia: Implications of Urban Function, Form, and Role. *Journal of Industrial Ecology* 11 (2): 61–81.

Lee, Taedong (2013). Global Cities and Transnational Climate Change Networks. *Global Environmental Politics* 13 (1): 108–127.

Lee, Taedong; van de Meene, Susan (2012). Who Teaches and Who Learns? Policy Learning Through the C40 Cities Climate Network. *Policy Sciences* 45 (3): 199–220.

Lefèvre, Benoît (2012). Incorporating Cities into the Post-2012 Climate Change Agreements. *Environment and Urbanization* 24 (2): 575–595.

Lindseth, Gard (2004). The Cities for Climate Protection Campaign (CCPC) and the Framing of Local Climate Policy. *Local Environment* 9 (4): 325–336.

Nakamura, Hidenori; Elder, Mark; Mori, Hideyuki (2010). *Mutual Learning Through Asian Intercity Network Programmes for the Environment.* Kamiyamaguchi: Institute for Global Environmental Strategies.

Nye, Joseph S.; Keohane, Robert O. (1971). Transnational Relations and World Politics: An Introduction. *International Organization* 25 (3): 329–349.

Ostrom, Elinor (2010). Polycentric Systems for Coping with Collective Action and Global Environmental Change. *Global Environmental Change* 20 (4): 550–557.

Parker, Paul; Rowlands, Ian H. (2007). City Partners Maintain Climate Change Action Despite National Cuts: Residential Energy Efficiency Programme Valued at Local Level. *Local Environment* 12 (5): 505–517.

Pattberg, Philipp; Stripple, Johannes (2008). Beyond the Public and Private Divide: Remapping Transnational Climate Governance in the 21st Century. *International Environmental Agreements* 8 (4): 367–388.

Risse-Kappen, Thomas, (ed.). (1995). *Bringing Transnational Relations Back*. In: Non-State Actors, Domestic Structures, and International Institutions. Cambridge, UK: Cambridge University Press.

Risse, Thomas (2013). Transnational Actors and World Politics. In: Carlsnaes, Walter; Risse, Thomas; Simmons, Beth A. *Handbook of International Relations*. Los Angeles, CA: Sage, 426–452.

Román, Mikael (2010). Governing From the Middle: The C40 Cities Leadership Group. *Corporate Governance* 10 (1): 73–84.

Romero Lankao, Patricia (2007). How Do Local Governments in Mexico City Manage Global Warming. *Local Environment* 12 (5): 519–535.

Sassen, Saskia (1994). *Cities in a World Economy*. Thousand Oaks, CA: Pine Forge Press.

Sassen, Saskia, (ed.). (2002). *Global Networks, Linked Cities*. New York: Routledge.

Schreurs, Miranda A. (2008). From the Bottom-Up: Local and Subnational Climate Change Policies. *The Journal of Environment & Development* 17 (4): 343–355.

Schroeder, Heike; Lovell, Heather (2012). The Role of Non-Nation-State Actors and Side Events in the International Climate Negotiations. *Climate Policy* 12 (1): 23–37.

Scott, Allen John, (ed.). (2001). *Global City-Regions: Trends, Theory, Policy*. Oxford: Oxford University Press.

Stern, Nicholas H. (2007). *The Economics of Climate Change: The Stern Review*. Cambridge, UK: Cambridge University Press.

Taylor, Peter J. (2004). *World City Network: A Global Urban Analysis*. London: Routledge.

Toly, Noah J. (2008). Transnational Municipal Networks in Climate Politics: From Global Governance to Global Politics. *Globalizations* 5 (3): 341–356.

UCLG (2013). *Organization: About UCLG*. Available at: www.uclg.org/en/organisation/about (accessed January 3, 2013).

UNFCCC (2007). *Report of the Conference of the Parties on Its Thirteenth Session, held in Bali from December 3 to December 15, 2007*. FCCC/CP/2007/6. Bonn: UNFCCC Secretariat.

UNFCCC (2010). *Report of the Conference of the Parties on Its Sixteenth Session, held in Cancun from November 29 to December 10, 2010. Addendum: Part Two: Action Taken by the Conference of the Parties at Its Sixteenth Session*. FCCC/CP/2010/7/Add.2. Bonn: UNFCCC Secretariat.

UNFCCC (2013). *Parties & Observers: Admitted* NGO. Available at: http://maindb.unfccc.int/public/ngo.pl (accessed February 5, 2013).

UNFCCC (2014). *FOCUS: Mitigation – NAMAs, Nationally Appropriate Mitigation Actions*. Available at: http://unfccc.int/focus/mitigation/items/7172.php (accessed August 1, 2014).

United Nations (1992). *Agenda 21: Earth Summit – The United Nations Program of Action from Rio*. New York: United Nations Department of Public Information.

United Nations Department of Economic and Social Affairs (2012). *World Urbanization Prospects: The 2011 Revision*. New York: United Nations.

United Nations Habitat (2011). *Cities and Climate Change: Global Report on Human Settlements 2011*. London: Earthscan.

United Nations Population Fund (2007). *State of World Population 2007: Unleashing the Potential of Urban Growth*. New York: United Nations Population Fund.

van Staden, Maryke; Klas, Christine (2010). ICLEI's Support for Local Climate Action: A Selection of Tools. In: van Staden, Maryke; Musco, Francesco. *Local Governments and Climate Change*. Dordrecht: Springer, 99–107.

World Commission on Environment and Development (1987). *Our Common Future*. Oxford: Oxford University Press.

Zimmermann, Monika; Van Begin, Gino; Vergara Cristobál, Irene (2010). The International Local Government Climate Roadmap. In: van Staden, Maryke; Musco, Francesco. *Local Governments and Climate Change*. Dordrecht: Springer, 79–89.

Notes

1 Numerous authors have analyzed transnational networks in the past two decades. For a recent overview, see the handbook article by Thomas Risse (Risse 2013).

2 The participating cities and counties were Ankara (Turkey), Bologna (Italy), Copenhagen (Denmark), Chula Vista (United States), Dade County (United States), Denver (United States), Hanover (Germany), Helsinki (Finland), Minneapolis (United States), Portland (United States), Saarbrücken (Germany), Saint Paul (United States), Toronto (Canada), and Toronto Metropolitan (Canada) (ICLEI 1993c).

3 Nationally Appropriate Mitigation Actions were adopted at the 2007 Conference of the Parties to the UNFCCC held in Bali as a set of certain climate policies to be implemented by national governments of emerging economies and developing countries on a voluntary basis with support of industrialized countries (UNFCCC 2014).

4 Personal interviews conducted on December 6, 2012 with Huey-Por Chang, Kaohsiung City, Taiwan; Nancy Lago, Buenos Aires, Argentina; Yuko Nishida, Tokyo Metropolitan Government, Japan; Rodrigo Perpétuo, Belo Horizonte, Brazil; and Sunil Pote, Thane Municipal Corporation, India, during the 18th Conference of the Parties to the UNFCCC held in Doha from November 26 to December 8, 2012.

5 Personal interview conducted on December 5, 2012 with Gino Van Begin, *ICLEI's Secretary General*, during the 18th Conference of the Parties to the UNFCCC held in Doha from November 26 to December 8, 2012.

6 Personal interview conducted on December 4, 2012 with Yunus Arikan, *ICLEI's Cities Climate Center Manager*, during the 18th Conference of the Parties to the UNFCCC held in Doha from November 26 to December 8, 2012.

7 The transnational city networks that started the Local Government Climate Roadmap were the C40 Group, ICLEI, Metropolis, UCLG, and the World Mayors Council on Climate Change (Zimmermann, Van Begin, and Vergara Cristobál 2010).

5 Private certification schemes

The Gold Standard for Carbon Offsets

Overview

Private certification schemes are a relatively new phenomenon in global affairs. Until the 1980s, standard-setting was still the almost exclusive domain of nation-states or governmental bodies. Yet, in the past two decades, we have witnessed the development of a great variety of private labels in global policy-making (Peters, Koechlin, and Fenner Zinkernagel 2009). These labels have emerged in several policy domains of world politics and now exist for numerous industries and commodities. They can, for instance, be found in the textile industry, the building sector, the food production and processing industry, the tourism sector, as well as in the forestry and fishery sectors (e.g. Font 2002; Bartley 2003; Gulbrandsen 2005; Raynolds, Murray and Heller 2007; Pérez-Lombard *et al.* 2009). In general, certification schemes define social and environmental standards for responsible corporate behavior and practices. By accepting and employing the standards of a certain certification scheme, corporations can enhance their credibility and showcase a particular social and environmental commitment to their customers and investors. In the absence of governmental regulations, certification is a voluntary process that corporations undergo to promote the quality of their goods and services. While the certification process usually accrues additional costs for corporations, the logic behind their participation in private certification schemes is that customers and investors pay a premium price for certified products. One of the most prominent examples of private certification schemes is the *International Fairtrade Certification Mark*. This standard-setting mechanism can be seen 'as an innovative certification and labeling initiative, which harnesses the power of the market to address social and environmental problems exacerbated by conventional global markets' (Taylor, Murray, and Raynolds 2005: 199). In the past few years, various similar initiatives have emerged in global environmental governance, such as the *Forest Stewardship Council*, the *Marine Stewardship Council*, the *Rainforest Alliance*, *EKOenergy*, and the *ISO 14001 Standard*.

The proliferation of private certification schemes in global environmental policy-making was caused by different factors (cf. O'Neill 2009: 178). One factor is that a number of environmental non-governmental organizations have broadened their strategies in recent years. They no longer only use protests to target harmful business performances, but have begun to collaborate with the business sector to improve the environmental standards applied by corporations. Another factor is that corporations increasingly seek to position themselves as environmentally sensitive producers. By adopting a green reputation, they aim at exploring new markets and reach new consumer groups. A third factor is that the international political context has been lately favorable for the emergence of private certification schemes. This became evident at the 2002 *World Summit on Sustainable Development* held in Johannesburg, which laid the foundation for various so-called *Type 2* partnerships for sustainable development, including numerous certification and labeling schemes (e.g. Glasbergen 2007).

Drawing on Ronnie Lipschutz and Cathleen Fogel, three different types of certification schemes can be distinguished: first-, second-, and third-party certification (cf. Lipschutz and Fogel 2002: 134). Under first-party certification, the most common and simplistic approach, the corporations themselves make claims about their product and develop their own quality standards. Since these claims are not verified, customers and investors have to rely on the corporation's reputation to evaluate the environmental soundness of the product. Second-party certification involves industry or trade associations, which formulate certain guidelines and establish an industry or sector-wide label promoting the quality of the product. The industry or trade associations require the respective corporations to adhere to the standards and sometimes also to submit reports on their performance. Accordingly individual corporations will not have a competitive advantage if they meet the industry or sector-specific standards. Finally, as the name implies, third-party certification is carried out by an independent body, often an environmental non-governmental organization or specialized auditing agency. In contrast to second-party certification, in this type of certification scheme the certifying entity usually develops its own guidelines that the producer has to meet in order to use the particular label. In many of these schemes, the independent certifier also conducts audits, and monitors the corporations' compliance with the defined standards. Obviously, third-party certification is the most credible and widely accepted type of certification scheme and has attracted great attention among scholars and policy-makers concerned with global environmental governance.

While classical approaches to international politics have not shown much interest in private certification schemes, several authors have recently taken up this topic and begun to analyze privately created standards in world politics. These authors focus on different aspects. For instance, some scholars have traced and compared the evolution of private standards in different policy domains of global affairs (Djelic and Sahlin-Andersson 2006; Büthe 2010; Büthe and Mattli 2011). Others have studied more theoretical matters, such as the accountability and legitimacy of private standard-setters (Bernstein and Cashore 2004; Chan and Pattberg 2008; Wheatley 2009), the rapid increase in private labeling initiatives in certain sectors (Bartley 2003), or the relation between private regulatory systems and traditional forms of public regulation (Mayer and Gereffi 2010). Still another group of authors have examined the impact and effectiveness of private certification schemes that have developed over the past decades (e.g. Clapp 1998; Auld, Gulbrandsen, and McDermott 2008; Marx and Cuypers 2010).

In recent years, several private certification schemes have also emerged in the subject area of climate change. Basically, these privately created standards help measure and manage the GHG emissions of individual corporations. While the range of private certification schemes in global climate governance is relatively broad, the vast majority of private standards has been developed for carbon markets, or more specifically, for carbon offset markets (Green 2013: 10–11). Therefore, this chapter focuses on this particular type of private standards. In general, two forms of carbon offset markets can be distinguished: the *compliance* market and the *voluntary* market for carbon offsets (Lovell 2010). In the compliance carbon offset market, better known as the *Clean Development Mechanism*, industrialized countries with GHG emission reduction obligations can meet their targets by investing in climate change mitigation projects in developing countries or emerging economies. In the voluntary carbon offset market, corporations, environmental groups, and individual consumers purchase GHG emission reductions mainly to highlight their environmental awareness and commitment. In these markets, private certification schemes provide standards for measuring the GHG emissions that are reduced or avoided through carbon offset projects. In some instances, they also set guidelines for the evaluation of projects in terms of their overall environmental or social impact. These so-called carbon offset standards are based on relatively complex methodologies because GHG emission reductions are an intangible commodity, which cannot easily be traded. Or, as Hoffmann has put it, 'in contrast to traditional commodities – minerals, grains, livestock, and so on – nothing tangible is being produced or changing hands. Instead what is changing hands are promises and permissions' (Hoffmann 2011: 125). Private carbon offset standards take on the difficult task of credibly measuring and certifying reduced or avoided GHG emissions and potential co-benefits. They play an important role and perform a major regulatory function in both forms of carbon offset markets. According to different authors, this development can be conceived as an illustrative instance of the shift from public towards private forms of authority in global climate governance (e.g. Bernstein *et al.* 2010).

Thus, in sum, various private certification schemes have emerged in different policy domains of world politics. These privately created standards have largely been neglected by classical approaches to international politics and only recently attracted the attention of scholars focusing on global affairs. As stated above, in the past few years, private certification schemes have become increasingly important for the measurement and management of GHG emission reductions and removals, particularly in carbon offset markets. The analysis in this chapter follows the same structure as the previous case study. First, I trace the emergence of private certification schemes concerned with the issue of climate change. After that, I examine how these certification schemes operate, summarize why they are regarded as important instruments in global climate governance, and put the discussion in context with the theoretical approaches presented in the third chapter of this study. Then, I concentrate on one private certification scheme and explore its interaction and interplay with the intergovernmental level. Drawing on the analytical framework outlined above, I specifically examine how the various operational activities of the *Gold Standard for Carbon Offsets* relate to the international climate regime. At the end of the case study, I again recapitulate the main findings from the empirical analysis and derive conclusions for the theoretical debate on the concept of authority in global climate governance.

The emergence of private certification schemes in global climate governance

The number of private certification schemes in the policy domain of climate change has steadily increased in the past few years (e.g. Capoor and Ambrosi 2008; Bernstein *et al.* 2010; Green 2013). As already mentioned, most privately created standards have been established for measuring how many GHG emissions are reduced or avoided through a certain climate change mitigation project. These private carbon offset standards are based on a specific methodology for calculating the achieved emission reductions or removals. Thereby, the main challenge for the certifying agency is to provide credible information about the quality of the particular project in terms of its potential to reduce or avoid GHG emissions, and to produce possible environmental and societal co-benefits. This applies to both compliance and voluntary carbon offset markets. However, there is a decisive difference between these two markets. In the compliance carbon offset market, an oversight body, the *Clean Development Mechanism's Executive Board*, was established by nation-states at the intergovernmental level in order to ensure the environmental integrity of carbon offsets. This body is supported by various committees, expert panels, and working groups, and has adopted highly bureaucratic procedures and methodologies, in particular for the approval of individual projects and the evaluation of project activities (Streck 2007). In the voluntary carbon offset market, by contrast, no such centralized institution exists that oversees and regulates the trade with carbon offsets (Gillenwater *et al.* 2007; Corbera, Estrada, and Brown 2009; Lovell 2010). This has led some observers to describe the voluntary offset market as the 'Wild West' of carbon offsetting (e.g. Farenthold and Mufson 2007). Most important for the focus of this chapter, in the absence of a central regulatory agency in this market, privately created standards seek to substitute the central steering body that national governments have put into operation in the Clean Development Mechanism. This point will be discussed in detail further below.

Three examples of private carbon offset standards that have attracted wider scholarly attention are the *Gold Standard for Carbon Offsets* (hereafter Gold Standard), the *Verified Carbon Standard*, and the *Climate, Community and Biodiversity Standards* (Bulkeley and Newell 2010: 97–98; Newell and Paterson 2010: 119–122). While all of these privately created standards perform a similar regulatory function in carbon offset markets, they focus on different market sectors and also pursue slightly different objectives. The Gold Standard is probably the best-known private certification scheme today for the measurement and management of GHG emissions. This standard was initiated in 2003 by the World

Wide Fund for Nature and two partner organizations to define premium or high-end carbon offsets for both compliance and voluntary offset markets (Bayon, Hawn, and Hamilton 2007: 120–121). It certifies carbon offset projects in the renewable energy, energy efficiency, waste management, and, most recently, also in the land use and forestry sectors and aims 'to ensure that they all demonstrate real and permanent greenhouse gas (GHG) reductions and sustainable development benefits in local communities' (Gold Standard Foundation 2013g). The Gold Standard utilizes relatively strict certification guidelines. All projects certified under this standard must adhere to rigorous *additionality* criteria and contribute to sustainable development in the countries that host the projects. In particular, the certification process stipulated by the Gold Standard requires consultation with local stakeholders that might be affected by a certain project activity. Because of its strict guidelines, the carbon offsets issued by the Gold Standard have been referred to as 'boutique carbon credits' (Bumpus and Liverman 2008: 146). Accordingly, they are sold at higher prices than most other carbon offsets.

The Verified Carbon Standard, previously known as the Voluntary Carbon Standard, is another prominent example of a private certification scheme for carbon offsets. This standard was jointly developed by the *Climate Group*, the *International Emissions Trading Association*, and the *World Economic Forum* and published in early 2006 (Bayon, Hawn, and Hamilton 2007: 120). The Verified Carbon Standard was created as a quality standard particularly for the voluntary carbon market. By adopting guidelines that are claimed to be equally robust like those of the compliance carbon market, the standard aims to give buyers and sellers confidence in the offsets generated in the voluntary carbon market (Bulkeley and Newell 2010: 98). In recent years, the Verified Carbon Standard has evolved into one of the most widely used certification schemes for voluntary carbon offsets and certifies climate change mitigation projects in numerous so-called *sectoral scopes*, including energy, chemical industry, transport, metal production, waste handling, agriculture, and forestry. The standard's objective is to provide 'a trusted, robust and user-friendly program that brings quality assurance to voluntary carbon markets' (Verified Carbon Standard Association 2013). According to Ricardo Bayon, Amanda Hawn, and Katherine Hamilton, the standard was primarily designed as a basic quality threshold rather than to compete with other more specialized standards, and seeks to establish a generally acknowledged benchmark for the growing but relatively heterogeneous voluntary carbon market (Bayon, Hawn, and Hamilton 2007: 120).

The Climate, Community and Biodiversity Standards represent a third well-known example of private certification schemes for carbon offset markets. The Climate, Community and Biodiversity Alliance, a partnership consisting of research institutions, private companies, and environmental non-governmental organizations, initiated the development of these standards.[1] They were released in 2005 and constitute the result of a two-year multistakeholder process marked by 'outside input from academia, business, environmental organizations, and development groups; field testing on four continents; and an independent peer review' (Bayon, Hawn, and Hamilton 2007: 122). The Climate, Community and

Biodiversity Standards can be utilized for the certification of projects in both the compliance and voluntary markets for carbon offsets and apply certification criteria that go beyond those usually employed in the compliance carbon market. They essentially emerged from concerns about the quality of carbon offset markets and place emphasis on the social dimension of carbon offsets (Bulkeley and Newell 2010: 98; Hoffmann 2011: 148). In particular, the Climate, Community and Biodiversity Standards seek to 'identify land-based projects that are designed and implemented using best practices to deliver robust and credible greenhouse gas reductions while also delivering net positive benefits to local communities and biodiversity' (Climate, Community and Biodiversity Alliance 2013). Carbon offset projects that intend to obtain and use the label of the Climate, Community and Biodiversity Standards have to fulfill 15 criteria in three categories: (i) the mitigation of climate change, (ii) the conservation of biodiversity, and (iii) the improvement of socio-economic conditions for local communities. In addition, the standards define a number of optional criteria, such as safety measures for workers or the involvement of stakeholders in project management. Depending on how many of these additional criteria are met, projects certified under the Climate, Community and Biodiversity Standards earn gold, silver, or standard certification status.

After having discussed prominent examples of private certification schemes, it is important to note that the various carbon offset standards do not operate in isolation from one another, but are, in fact, closely interlinked. Their relationship is essentially characterized by two distinct features: *cooperation* and *competition* (cf. Hoffmann 2011: 146–148). On the one hand, only a small group of people are engaged in developing carbon offset standards, and these people often work for more than one standard-setting organization. Hence, there is obviously substantial exchange and communication between the different standards. Moreover, some carbon offset standards are also functionally connected. In 2012, for instance, the Verified Carbon Standard and the Climate, Community and Biodiversity Standards started a collaborative effort to simplify the processes for project approval under both standards (Verified Carbon Standard Association 2012). This enables project developers to receive carbon offsets tagged with a label for good societal and environmental performance. On the other hand, despite the non-profit nature of the vast majority of carbon offset standards, there is also rivalry among them. The various standard-setting organizations seek to position themselves as the best option for project developers and purchasers of carbon offsets. They compete particularly over the quality of offsets, efficient certification processes, and, due to their market orientation, naturally also over market share (Kollmuss, Zink, and Polycarp 2008: 14).

According to different scholars, the competition between standard-setting organizations involved in carbon offset markets can generate a 'race to the top' and enhance the quality of carbon offset projects (e.g. Corbera, Estrada, and Brown 2009: 33; Bulkeley and Newell 2010: 96; Hoffmann 2011: 148). Moreover, a number of partnerships between non-profit organizations have emerged in the past few years that seek to improve the credibility and robustness of carbon offsets, such as the *Offset Quality Initiative* established in 2007 or the *International Carbon Reduction and Offset Alliance* launched in 2008 (Leonard 2009: 88–89). The aim of these initiatives is to provide information and guidance for participants in the voluntary carbon market (International Carbon Reduction and Offset Alliance 2013; Offset Quality Initiative 2013). In addition, the United Kingdom Department for Environment, Food and Rural Affairs has established certain rules and regulations for carbon offsetting in order to raise consumers' confidence in the environmental integrity of offsets traded in the voluntary market for carbon offsets under British legislation (Lovell 2010: 360–361). The combined effect of these developments has put considerable pressure on the voluntary offset market in the past few years, particularly on private certification schemes to produce high-quality carbon offsets (e.g. Hamilton *et al.* 2009).

Interestingly, while the first privately created standards for carbon offset markets have been in operation since the early 2000s, most private carbon offset standards were created after the Kyoto Protocol entered into force in 2005 (Green 2013: 8). A few years earlier, nation-states had adopted the modalities and procedures for the Clean Development Mechanism at the 2001 Conference of the Parties to the UNFCCC held in Marrakesh (UNFCCC 2001). This detailed set of rules agreed upon by nation-states in international climate negotiations laid the foundation for the first carbon offset project registered under the Clean Development Mechanism in late 2004 (UNFCCC 2004). Evidently, many private certification schemes have taken the methodologies and practices of the compliance offset market as a point of reference and modeled their guidelines on those of the Clean Development Mechanism (e.g. Lovell 2010: 357). Here, the interrelationship between privately created standards for the measurement and management of GHG emissions with the intergovernmental level becomes obvious. In the following sections of this chapter, I further discuss this point and explore the interaction and interplay between one private certification scheme (i.e. the Gold Standard) and the international climate regime.

Private certification schemes and climate change

Several authors have pointed out that the measurement and management of GHG emissions is a highly complex task (e.g. Corbera, Estrada, and Brown 2009). In general, private certification schemes operating in carbon offset markets have to ensure the environmental integrity of carbon offset projects and demonstrate the robustness of GHG emission reductions or removals. As indicated above, a particular challenge for certification schemes is that carbon offsets are 'an intangible economic commodity that represents the avoidance or sequestration of GHG emissions' (Gillenwater *et al.* 2007: 85). Carbon offsets can be generated from various types of climate change mitigation projects, involving, for instance, the substitution of fossil fuels with renewable energy sources, the installation of energy-efficient technologies, the planting of trees to sequester and store carbon dioxide, and the burning of methane from landfills. The logic behind carbon offset projects is based on two key principles. First, the location of GHG emissions is irrelevant to their contribution to climate change (e.g. Lovell 2010: 353). Put differently, it does not matter where GHG emission reductions or removals take place. Second, GHG emission savings are easier to achieve in countries with large-scale climate change mitigation potentials. More specifically, opportunities for implementing low-carbon energy systems or carbon sequestration programs are for various reasons much less costly in developing countries and emerging economies (e.g. Bumpus and Liverman 2008: 133). From this perspective, it can be economically rational for individual actors to invest in carbon offset projects instead of reducing GHG emissions from their own activities. Proponents of carbon offset markets argue that offsetting also benefits the society as a whole 'because more emissions can be reduced for a given expenditure of resources' (Gillenwater *et al.* 2007: 85). In addition, carbon offset projects potentially contribute to sustainable development in the countries hosting the projects by delivering co-benefits, such as cheaper and healthier energy systems, environmental protection, and new jobs for the local population (Liverman, 2010: 130). Thus, in essence, the idea of carbon offsetting is premised on the power of the market to identify and implement low-cost emission reduction options, while (at best) simultaneously promoting sustainable development in developing countries and emerging economies.

Basically, in order to function, five issues need to be governed in carbon offset markets (cf. Goodward and Kelly 2010). First, the GHG emission reductions or removals must be *real*. This means that a carbon offset project has to lead to a net decrease of GHG emissions in the atmosphere, relative to a 'business-as-usual' baseline scenario. In practice, the emissions that can be avoided or sequestered by a certain carbon offset project are quantified against the hypothetical assumption that the project had not been implemented. Second, the GHG emission reductions or removals must be *permanent*. This means that the emission reductions achieved through a carbon offset project are not reversed over time. The issue whether emission reductions are permanent concerns especially afforestation and reforestation projects, which bear the difficult task of safeguarding against the future removal or destruction of the planted trees. Third, the GHG emission reductions or removals must be *additional*. This means that the carbon offset project has to generate emission reductions or lead to removals that would not have happened without the revenues generated from carbon offsets. For instance, if an industrial plant was upgraded with energy-efficient technologies entirely for economic reasons (i.e. cost savings) and thereby a certain amount of GHG emissions were saved, the emission reductions would, at least in a strict understanding, not be considered additional. The concept of additionality is probably the most complex and controversial issue in carbon offset markets because of the methodological difficulties in determining whether a project was implemented due to the incentive provided by the carbon offset market or would have happened anyway. Fourth, the GHG emission reductions or removals must be *verifiable*. This means that the GHG emission reductions can be monitored to ensure that they actually occur as stipulated in the project development plan. Fifth, the GHG emission reductions or removals must be *enforceable*. This means that carbon offsets generated from a carbon offset project can be sold only once.

Therefore, carbon offsets have to be tracked and clear ownership needs to be defined, usually through a certain GHG emissions registry. While these five issues are widely acknowledged and accepted among the participants in carbon offset markets, in practice there are various ways in which they are interpreted and implemented. This particularly concerns the issue of additionality. According to Charlotte Streck, '[t]here is no uniform or proven way to test additionality. Existing mandatory and voluntary carbon standards apply at least [a] dozen different interpretations, tests and criteria for proving the additionality of emission reductions' (Streck 2010: 13). Moreover, the issues sketched above cannot easily be applied to all types of climate change mitigation projects. Certain project types, for example carbon sequestration programs, face particular challenges when tested against the quantification, verification, and enforcement criteria of carbon offset markets (Broekhoff and Zyla 2008).

As stated above, two distinct forms of markets for carbon offsets have emerged over the past few years. From a general point of view, the functions performed by private certification schemes are relatively similar in both the compliance and voluntary offset markets. Yet, a closer look reveals that private standard-setting organizations undertake different tasks in the two forms of carbon offset markets. Although a number of private carbon offset standards operate in both market forms, they serve different purposes in the compliance and voluntary carbon markets. Therefore, the following sections analyze the role of private carbon offset standards consecutively, at first in the compliance offset market and then in the voluntary offset market.

Private carbon offset standards in the compliance offset market

On the one hand, there is the Clean Development Mechanism established by national governments with the Kyoto Protocol in 1997 as one of three flexible instruments to lower the overall economic costs of achieving GHG emission reductions.[2] The Clean Development Mechanism has often been referred to as the 'Kyoto surprise,' since it emerged late in the negotiation process and evolved into a key instrument in global climate governance (Werksman 1998; Werksman and Cameron 2000; Streck and Lin 2008). The Clean Development Mechanism is commonly known as the compliance offset market because the carbon offsets generated under this mechanism can be used to fulfill national GHG emission reduction targets negotiated at the intergovernmental level. In particular, the mechanism is based on the idea of allowing companies from industrialized countries with GHG emission reduction obligations under the Kyoto Protocol (i.e. Annex 1 countries) to gain *Certified Emission Reductions* by investing in projects that reduce or avoid emissions in less-developed countries (i.e. non-Annex 1 countries). The purpose of the Clean Development Mechanism, which is defined in Article 12 of the Kyoto Protocol, is twofold: (i) the mechanism aims to reduce the costs for Annex 1 countries to meet their emission reduction targets, and (ii) it is supposed to assist non-Annex 1 countries in achieving sustainable development (UNFCCC 1997: Article 12). The Clean Development Mechanism has a relatively hierarchical structure (Corbera, Estrada, and Brown 2009: 32). The supreme oversight body in this mechanism is the Executive Board, which acts 'under the authority and guidance' of the Conferences of the Parties to the UNFCCC serving as the Meeting of the Parties to the Kyoto Protocol to which it is 'fully accountable' (UNFCCC 2001: 27). The members of the Executive Board make various regulatory decisions, including the accreditation of third-party certifiers, the approval of methodologies, the registration of projects, and the issuance of carbon offsets. Hence, this intergovernmental institution has the final say on whether or not a certain carbon offset project will be implemented, and makes the final decision as to how many carbon offsets are attributed to an individual project activity. In these tasks, the Executive Board members are supported by a wide range of committees, expert panels, and working groups (Streck 2007: 93). A particular influential expert panel is the so-called *Meth Panel*, which develops guidelines for the methodologies used by private auditing corporations to assess the project activities (UNFCCC 2013b). This underscores the fact that the Clean Development Mechanism incorporates a rigorous regulatory framework 'to define credits strictly and establish standards of quality through project methodologies' (Lovell 2010: 354).

Investors' motivations for purchasing carbon offsets under the Clean Development Mechanism are clear. Governments and companies with GHG emission reduction obligations that are unwilling or unable to save emissions from their own activities invest in carbon offset projects to meet their particular targets. Hence, the demand for these emission reductions is driven by the individual commitments made by industrialized countries under the Kyoto Protocol (Bumpus and Liverman 2008: 132). Since its introduction, the Clean Development Mechanism has generated nearly 11,000 projects, of which approximately 6,900 were registered with the UNFCCC Secretariat by June 2013 (United Nations Environment Programme Risø Centre 2013). The different projects have led to a significant amount of GHG emission reductions. By mid-2013, approximately 1,335 million Certified Emission Reductions had been issued by the Executive Board, each representing one ton of avoided or sequestered CO_2e (UNFCCC 2013a).[3] Taking these figures into account, different scholars have acknowledged that the Clean Development Mechanism has provided a cost-effective way for industrialized countries to adhere to their GHG emission reduction obligations under the Kyoto Protocol (e.g. Pattberg and Stripple 2008: 375; Fuhr and Lederer 2009: 331–332; Lederer 2010: 19).

Yet, despite the relatively tight regulatory oversight and the achievement of cost-effective emission reductions, the Clean Development Mechanism has been heavily criticized for various reasons in recent years (cf. Paulsson 2009). One of the recurrent criticisms is that the market-based instrument prioritizes cheap emission reductions achieved by industrialized countries, while it does not place enough value on the promotion of sustainable development in developing countries (e.g. Ellis *et al.* 2007; Lövbrand, Rindefjäll, and Nordqvist 2009; Stripple 2010; Subbarao and Lloyd 2011; Karakosta *et al.* 2013). Due to the lack of a common definition of sustainable development, the countries that host the climate change mitigation projects have 'to confirm whether a clean development mechanism project activity assists it in achieving sustainable development' (UNFCCC 2001: 20). Hence, in practice, the host countries of the projects decide how strictly they define and implement the sustainable development criteria for carbon offset projects (Corbera, Estrada, and Brown 2009: 33; Liverman 2010: 136; Evans 2011: 47–48). While this enables the host countries to determine how sustainable development could be interpreted and achieved in their national contexts, it brings them into a difficult situation because they have to reconcile their desire for investments with national sustainable development goals (Liverman 2010: 136). The problem is that if they establish strict sustainable development guidelines for carbon offset projects, they will risk deterring project developers from investing in their countries. Most developing countries, therefore, are not able or willing to adopt effective rules and procedures to ensure that the different projects promote sustainable development and improve the socio-economic conditions for local communities (Olsen 2007; Sutter and Parreno 2007; Olsen and Fenhann 2008).

In response to that, private certification schemes have emerged that seek to overcome this regulatory deficit. A number of private standard-setting organizations have developed guidelines for the promotion of sustainable development through climate change mitigation projects. In particular, private certification schemes apply additional screens and evaluate the carbon offset projects against a certain set of social and environmental criteria (e.g. Headon 2009; Liverman 2010; Evans 2011). If the project activity is in accordance with these criteria, the private standard-setting organization will assign a label to the carbon offset project. This label should guarantee that the respective project activity is in accordance with the rules and procedures of the Clean Development Mechanism and at the same time contributes to sustainable development and improves the socio-economic conditions for local communities in the host country of the project. In recent years, some private standard-setting organizations have collaborated and exchanged information with both the Clean Development Mechanism's Executive Board and the UNFCCC Secretariat. For instance, in 2011, the Executive Board launched a call for public input to gain practical insights from private standard-setting organizations and other stakeholders. More precisely, the Executive Board aimed at getting expert advice on how co-benefits could be achieved and negative impacts avoided through adequate certification processes (UNFCCC 2011a).

Private carbon offset standards in the voluntary offset market

On the other hand, there is the voluntary carbon offset market that largely emerged in parallel with the compliance offset market (Bumpus and Liverman 2008: 132–133). While the two forms of carbon offset markets have many similarities, they also differ in a number of relevant aspects (Corbera, Estrada, and Brown 2009: 27). The basic idea of the voluntary offset market is that all entities without GHG emission reduction obligations can voluntarily compensate for their emissions by purchasing *Voluntary Emission Reductions* generated through carbon offset projects. These projects are predominantly located in countries that do not have GHG emission reduction targets. The voluntary carbon offset market is entrenched in the concept of 'carbon neutrality.' This term 'signifies that there is no carbon burden upon the earth as a result of the activities performed by the company or the individual' (Dhanda and Hartman 2011: 121). In the past few years, several industrial and service companies have made the decision to become carbon neutral, mostly for philanthropic or marketing reasons. A prominent example in this regard is the HSBC bank, which became the first carbon neutral bank in 2004. Although the bank undertook different measures to prevent GHG emissions from its own activities, it was able to achieve the status of carbon neutrality ultimately only through buying a considerable amount of offsets from the voluntary carbon market (Bayon, Hawn, and Hamilton 2007: 95–99). Because of the difficulties of tracking and quantifying the emissions associated with the various sorts of corporate activity, the concept of carbon neutrality is controversial and in recent years many companies have shied away from making claims about carbon neutrality (Newell and Paterson 2010: 117).

Unlike the Clean Development Mechanism, which sets comparatively detailed rules and procedures for the approval of carbon offset projects, the structure of the voluntary carbon market is much more diverse and flexible (Lovell 2010: 354). While an intergovernmental body to ensure the environmental integrity of the project activities regulates the compliance offset market, no central regulatory instrument exists in the market for voluntary carbon offsets. Consequently, the voluntary carbon market is less bureaucratic and has lower transaction costs than the compliance offset market. In particular, the flexibility of the voluntary offset market avoids bottlenecks in the project approval process and offers considerable room for the innovation of methodologies that can benefit both the buyers and the suppliers of carbon offsets (Bayon, Hawn, and Hamilton 2007: 13). Moreover, there is also no commonly agreed-upon standard to which project developers adhere when they design and implement carbon offset projects (Gillenwater *et al.* 2007: 86; Brohe, Eyre, and Howarth 2009: 280; Dhanda and Hartman 2011: 128). In response, many different private carbon standards have evolved in the past few years that compete with each other for market share and seek to establish the credibility of voluntary carbon offsets. The voluntary carbon market has hence been framed as an illustrative instance of a privately created governance arena 'with the potential to mitigate climate change largely independent of state action' (Pattberg and Stripple 2008: 378).

In the voluntary carbon market, the motivations of consumers to purchase carbon offsets are more complex than in the Clean Development Mechanism. The motives of buyers of voluntary carbon offsets range from the intention to enhance their public image and the expectation to gain first-mover advantages to real concerns about the environment (e.g. Taiyab 2006: 15–19; Bulkeley and Newell 2010: 95; Newell and Paterson 2010: 115–116). Private corporations purchase the vast majority of carbon offsets in the voluntary offset market. They account for about 80 percent of the offsets generated through voluntary climate change mitigation projects. Non-governmental organizations constitute the second largest demand group, buying 13 percent of the offsets, whereas only 5 percent of the demand is driven by individual consumers who compensate, for instance, for the GHG emissions caused by personal air travel (Bulkeley and Newell 2010: 94). The precise size of the voluntary offset market is difficult to determine, since a common registry or tracking system has not (yet) been established. According to Molly Peters-Stanley and Katherine Hamilton, the volume of the voluntary carbon market can be estimated at approximately 95 million tons of CO_2e in 2011 (Peters-Stanley and Hamilton 2012: 9). While the market for voluntary carbon offsets has grown rapidly in recent years, from the amount of USD 48 million in 2005 to USD 576 million in 2011, it still constitutes only a fraction of the size of the compliance carbon offset market (Bayon, Hawn, and Hamilton 2007: 14; Corbera, Estrada, and Brown 2009: 28; Newell and Paterson 2010: 112).

Over the past few years, the voluntary offset market has come under critical scrutiny. Many scholars emphasize that the voluntary offset market lacks standardization, transparency, and consistent rules for project approvals (e.g. Schiermeier 2006: 977; Bayon, Hawn, and Hamilton 2007: 12; Gillenwater *et al.* 2007: 86; Lovell 2010: 357; Stripple and Lövbrand 2010: 173). Moreover, authors have pointed out that the voluntary offset market is 'unlikely to deliver substantive GHG emissions reduction and deviate[s] attention from changing lifestyles and energy consumption patterns in developed countries' (Corbera, Estrada, and Brown 2009: 26). In addition, environmental advocacy groups and the media have recently published reports that fundamentally question whether voluntary carbon offset projects contribute to sustainable development in the countries hosting the projects (e.g. Ma'anit 2006; Harvey 2007; Revkin 2007; Smith 2007; Gilbertson and Reyes 2009). They have reported that planted trees are cut down soon after completion of the crediting process, that projects do not benefit the local communities, and that project developers employ neo-colonial practices when conducting a project (Liverman 2010: 138). In contrast to the Clean Development Mechanism, in the voluntary offset market the governments of the host countries usually do not approve whether a certain project activity promotes sustainable development. The extent to which voluntary carbon offset projects deliver co-benefits to the host country is thus left entirely to the market. Therefore, private carbon offset standards play a fundamental role in the voluntary offset market. They face the challenge of adequately calculating how many GHG emissions are reduced or avoided through a certain project activity and in many cases also to assess the project's sustainable development benefits (Gillenwater *et al.* 2007: 86; Bumpus and Liverman 2008: 132–133; Dhanda and Hartman 2011: 128–130). Due to the lack of a centralized regulatory instrument, the different private carbon offset standards vary considerably in terms of their stringency and scope. While some standards closely resemble the detailed rules and procedures, as well as the relatively complex methodologies used in the compliance offset market, others are less demanding to simplify the administrative processes and allow as many offsets as possible to enter the market (Kollmuss, Zink, and Polycarp 2008: 2). Most importantly for the focus of this chapter, as Heather Lovell notes, the more similar the voluntary carbon offset standards are to the regularities in the compliance offset market, the better is their perceived quality (Lovell 2010: 357). While this aspect is further discussed in the following sections, it is important to underline here that private carbon offset standards are, in fact, the only instrument that can ensure the credibility of the voluntary carbon offset market and allow customers to gain confidence in the offsets they purchase.

The relevance of private certification schemes

In general, carbon markets have experienced considerable rates of growth in the past few years and are at the center of the scholarly debate on adequate policy instruments to foster transformative changes towards a low-carbon economy (e.g. Yamin 2005; Callon 2009; MacKenzie 2009; Bernstein *et al.* 2010; Stephan and Paterson 2012). Based on the logic of *commensuration* and *commodification*, carbon markets turn air pollution into quantities on a common metric and attach a price to GHG emissions (Levin and Espeland 2002: 121). In this way, promises and permissions to emit GHGs become a commodity that can be traded. Given the general move towards market-based instruments in contemporary global politics, especially in the field of environmental regulation, the inclusion of markets in the global response to climate change does not come as a great surprise (Bernstein *et al.* 2010: 164; Newell and Paterson 2010: 34; Hoffmann 2011: 123). Despite the critique expressed by various authors who question the effectiveness and legitimacy of carbon markets (e.g. Wara 2007; Paterson 2010; Böhm, Misoczky, and Moog 2012), market-based instruments have, with certain restrictions, flourished over the past decade and are widely perceived as an indispensable tool to address the problem of climate change (e.g. IPCC 2007; Stern 2007; Eliasch 2008; The World Bank 2011; UNFCCC 2012a). As mentioned earlier, carbon offset markets are a particular type of carbon market and can be subdivided into the compliance and voluntary offset markets. The compliance offset market represents 'one of the international climate regime's core strategies for reducing greenhouse gas emissions in the developing world' (Liverman 2010: 130). Although still relatively small in size, several authors regard the voluntary carbon offset market as a promising new mode of climate governance and place considerable hopes in this market (e.g. Bayon, Hawn, and Hamilton 2007; Guigon, Bellassen, and Ambrosi 2009; Peters-Stanley and Hamilton 2012). Essentially, these two forms of carbon offset markets share the same conceptual basis, but have fundamentally different regulatory structures (Bumpus and Liverman 2008: 128).

Thus, as the previous depiction in this chapter has shown, private certification schemes play an important role in both forms of carbon offset markets. In the Clean Development Mechanism, private carbon offset standards assign labels to those climate change mitigation projects, which successfully contribute to sustainable development or biodiversity conservation in the host countries of the projects. In the voluntary offset market, privately created standards perform a crucial regulatory function and seek to ensure the societal and environmental effectiveness of voluntary carbon offset projects. Various authors have argued that private certification schemes have the potential to meet the challenges associated with the measurement and management of GHG emissions and to thereby enhance the credibility of carbon offset markets. For instance, they contend that private standard-setting initiatives might initiate a 'race to quality' in carbon offset markets (Bulkeley and Newell 2010: 96). Others point out that privately created standards can accelerate and improve the sustainable development benefits achieved through carbon offset projects in both the compliance and voluntary offset markets (Peskett, Luttrell, and Iwata 2007: 6; Bumpus and Liverman 2008: 148; Liverman 2010: 139). And still others claim that private standard-setting organizations have become a central feature in voluntary carbon offset trading and will shape future market-based instruments (Pattberg and Stripple 2008: 378; Newell and Paterson 2010: 125; Hoffmann 2011: 148).

Link to the theoretical background

The preceding sections have shown that several scholars recognize private certification schemes to be important instruments in global climate governance. A number of these scholars assert that privately created standards for the measurement and management of GHG emissions operate as climate governance arrangements beyond the authority of state-based forms of governance (e.g. Bäckstrand 2008; Pattberg and Stripple 2008; Andonova, Betsill, and Bulkeley 2009). This group of authors holds that the emergence of private certification schemes in the policy domain of climate change generates a shift of authority from existing modes of multilateral treaty-making towards sub- and non-state actors. They suggest that private standard-setting initiatives have adopted essential functions in the voluntary carbon market, which could be seen as a governance arena with practically no link to the intergovernmental level. Hence, these scholars maintain that existing modes of inter-state cooperation are increasingly challenged through the emergence of a private realm of climate governance. However, I put forward the argument that only a few scholars have thus far empirically investigated the relationship between the various privately created standards for the measurement and management of GHG emissions and the international climate regime. While the various case studies on private certification schemes have contributed to our knowledge about their role and function in the global response to climate change, scholars have not sufficiently analyzed the interaction and interplay between privately created standards and the intergovernmental level. Consequently, this case study does not stop at the description of the emergence of private certification schemes in the issue area of climate change. In fact, it also analyzes the wider implications associated with this development for global climate governance. Using the theoretical background and analytical framework described in the third chapter of this book, the present chapter particularly studies the interrelationship between the Gold Standard and the international climate regime. In this analysis, the Gold Standard is perceived as an illustrative instance of a *non-profit* climate governance arrangement. As in the previous chapter, at the outset of the case study, I provide an overview of the

Gold Standard, including its main fields of application, organizational structure, and perception in the literature. Then, I call to mind the three conceptual assumptions about the interaction and interplay between transnational governance arrangements and the international climate regime and investigate how the Gold Standard's different operational activities relate to existing modes of interstate cooperation.

The Gold Standard for Carbon Offsets and the international climate regime

Overview of the Gold Standard

The World Wide Fund for Nature established the Gold Standard in collaboration with *Helio International* and *SouthSouthNorth* in 2003 to create a 'best practice' benchmark standard for the evaluation of climate change mitigation projects. Basically, the Gold Standard aims to assure that the projects under its label meet certain environmental integrity criteria and deliver societal co-benefits in the countries that host the projects (Andonova, Betsill, and Bulkeley 2009: 65). This shall guarantee that the different project activities not only reduce or avoid GHG emissions, but also promote sustainable development in developing countries and emerging economies. According to its own website, the Gold Standard is endorsed and supported by over 80 non-governmental organizations and employed by numerous national governments, multinational corporations, and United Nations agencies (Gold Standard Foundation 2013g). As of 2012, more than 750 carbon offset projects in over 60 countries had completed or were undergoing Gold Standard certification, which accounts for approximately 65 million tons of avoided or removed CO_2e by 2015 (Gold Standard Foundation 2012h). National governments, companies, and non-governmental organizations, seeking to showcase their particular environmental commitment, mainly purchase the Gold Standard certified offsets.

Main fields of application

According to Bayon, Hawn, and Hamilton, the Gold Standard was originally designed to improve the quality of carbon offset projects in the compliance offset market (Bayon, Hawn, and Hamilton 2007: 121). The intention of the organizations that created the Gold Standard was to overcome the shortcomings of the Clean Development Mechanism that had failed to establish adequate sustainable development criteria for the evaluation of climate change mitigation project activities. In 2007, the Clean Development Mechanism's Executive Board issued the first Certified Emission Reductions for a project, which was reviewed by the Gold Standard (Gold Standard Foundation 2007). Due to the premium type of offsets, there is a significant price difference between the offsets generated through Gold Standard certified projects and offsets without the Gold Standard label. The prices for Gold Standard offsets in the Clean Development Mechanism were occasionally 25 percent higher than the average offset prices in the past few years (Boyd and Salzman 2011: 89). Recently, the Gold Standard has received widespread recognition among national governments. For instance, in 2009 the British Government announced that it would purchase only those carbon offsets for its air and train travel that were generated through Clean Development Mechanism projects carrying the Gold Standard label. This should accelerate the demand for Gold Standard certified projects (Murray 2009). Two years later, the German Government engaged with the Gold Standard Foundation under its *International Climate Initiative* in order to bring climate change mitigation projects to underrepresented regions, such as sub-Saharan Africa (Gold Standard Foundation 2011c). Furthermore, in May 2013 the Swiss Government decided to recognize Gold Standard certified offsets as the only type of offsets automatically eligible as Certified Emission Reductions within its national emission trading scheme (Swiss Federal Office for the Environment 2013). Beyond that, according to Wolfgang Sterk and colleagues, at least 15 national governments, mostly from emerging economies and developing countries, build on the Gold Standard to evaluate whether a certain project activity in the compliance offset market contributes to sustainable development in their countries (Sterk *et al.* 2009).

In 2006, the Gold Standard was also launched for the evaluation of voluntary carbon offset projects (Kollmuss, Zink, and Polycarp 2008: 54). Two years later, the first Voluntary Emission Reductions for a project activity were issued and transferred to the Gold Standard's Registry (3Degrees 2008). Today, about 60 percent of the overall number of Gold Standard certified project activities are voluntary climate change mitigation projects (Gold Standard Foundation 2013e). As with the Gold Standard for the Clean Development Mechanism, the voluntary carbon offsets issued by the Gold Standard Foundation are traded for a premium price, which has been as much as 100 percent above the price of voluntary carbon offsets that do not have the Gold Standard label (Kollmuss *et al.* 2010: 150). In response to criticisms about the quality of voluntary carbon offsets, a number of organizations, such as My*Climate*, opted to solely invest in project activities that adhere to the rules and procedures established by the Gold Standard (Newell and Paterson 2010: 119–121). This illustrates the fact that different actors perceive the Gold Standard as a high-quality certification scheme that provides guidelines and standardized procedures for assessing climate change mitigation projects in both the compliance and voluntary carbon markets.

Organizational structure

The Gold Standard Foundation, which is based in Geneva, is a non-profit organization that consists of several administrative bodies with different responsibilities. The day-to-day management of the organization is handled by the *Gold Standard Secretariat* that currently employs a core staff of about 30 people (Gold Standard Foundation 2013b). Their tasks include the certification and registration of carbon offset projects, the issuance of carbon offsets, and the maintenance of Gold Standard criteria for the evaluation of project activities (Kollmuss *et al.* 2010: 149). The Gold

Standard Foundation Board, which comprises several members from partner organizations, provides the financial oversight and strategic development. Most interestingly for the focus of this chapter is the *Gold Standard Technical Advisory Committee*. This committee currently has twelve members that deliver expert advice and strategic input to further develop the Gold Standard (Gold Standard Foundation 2013a). In particular, they evaluate and approve projects, adopt new methodologies, and regularly update the rules and procedures for the certification process. Hence, they play a similar role to that of the members of the Executive Board in the Clean Development Mechanism (Kollmuss *et al.* 2010: 149).

Perception in the literature

Many authors conceive the Gold Standard as a well-functioning carbon offset standard. Several of them describe the Gold Standard as one of the most credible standards currently in operation in carbon offset markets (e.g. Taiyab 2006: 11; Kollmuss, Zink, and Polycarp 2008: 57; Brohe, Eyre, and Howarth 2009: 281). They highlight that, in some respect, the Gold Standard's rules and procedures go beyond those of the Clean Development Mechanism, which renders Gold Standard certified project activities suitable to deliver societal and environmental co-benefits in the host countries of the projects (e.g. Boyd and Salzman 2011). In this context, a number of studies indicate that Gold Standard certified projects have, at least in the Clean Development Mechanism, led to measurable contributions to sustainable development in the project host countries (Muller 2008; Nussbaumer 2009; Drupp 2011). Moreover, Beth Evans states that the comparatively strict sustainable development criteria of the Gold Standard might 'positively influence southern states' perceptions of the CDM's [Clean Development Mechanism's] legitimacy in a number of ways' (Evans 2011: 52). In addition, scholars claim that the Gold Standard with its widely accepted rules and procedures for the evaluation of carbon offset projects might also engage those national governments in climate change mitigation efforts that do not have binding obligations under the Kyoto Protocol (e.g. Newell and Paterson 2010: 126).

However, in recent years, a number of authors have also pointed to some problems that constrain the efficiency of the Gold Standard. These scholars emphasize that the Gold Standard builds upon highly complicated rules and procedures and hence involves a rather bureaucratic approval process, which closely resembles the one under the Clean Development Mechanism (Peskett, Luttrell, and Iwata 2007). This might deter potential project developers who prefer greater flexibility when choosing a certain project type and approval methodologies. Other scholars point out that the Gold Standard has, until recently, received only limited application and might merely occupy a small niche in carbon offset markets (Headon 2009: 148–149; Sterk and Wittneben 2009: 281; Evans 2011: 53). And, more fundamentally, still other authors contend that due to the market approach used by the Gold Standard and the related dependence on consumer behavior, private carbon offset standards cannot adequately contribute to solving the problem of climate change (Evans 2011: 53). These different assessments of the Gold

Standard have delivered important insights. Yet, this book puts forward the argument that the role and function of the Gold Standard in global climate governance needs to be viewed in the context of the norms and rules stipulated in international climate agreements. Consequently, the remainder of this chapter examines the Gold Standard's relationship to the international climate regime.

Conceptual assumptions and theoretical expectations

After having provided an overview of the Gold Standard's main fields of application, organizational structure, and perception in the literature, next I tie the case study to the analytical framework of this book. Based on the three conceptual assumptions outlined in the research design, the following sections explore the Gold Standard's interaction and interplay with the international climate regime. The first conceptual assumption portrays a *conflictive relationship* between transnational climate initiatives and the international climate regime. It suggests that transnational governance arrangements depart from the ultimate objective and basic principles of the UNFCCC and weaken the norms and rules stipulated in international climate agreements. Accordingly, in the case study in this chapter, I would expect that the Gold Standard aims to establish its own procedures and methodologies as alternative guidelines to the norms and rules agreed upon by nation-states at the intergovernmental level. The second conceptual assumption portrays a *complementary relationship* between transnational climate initiatives and the international climate regime. It implies that the emergence of transnational governance arrangements leads to a division of responsibilities between sub- and non-state actors and the UNFCCC, thereby strengthening the norms and rules set out in international climate agreements. Consequently, in the particular case analyzed here, I would expect that the Gold Standard enhances both the environmental and societal effectiveness of carbon offset markets set out in international climate agreements. And the third conceptual assumption portrays a *dependency relationship* between transnational climate initiatives and the international climate regime. It supposes that transnational governance arrangements are a side issue to the UNFCCC process and rely on the norms and rules anchored in international climate agreements. Hence, in the present case study, I would expect that the Gold Standard remains largely dependent on the international regulatory framework to contribute to the promotion of societal and environmental co-benefits in emerging economies and developing countries. Again, these conceptual assumptions and theoretical expectations guide the following analysis and help identify relevant empirical findings (see Table 5.1). In the final section of this chapter, I come back to this analytical framework and draw conclusions for the debate on the concept of authority in global climate governance.

The Gold Standard's main operational activities

The analysis of the relationship between the Gold Standard and the international climate regime is structured around the three main operational activities of the

Table 5.1 Conceptual assumptions and theoretical expectations for the empirical analysis of the relationship between the Gold Standard and the international climate regime

Conceptual assumptions	*The Gold Standard: Theoretical expectations*
Conflictive relationship	The Gold Standard aims to establish its own procedures and methodologies as alternative guidelines to the norms and rules agreed upon by nation-states at the intergovernmental level
Complementary relationship	The Gold Standard enhances both the environmental and societal effectiveness of carbon offset markets set out in international climate agreements
Dependency relationship	The Gold Standard remains to a large extent dependent on the international regulatory framework to contribute to the promotion of societal and environmental co-benefits in emerging economies and developing countries

Gold Standard Foundation. First, I analyze the role played by the Gold Standard in the Clean Development Mechanism. After that, I study its function in the voluntary carbon offset market. And then, I focus the analysis on the involvement of the Gold Standard Foundation in the UNFCCC conferences.

The Gold Standard in the compliance offset market

As stated above, the Clean Development Mechanism has two purposes. The project-based mechanism aims to lower the compliance costs of industrialized countries, while at the same time assisting developing countries and emerging economies to achieve sustainable development. After concerns were raised about the shortcomings of the Clean Development Mechanism, the Gold Standard was established in order to enhance the environmental and social integrity of the market-based instrument. Essentially, the Gold Standard builds on the regulatory framework of the compliance offset market and employs a number of additional screens for the evaluation of project activities (Bayon, Hawn, and Hamilton 2007: 121). This section discusses the most important requirements that all Gold Standard certified projects have to meet before they can be tagged with the Gold Standard label.

PROJECT TYPE SCREEN

First, and most basically, projects undergoing Gold Standard certification have to pass a *project type screen*. This means that projects must supply renewable energy, introduce energy efficiency, or involve waste handling activities that deliver an energy service (Gold Standard Foundation 2012f: 23–24).[4] The logic of this requirement is that renewable energy and energy efficiency projects are more likely to contribute to long-term changes of the energy sector in the countries hosting the carbon offset projects than other project types (Pearson 2007; Schneider 2007; Olsen and Fenhann 2008). By restricting the project type, the Gold Standard seeks to guarantee that the individual project activity benefits the host countries of the projects. For the same reason, the Gold Standard also limits the type of eligible GHGs. Only those project activities are eligible for Gold Standard registration that involve the reduction of carbon dioxide, methane, or nitrous oxide (Gold Standard Foundation 2012f: 23). Project activities based on the destruction of industrial GHGs like *trifluoromethane* (hereafter HFC-23) are therefore excluded *a priori* from the approval process and cannot be accepted as Gold Standard certified projects. Moreover, carbon offset projects have to meet two other general requirements before they can be considered eligible for registration under the Gold Standard. First, the Gold Standard demands that the respective project activity are not publicly announced prior to receiving any payment for the project through the Clean Development Mechanism (Gold Standard Foundation 2012f: 22). The idea behind this clause is that a project announced before receiving the support of the market-based mechanism could principally have been implemented without the revenues from carbon offsets. Second, the Gold Standard also requires that the particular project activity do not receive funds declared as *Official Development Assistance* (Gold Standard Foundation 2012f: 26–27). This shall prevent the relabeling of previously planned development projects as climate change mitigation projects. In addition, the Gold Standard sets a number of specific criteria for certain project types. For instance, the Gold Standard does not allow hydropower projects to be implemented in high conservation value areas, requires a certain declaration from project developers that deploy genetically modified organisms, and decides on a case-by-case basis about the feasibility of projects related to the production of biofuels.[5]

ADDITIONALITY SCREEN

Second, projects undergoing Gold Standard certification have to pass a rigorous *additionality screen*. This means that projects must demonstrate that they lead to GHG emission reductions or removals, which would not have occurred without the respective project activity. As stated above, the concept of additionality is highly contested and various methodologies exist for ascertaining whether an individual project generates *additional* GHG emission reductions (Streck 2010). The key problem is that an additionality test always involves a counterfactual scenario that gives rise to methodological problems. In the past few years, the Clean Development Mechanism's Executive Board has developed a detailed methodological tool for the demonstration and assessment of whether a project can be considered additional (UNFCCC 2012c). This tool provides a stepwise approach. At the outset, the project developer can prove that the proposed project is the first of its kind and in this way demonstrate the additionality of the project. After that, the project developer has to identify realistic and credible alternatives to the proposed project. These alternative scenarios must deliver outputs or services that can be compared to those of the proposed project, but produce considerably higher GHG emissions. In the next two steps, the project developer can either show that the proposed project is not financially and economically attractive in its own right or determine at least one barrier that prevents the implementation of the proposed project activity without the support of the Clean Development Mechanism. Finally, the project developer has to demonstrate that the proposed project activity is not common practice in the project host country. Most relevant for the focus of this chapter, the Gold Standard employs the rules and procedures of the Clean Development Mechanism and demands from project developers the use of the most up-to-date versions of the various specific additionality guidelines provided by the UNFCCC Secretariat (Gold Standard Foundation 2012f: 31–32). Hence, Gold Standard certified projects under the Clean Development Mechanism have to use UNFCCC-approved methodologies to demonstrate and assess project additionality. This underlines the close connection between the Gold Standard and the norms and rules of the international climate regime.

SUSTAINABLE DEVELOPMENT SCREEN

Third, projects undergoing Gold Standard certification have to pass a *sustainable development screen*. This means that projects must fulfill a number of sustainability criteria in order to be eligible for the Gold Standard label. This screen is relatively complex and can be regarded as the core element of the Gold Standard. Basically, it consists of four components. At first, project developers have to undertake a *'Do No Harm' Assessment* to identify any negative social, environmental, or economic impact that could be caused by the proposed project activity (Gold Standard Foundation 2012f: 33–34). This assessment is based on eleven safeguarding principles, which are derived from the Millennium Development Goals of the *United Nations Development Programme*.[6] Project activities that violate any of these principles are not eligible for Gold Standard registration. After the completion of this self-assessment, project developers have to demonstrate through a detailed impact assessment that the proposed project provides clear benefits to sustainable development in the project host countries (Gold Standard Foundation 2012f: 34). In particular, projects applying for the Gold Standard are tested against a number of predefined globally applicable indicators (e.g. air quality, biodiversity, livelihoods of the population, human and institutional capacities, and technology transfer) in three categories, namely (i) environment, (ii) social development, and (iii) economic and technological development. The different indicators are rated on a scale from *major negative impact (-1)* and *neutral impact (0)* to *major positive impact (+1)*. The result of this assessment is an individual *Sustainable Development Matrix* for each project (Gold Standard Foundation 2012c). In order to qualify for Gold Standard registration, the proposed project must score positively (+1) in at least two categories and be neutral (0) in the third category. Project activities that do not meet the minimum scoring requirements are not eligible for Gold Standard registration and have to alter and improve the project design document. A third element of the sustainability assessment required by the Gold Standard is a two-step consultation process with relevant stakeholders (Gold Standard Foundation 2012f: 36–38). The first consultation round includes a presentation of the project design and a discussion of potential impacts with local stakeholders. While this first step of the consultation process is comparable to the stakeholder consultation required under the UNFCCC, the Gold Standard gives particular guidance on how to organize and implement the consultation with the stakeholders. In particular, the Gold Standard stipulates that project developers *proactively* invite local and global stakeholders, including all non-governmental organizations that are based in the respective country and support the Gold Standard to provide comments on the proposed project activity (Gold Standard Foundation 2012f: 36). During a second consultation round, stakeholders can provide feedback on how their comments were taken into account by the project developer in the revised project design document. The stakeholder feedback round must last for at least two months. During this period, the project design document must be made publicly available (Gold Standard Foundation 2012g: 54). Finally, the Gold Standard's sustainable development screen requires the completion of a *Sustainability Monitoring Plan* to scrutinize the particular impact of a proposed project activity and 'verify if the project indeed contributes to sustainable development and/or prevents severe negative environmental, social and/or economic impacts' (Gold Standard Foundation 2012f: 35). In this final process, project developers have to identify certain parameters and test them against the individual Sustainable Development Matrix of the project to evaluate its performance over the whole crediting period. This requirement gives special weight to the sustainable development needs of developing countries and emerging economies vis-à-vis the economic and environmental priorities of industrialized countries (Evans 2011: 51).

THIRD-PARTY VALIDATION AND VERIFICATION

Beyond these three screens, the Gold Standard also requires third-party validation and verification of the project activities undertaken by specialized private auditing companies. These so-called *Designated Operational Entities* are officially accredited under the UNFCCC Secretariat, and their function in the Clean Development Mechanism was defined in the Marrakesh Accords at the 2001 Conference of the Parties to the UNFCCC (UNFCCC 2001: 30–32). Basically, the private auditors have two functions: In the validation process, they assess whether a proposed project meets the requirements for registration under the Gold Standard. This means that the auditor evaluates whether the proposed project will likely fulfill the Gold Standard eligibility criteria. In the verification phase, they periodically review the project activity and measure the GHG emission reductions that have been achieved through a certain project. Hence, the private auditing companies are entrusted with the important task of monitoring whether the project developers meet the different requirements stipulated by the Gold Standard. In addition, the Technical Advisory Committee of the Gold Standard oversees the whole certification process from the initial project registration to the final issuance of offsets. This committee delivers technical expertise, approves methodologies, and supports the further development of the Gold Standard rules and procedures (Gold Standard Foundation 2013a). Its role can therefore be compared to that of the Executive Board in the Clean Development Mechanism. The third-party check by the private auditor company and the oversight through the Technical Advisory Committee shall ensure that 'the fundamental principles of The Gold Standard are followed and documented to the best extent possible' (Gold Standard Foundation 2012f: 13).

THE GOLD STANDARD'S CURRENT SITUATION IN THE COMPLIANCE OFFSET MARKET

In late 2012, the Clean Development Mechanism celebrated its one-billionth Certified Emission Reduction and highlighted its positive impact on the promotion of sustainable development in developing countries (UNFCCC 2012b). In recent years, however, the market-based instrument has run into a serious crisis and some observers have already reported on the imminent collapse or extinction of the Clean Development Mechanism (e.g. Gronewold 2009; Goswami 2012; Harvey 2012). The main problem of the Clean Development Mechanism is the extremely low price for carbon offsets resulting from a rapidly decreasing demand for carbon offset projects, which can be ascribed to a number of factors. First, and most important, due to the lack of an ambitious international climate agreement and the withdrawal of several industrialized countries from the Kyoto Protocol's second commitment period, national governments are no longer forced to invest in carbon offset projects to meet their GHG emission reduction targets (e.g. Newell 2012: 136). Second, because of the financial crisis and the associated decline in economic activity with fewer GHG emissions, several industrialized countries did not exhaust their Kyoto quota. This has led to an over-supply of offsets in the carbon market (e.g. Marcu 2012: 2). Third, a series of scandals around the market-based mechanism, including instances of fraud, conflicts of interests and collusion, as well as outright corruption, have shattered the confidence of many actors in carbon offset markets (e.g. Böhm and Dhabi 2009; Lund 2010; Transparency International 2011).

This development has obviously affected the work of the Gold Standard and made it more difficult for the carbon offset standard to achieve its self-proclaimed objectives. The problem of the Gold Standard is that it largely relies on the demand for high-quality carbon offsets that are sold at higher prices than non-certified carbon offsets (Levin, Cashore, and Koppel 2009: 787). Due to the unsure future of the Clean Development Mechanism, the demand for such offsets has considerably declined, raising serious problems for the Gold Standard. In a personal interview, Adrian Rimmer, the Gold Standard Foundation's *Chief Executive Officer*, acknowledged that 'we need a clear sense of direction sent from the negotiations to boost the carbon market to work.'[7] In a similar vein, a number of investors and project developers noted that the demand for high-quality offsets can only be revived through a large-scale reform of the compliance offset market or the introduction of similar mechanisms.[8] This indicates that, without a far-reaching international climate agreement and the establishment of adequate instruments that create and accelerate a significant demand for premium carbon offsets, the contribution of the Gold Standard to the global response to climate change remains limited.

The Gold Standard in the voluntary carbon offset market

Three years after the initial publication of the Gold Standard rules and procedures for the Clean Development Mechanism, the Gold Standard also launched separate guidelines for the voluntary offset market (Gold Standard Foundation 2006). Hence, the Gold Standard has relatively quickly broadened its operational activities to the voluntary market for carbon offsets. In this type of offset market, the Gold Standard aims at ensuring 'that offsetting emissions is not a zero-sum [Public Relations] stunt, but real engagement with real impact' (Kollmuss *et al.* 2010: 149). Interestingly, since the most recent update of the Gold Standard rules and procedures published in 2012, the Gold Standard no longer releases two different manuals for the two forms of offset markets. Instead, the Gold Standard Foundation has combined the guidelines for projects undergoing Gold Standard certification in both the compliance and voluntary offset markets. The remaining criteria for voluntary offset projects are now merely described in certain paragraphs. This underlines the great similarity between the Gold Standard for the Clean Development Mechanism and the voluntary offset market. In the following sections, I first examine the similarities of the Gold Standard requirements for the compliance and voluntary offset markets. Then, I point to the most relevant differences between them and delineate the current situation of the Gold Standard in the voluntary offset market.

SIMILARITIES TO THE GOLD STANDARD FOR THE COMPLIANCE OFFSET MARKET

In general, the Gold Standard requirements for the certification of projects under the Clean Development Mechanism also apply to projects in the voluntary carbon market. This means that voluntary offset projects seeking to obtain the Gold Standard label have to pass all three screens described above. At first, voluntary project activities have to adhere to the Gold Standard's project eligibility screen. This also entails that project developers of voluntary projects send a letter to the public administration of the project host country in order to communicate the launch of the project (Gold Standard Foundation 2012g: 47). After that, voluntary offset projects have to pass the rigorous additionality screen of the Gold Standard that principally follows the rules and procedures of the Clean Development Mechanism (Gold Standard Foundation 2012f: 31–32). And then, voluntary projects have to prove that they meet the requirements of the sustainable development screen and demonstrate that the project activity leads to co-benefits and avoids negative impacts in the project host country (Gold Standard Foundation 2012f: 32–35). In addition, voluntary offset project activities certified by the Gold Standard must also be validated and verified by a third-party private auditing company. The external validation and verification requirements of the Gold Standard for projects in the compliance and voluntary offset markets are largely identical (Kollmuss *et al.* 2010: 153). In the absence of a centralized body that supervises the voluntary offset market, third-party validation and verification is an indispensable element for ensuring that the project activities generate real, permanent, and additional GHG emission reductions. Beyond that, the Gold Standard's Technical Advisory Committee that evaluates and approves all project activities and methodologies used in the voluntary offset market oversees the certification process. The Technical Advisory Committee and the Gold Standard's Secretariat, as well as the non-governmental organizations supporting the Gold Standard, can also require clarifications and corrections from the project developer after the verification report has been published (Gold Standard Foundation 2012f: 46).

This shows that the Gold Standard's rules and procedures for voluntary offset projects very much resemble those for the compliance offset market. Most important for the focus of this case study, the Gold Standard for the voluntary offset market is largely modeled on the regulatory framework of the Clean Development Mechanism and builds upon many of the methodologies developed for the compliance offset market (Stripple and Lövbrand 2010: 175–176). This is in line with more general findings that the voluntary offset market is closely coupled to the Clean Development Mechanism. Some scholars have even pointed out that the voluntary market lives in the 'shadow' of the compliance market (Bulkeley and Newell 2010: 101; Newell and Paterson 2010: 125; Lederer 2012: 533). A further example that illustrates the great similarity between the compliance and voluntary offset markets is the establishment of a registry for voluntary offset projects certified by the Gold Standard. While the Clean Development Mechanism demands that all Certified Emission Reductions are issued and tracked through a central registry, the Gold Standard Foundation has followed this practice and installed a registry for its voluntary offset projects in order to ensure 'the transparency, quality, reliability and security of these carbon commodities for the marketplace' (Gold Standard Foundation 2013f). Against this background, it can be argued that private carbon offset standards have rendered the structure of the voluntary offset market very similar to the regulatory framework of the Clean Development Mechanism. In particular, the supply chains in the voluntary offset market apparently follow those in the compliance offset market (Stripple and Lövbrand 2010: 175). This suggests that the rules and procedures created at the intergovernmental level for the compliance offset market have been copied by private certification schemes and extended their impact beyond their initial reach.

DIFFERENCES IN THE GOLD STANDARD FOR THE VOLUNTARY OFFSET MARKET

As noted above, until 2009, the Gold Standard still published two separate manuals and toolkits for the development of projects in the compliance and voluntary offset markets. In mid-2012, however, the Gold Standard released a combined set of rules and procedures for the evaluation of climate change mitigation projects in both types of offset markets. While this underscores the increasing similarity between the Gold Standard rules and procedures for the compliance and voluntary offset markets, some special requirements and simplified procedures remain in place for the certification of voluntary offset projects. First, while voluntary offset projects may, in principle, be conducted in any country, the Gold Standard contains specifications for those project activities located in countries with legally binding GHG emission targets. In such cases, the project developer has to prove that the achieved Voluntary Emission Reductions are backed by the retirement of an equivalent amount of national GHG emission allowances under the Kyoto Protocol before the Gold Standard can issue credits for voluntary offset projects (Gold Standard Foundation 2012f: 23). Second, while Clean Development Mechanism projects certified by the Gold Standard must employ the methodologies approved by the Clean Development Mechanism's Executive Board to demonstrate and assess project additionality, voluntary carbon offset projects can use either the UNFCCC-approved methodologies or a specific Gold Standard methodology (Gold Standard Foundation 2012f: 32). Moreover, voluntary offset projects that apply for the Gold Standard label can develop new methodologies for the evaluation of the environmental integrity of carbon offset projects to be approved by the Gold Standard's Technical Advisory Committee. Interestingly, this has resulted in the development of several innovative methodologies and techniques used for the certification of climate change mitigation projects. In particular, the Gold Standard currently has twelve methodologies in operation for the voluntary offset market, most of them in the energy sector, which were created in collaboration with individual project developers (Gold Standard Foundation 2013c). Some of these methodologies were designed especially to make the revenues of carbon offset markets more accessible to the least-developed countries. These innovations might, in turn, influence the rules and procedures of the compliance offset market and improve the regulatory structure of the Clean Development Mechanism (Harris 2007; Guigon, Bellassen, and Ambrosi 2009; Hoffmann 2011). This underscores the pioneer character of private certification schemes in global climate governance. Third, while climate change mitigation projects certified by the Gold Standard have to show clear sustainable development benefits, the requirements for voluntary offset projects are slightly less demanding. For instance, in contrast to the requirements for the certification of projects under the Clean Development Mechanism, no global stakeholder consultation is required for voluntary offset projects (Gold Standard Foundation 2012g: 57). In addition, voluntary *micro-scale* project activities do not have to be validated and verified by a private auditing company, but can opt for a simplified validation and verification process (Gold Standard Foundation 2012f: 40 and 44).[9] This enables those project activities with a very small size to obtain the Gold Standard label without bearing unreasonably high expenditures for third-party validation and verification procedures (Kollmuss *et al.* 2010: 154).

THE GOLD STANDARD'S CURRENT SITUATION IN THE VOLUNTARY OFFSET MARKET

The recent trends in the market for voluntary carbon offsets indicate that it suffers from the current crisis and uncertain future of the Clean Development Mechanism. While the volume and value of the voluntary carbon offset market has grown rapidly in the past few years, the growth rates have recently stagnated and the market value has decreased by approximately 11 percent in 2012 (Peters-Stanley and Yin 2013: 10). As in the compliance offset market, there is a trend towards lower offset prices in the voluntary offset market, although the prices for Voluntary Emission Reductions have not fallen as dramatically as those for Certified Emission Reductions in the Clean Development Mechanism. One of the key problems of the voluntary offset market is that because of the over-supply and low price of Certified Emission Reductions, many project developers try to sell the offsets generated from their projects in the voluntary market (e.g. Vitelli 2013). As a result, the prices for carbon offsets also decline considerably in the voluntary carbon market. This shows once again the close relationship between the Clean Development Mechanism and the voluntary offset market. Moreover, due to the lack of signs that an ambitious international climate agreement might soon be adopted, the voluntary offset market is currently not very attractive for corporations seeking to prepare for the introduction of legally binding GHG emission reduction obligations. In particular, according to Peter Newell, '[e]ven carbon market entrepreneurs are casting doubt on whether future investments in carbon markets are worth their while in the absence of serious targets to maintain interest in them' (Newell 2012: 136).

The Gold Standard for the voluntary offset market might particularly be affected by the downward trend in the prices for voluntary carbon offsets. As a high-quality private carbon offset standard, the Gold Standard relies on private and public investors that pay a premium price for carbon offsets to showcase their particular environmental commitment. The 2013 Voluntary Carbon Market report commissioned by *Ecosystem Marketplace* and *Bloomberg New Energy Finance* stated that the price decline of offsets in the voluntary carbon market was 'most apparent in the high-priced offset range (\$10+/tCO_2e) where the volume of offsets contracted at these prices fell by 46%' (Peters-Stanley and Yin 2013: 12). Furthermore, the low carbon price in the voluntary offset market might allow particularly cheap offsets with questionable environmental and social integrity to gain ground and at the same time damage the credibility of the market. In consequence, the oversupply and recent price decline of offsets in the compliance carbon market could lead to a 'suffocation of the supply of innovative Gold Standard and Verified Carbon Standard projects designed specifically for voluntary carbon market buyers' (Crouch 2012: 3).

The Gold Standard Foundation at the UNFCCC conferences

Shortly after the release of the Gold Standard rules and procedures for the voluntary offset market in mid-2006, the Gold Standard Foundation was officially accredited as a non-governmental observer organization by the UNFCCC

Secretariat (UNFCCC 2007). Since then, the Gold Standard Foundation has been increasingly engaged in the UNFCCC conferences and tried to exert influence at the intergovernmental level in a variety of ways. Most obviously, the Gold Standard Foundation has delivered a number of submissions, comments, and recommendations to the international climate negotiations, in which it provided input and insights from its practical experiences on different aspects related to the certification of climate change mitigation projects (e.g. UNFCCC 2009; 2010; 2011b). As Adrian Rimmer underlined in a personal interview:

> The Gold Standard Foundation has been participating in the policy dialogue with the [Clean Development Mechanism's] Executive Board and proactively engaged with the [UNFCCC] Secretariat in order to improve the mechanism and represent the interests of the larger NGO [non-governmental organization] community at the international level.[10]

In particular, the Gold Standard Foundation has devoted a great deal of effort to laying emphasis on the goal of sustainable development in the regulatory framework of the Clean Development Mechanism (Gold Standard Foundation 2011a). Beyond that, the Gold Standard has organized a number of official side-events and other activities during the UNFCCC conferences, often in collaboration with other non-governmental organizations, such as *Fairtrade International* or the *Forest Stewardship Council* (Gold Standard Foundation 2012d; 2012e). On these occasions, representatives of the Gold Standard Foundation have repeatedly highlighted the usefulness of the market-based approach for promoting low-carbon growth and achieving sustainable development goals in emerging economies and developing countries. They also called for a reform of the Clean Development Mechanism and urged the negotiators to agree on a far-reaching international agreement with legally binding GHG emission reduction targets to accelerate climate funding and the development of carbon markets (Gold Standard Foundation 2011b). In addition, the Gold Standard Foundation has conducted numerous informal meetings at UNFCCC conferences in recent years with project developers, other private certification initiatives, and members of different national delegations. Thereby, the Gold Standard Foundation seeks to underscore its ability to certify high-quality carbon offset projects and to persuade national governments of the necessity to reflate the global carbon market. This is also reflected in a statement by Tanya Petersen, the Gold Standard Foundation's *Director of Marketing and Communications*, who noticed: 'We seek to demonstrate that high-quality standards for CDM [Clean Development Mechanism] projects can be an addition to the process. (...) But we rely on a strong regulatory scheme that produces a demand for carbon credits.'[11] Thus, it can be stated that the Gold Standard Foundation devotes great efforts to improve the compliance carbon offset market and increasingly pushes for an international market-based instrument that would secure a continuing stable demand for the generation of carbon offsets.

Summary

This case study examined the interaction and interplay between a private certification scheme and the international climate regime. Now, I come back to the analytical framework and sum up the main findings from the case study carried out in this chapter. First, as in the previous case study, no evidence was found in support of the assumption that the operational activities of the Gold Standard conflict with the international climate regime. The Gold Standard Foundation does not seek to establish its own procedures and methodologies as alternative guidelines to the norms and rules established through multilateral treaty-making. In fact, the analysis has shown that the Gold Standard largely builds on the regulatory framework created at the intergovernmental level.

Second, the case study provided some findings in support of the assumption that the operational activities of the Gold Standard complement existing modes of inter-state cooperation. It has become apparent that the Gold Standard contributes to the implementation of the norms and rules anchored in international climate agreements. In particular, the Gold Standard certifies carbon offset projects that deliver environmental and social co-benefits in the project host countries. In this way, the Gold Standard helps accomplish the goals of the Clean Development Mechanism as well as the ultimate objective of the UNFCCC. Most interestingly in this regard is that a number of criteria developed by the Gold Standard go beyond those stipulated by nation-states at the intergovernmental level. The Gold Standard has established stricter requirements for project eligibility than international climate agreements and assigns its label only to those climate change mitigation projects that generate significant sustainable development benefits in the project host countries. Moreover, the Gold Standard supports the development of innovative methodologies for the evaluation of carbon offset projects, especially in the voluntary offset market. In the absence of a centralized regulatory oversight in the voluntary offset market, private carbon offset standards are *de facto* solely responsible for ensuring the environmental integrity of offsets and demonstrating the robustness of GHG emission reductions or removals. In addition, the methodologies developed by the Gold Standard might in the long run also improve the validation and verification processes applied in the compliance offset market. Accordingly, private certification schemes can be regarded as pioneers in the policy domain of climate change.

Thirdly, the case study also provides strong evidence that the Gold Standard relies to a large extent on a functioning global offsetting scheme to be set up by national governments at international climate conferences. The analysis has demonstrated that the Gold Standard builds upon the regulatory framework of the Clean Development Mechanism, which was adopted with the Marrakesh Accords, and uses the rules and procedures created by the Clean Development Mechanism's Executive Board for the evaluation of project activities. The uncertain future of the Clean Development Mechanism and the associated decline of the price for carbon offsets has affected the Gold Standard and made it difficult for the private carbon offset standard to achieve its self-proclaimed objectives. Without the establishment of an international mechanism that generates an incentive for purchasers to invest in carbon offset projects, the contribution of the Gold Standard in the global response to climate change remains arguably limited. Furthermore, the Gold Standard for the voluntary market is largely modeled on the rules and procedures of the Clean Development Mechanism. Voluntary carbon offset projects applying for Gold Standard certification employ many of the methodologies developed for the compliance market and are required to adhere to very similar criteria as the projects in the Clean Development Mechanism. This indicates that the voluntary carbon market is closely coupled to the Clean Development Mechanism. The recent oversupply and declining prices of carbon offsets in the compliance market therefore considerably depress the demand for high-quality projects in the voluntary offset market. For these reasons, the Gold Standard Foundation has recently devoted much effort towards the reform of the existing regulatory framework of the Clean Development Mechanism and pushed for new measures to introduce an efficient international market-based instrument. These findings imply that the operational activities of the Gold Standard to address the problem of climate change are highly dependent on the norms and rules of the international climate regime. Thus, it can be stated that the potential of private carbon offset standards to contribute to the global response to climate change is largely restricted by the lack of a mechanism that would secure a continuing stable demand for investments in carbon offset projects (see Table 5.2).

Conclusions

This case study has pointed out that the Gold Standard plays a crucial role in global climate governance. It is clear that the different operational activities of the Gold Standard Foundation have led to the implementation of the norms and rules anchored in international climate agreements. Consequently, the Gold Standard can be viewed as complementary to existing modes of inter-state cooperation. Moreover, the activities undertaken by private certification schemes might ultimately improve the regulatory structure of the compliance and voluntary offset markets through the application of stringent guidelines and the development of innovative methodologies for the evaluation of carbon offset projects.

As in the previous case study, however, the analysis in this chapter has also shown that the effective operation of the Gold Standard in addressing the problem of climate change is strongly dependent on the existence of an international regulatory framework established in international climate negotiations. Based on the case study in this chapter, it can be argued that the Gold Standard will only contribute to the promotion of societal and environmental co-benefits in emerging economies and developing countries if there is a significant demand for carbon offset projects. Such a demand can be created and accelerated through a reform of the Clean Development Mechanism or the establishment of a similar instrument. Yet, in the absence of a regulatory structure that obligates national governments to meet GHG emission reduction targets, the role and function of the Gold Standard in the global response to climate change remains ambiguous. Most

Table 5.2 Main findings from the analysis of the relationship between the Gold Standard and the international climate regime

Conceptual assumptions	*The Gold Standard: Main findings*
Conflictive relationship	No indication
Complementary relationship	The Gold Standard contributes to the implementation of the norms and rules of the international climate regime by certifying carbon offset projects, which deliver significant sustainable development benefits to developing countries and emerging economies
	The Gold Standard Foundation supports the development of innovative methodologies for the evaluation of carbon offset projects, especially in the voluntary market. These methodologies might also improve the validation and verification processes applied in the compliance offset market
Dependency relationship	The demand for carbon offset projects under the Clean Development Mechanism certified by the Gold Standard is highly dependent on a functioning global offsetting scheme
	The Gold Standard for the voluntary market is also adversely affected by the current crisis of the Clean Development Mechanism, particularly the declining demand for high-quality carbon offsets
	For these reasons, the Gold Standard Foundation strongly advocates a reform of the compliance offset market and pushes for new measures to introduce an efficient international market-based instrument

relevant for the focus of this book, this finding does not only apply to the Gold Standard for the compliance offset market, which naturally must synchronize its certification process with the norms and rules of the international climate regime. This case study has demonstrated that the Gold Standard for the voluntary offset market comprises numerous elements and detailed provisions originally designed for the compliance offset market. The rules and procedures negotiated by national governments for the Clean Development Mechanism have been copied by private certification schemes and obviously extended their impact beyond their initial reach. This suggests that private certification schemes for the measurement and management of GHG emissions have to build upon an adequate framework in order to unfold their full potential for mitigating climate change. In other words, only if nation-states provide the necessary basis will privately created standards be able to effectively tackle the problem of climate change.

Returning to the theoretical background of this study, it can be concluded that the Gold Standard Foundation has adopted an authoritative task in global climate governance. The analysis underlined that the Gold Standard has created rules and procedures for ensuring the credibility of both the voluntary and compliance offset markets. More precisely, the Gold Standard has developed criteria for the evaluation of climate change mitigation projects that go beyond those established by nation-states in international climate negotiations. In addition, the Gold Standard Foundation is involved in the continuous development of innovative methodologies for the certification of carbon offset projects. These methodologies might also influence the rules and procedures of the compliance offset market. It can therefore be argued that the Gold Standard has gained rule-setting authority in carbon markets that is widely acknowledged among the participants in carbon offset markets. Nevertheless, what has also become clear in the analysis is that the function of the Gold Standard in global climate governance does not embody a substitute for the norms and rules of the international climate regime and in no way leads to a shift of authority away from multilateral treaty-making towards private standard-setting initiatives. In fact, the case study in this chapter has underscored that the rules and procedures established at the intergovernmental level have a significant and often overlooked impact on privately created standards for the measurement and management of GHGs. Thus, the emergence of private certification schemes in the issue area of climate change does not challenge state-based forms of governance, but has reaffirmed the centrality of the international climate regime.

References

3Degrees (2008). *First-Ever Transfer on Gold Standard Voluntary Carbon Reduction Registry Conducted by 3Degrees. Press Release, May 13.* San Francisco, CA: 3Degrees.

Andonova, Liliana B.; Betsill, Michele; Bulkeley, Harriet (2009). Transnational Climate Governance. *Global Environmental Politics* 9 (2): 52–73.

Auld, Graeme; Gulbrandsen, Lars H.; McDermott, Constance L. (2008). Certification Schemes and the Impacts on Forests and Forestry. *Annual Review of Environment and Resources* 33: 187–211.

Bäckstrand, Karin (2008). Accountability of Networked Climate Governance: The Rise of Transnational Climate Partnerships. *Global Environmental Politics* 8 (3): 74–102.

Bartley, Tim (2003). Certifying Forests and Factories: States, Social Movements, and the Rise of Private Regulation in the Apparel and Forest Products Fields. *Politics & Society* 31 (3): 433–464.

Bayon, Ricardo; Hawn, Amanda; Hamilton, Katherine (2007). *Voluntary Carbon Markets: An International Business Guide to What They Are and How They Work.* London: Earthscan.

Bernstein, Steven; Betsill, Michele; Hoffmann, Matthew; Paterson, Matthew (2010). A Tale of Two Copenhagens: Carbon Markets and Climate Governance. *Millennium: Journal of International Studies* 39 (1): 161–173.

Bernstein, Steven; Cashore, Benjamin (2004). Non-State Global Governance: Is Forest Certification a Legitimate Alternative to a Global Forest Convention? In: Kirton, John; Trebilcock, Michael. *Hard Choices, Soft Law: Combining Trade, Environment, and Social Cohesion in Global Governance.* Aldershot: Ashgate, 33–64.

Böhm, Steffen; Dhabi, Siddhartha, (eds). (2009). *Unpacking the Offset: The Political Economy of Carbon Markets.* London: MayFly.

Böhm, Steffen; Misoczky, Maria Ceci; Moog, Sandra (2012). Greening Capitalism? A Marxist Critique of Carbon Markets. *Organization Studies* 33 (11): 1617–1638.

Boyd, William; Salzman, James (2011). The Curious Case of Greening in Carbon Markets. *Environmental Law* 41 (1): 73–94.

Broekhoff, Derik; Zyla, Kathryn (2008). *Outside the Cap: Opportunities and Limitations of Greenhouse Gas Offsets*. Washington, DC: World Resources Institute.

Brohe, Arnaud; Eyre, Nick; Howarth, Nicholas (2009). *Carbon Markets: An International Business Guide*. London: Earthscan.

Bulkeley, Harriet; Newell, Peter (2010). *Governing Climate Change*. London: Routledge.

Bumpus, Adam G.; Liverman, Diana M. (2008). Accumulation by Decarbonization and the Governance of Carbon Offsets. *Economic Geography* 84 (2): 127–155.

Büthe, Tim (2010). Private Regulation in the Global Economy: A (P)Review. *Business and Politics* 12 (3): Article 2.

Büthe, Tim; Mattli, Walter (2011). *The New Global Rulers: The Privatization of Regulation in the World Economy*. Princeton, NJ: Princeton University Press.

Callon, Michel (2009). Civilizing Markets: Carbon Trading between In Vitro and In Vivo Experiments. *Accounting Organizations and Society* 34 (3–4): 535–548.

Capoor, Karan; Ambrosi, Philippe (2008). *State and Trends of the Carbon Market 2008*. Washington, DC: The World Bank.

Chan, Sander; Pattberg, Philipp (2008). Private Rule-Making and the Politics of Accountability: Analyzing Global Forest Governance. *Global Environmental Politics* 8 (3): 103–121.

Clapp, Jennifer (1998). The Privatization of Global Environmental Governance: ISO 14000 and the Developing World. *Global Governance* 4 (3): 295–316.

Climate, Community and Biodiversity Alliance, (2013). *CCB Standards*. Available at: www.climate-standards.org/ccb-standards/ (accessed May 22, 2013).

Corbera, Esteve; Estrada, Manuel; Brown, Katrina (2009). How Do Regulated and Voluntary Carbon-Offset Schemes Compare? *Journal of Integrative Environmental Sciences* 6 (1): 25–50.

Crouch, Oliver (2012). *Will the Predicted 'Death' of the CDM Prove Fatal for the Voluntary Carbon Market? News from November 7*. London: The Carbon Neutral Company.

Dhanda, K. Kathy; Hartman, Laura P. (2011). The Ethics of Carbon Neutrality: A Critical Examination of Voluntary Carbon Offset Providers. *Journal of Business Ethics* 100 (1): 119–149.

Djelic, Marie-Laure; Sahlin-Andersson, Kerstin, (eds). (2006). *Transnational Governance: Institutional Dynamics of Regulation*. Cambridge, UK: Cambridge University Press.

Drupp, Moritz A. (2011). Does the Gold Standard Label Hold Its Promise in Delivering Higher Sustainable Development Benefits? A Multi-Criteria Comparison of CDM Projects. *Energy Policy* 39 (3): 1213–1227.

Eliasch, Johan (2008). *Climate Change: Financing Global Forests: The Eliasch Review*. London: Earthscan.

Ellis, Jane; Winkler, Harald; Corfee-Morlot, Jan; Gagnon-Lebrun, Frédéric (2007). CDM: Taking Stock and Looking Forward. *Energy Policy* 35 (1): 15–28.

Evans, Beth Jean (2011). Implications of the Gold Standard Certification Scheme for the Perceived Legitimacy of the Clean Development Mechanism. *Inquiry and Insight: University of Waterloo's Graduate Journal of Political Science* 4 (1): 43–59.

Farenthold, David A.; Mufson, Steven (2007). Cost of Saving the Climate Meets Real-World Hurdles. *Washington Post*, August 16.

Font, Xavier (2002). Environmental Certification in Tourism and Hospitality: Progress, Process and Prospects. *Tourism Management* 23 (3): 197–205.

Fuhr, Harald; Lederer, Markus (2009). Varieties of Carbon Governance in Newly Industrializing Countries. *Journal of Environment & Development* 18 (4): 327–345.
Gilbertson, Tamra; Reyes, Oscar (2009). *Carbon Trading: How It Works and Why It Fails*. Uppsala: Dag Hammarsköld Foundation.
Gillenwater, Michael; Broekhoff, Derik; Trexler, Mark; Hyman, Jasmine; Fowler, Rob (2007). Policing the Voluntary Carbon Market. *Nature Reports Climate Change* 6: 85–87.
Glasbergen, Pieter (2007). Setting the Scene: The Partnership Paradigm in the Making. In: Glasbergen, Pieter; Biermann, Frank; Mol, Arthur P. J. *Partnerships, Governance and Sustainable Development: Reflections on Theory and Practice*. Cheltenham: Edward Elgar, 1–27.
Gold Standard Foundation (2006). *The Gold Standard Voluntary Emission Reductions (VERs): Manual for Project Developers*. Geneva: The Gold Standard Foundation.
Gold Standard Foundation (2007). *First CERs From GS Validated Project*. *Press Release, March 14*. Geneva: The Gold Standard Foundation.
Gold Standard Foundation (2011a). *CDM Executive Board Call for Public Input on the Inclusion of Co-Benefits and Negative Impacts in CDM Documentation: The Gold Standard Foundation Submission*. Geneva: The Gold Standard Foundation.
Gold Standard Foundation (2011b). *COP17 Special Edition*. *Newsletter Q4 2011*. Geneva: The Gold Standard Foundation.
Gold Standard Foundation (2011c). *The Gold Standard: Preparing to Expand the Carbon Market in Under-Represented Regions*. *Press Release, May 27*. Geneva: The Gold Standard Foundation.
Gold Standard Foundation (2012a). *Annex C: Guidance on Project Eligibility*. Geneva: The Gold Standard Foundation.
Gold Standard Foundation (2012b). *Annex H: Guidance Questions for the 'Do No Harm' Assessment*. Geneva: The Gold Standard Foundation.
Gold Standard Foundation (2012c). *Annex I: Guidance on SD Indicators*. Geneva: The Gold Standard Foundation.
Gold Standard Foundation (2012d). *Collaborating at COP18: Gold Standard & FSC*. *Press Release, December 2*. Geneva: The Gold Standard Foundation.
Gold Standard Foundation (2012e). *The Gold Standard and Fairtrade International Announce New Collaboration*. *Press Release, November 30*. Geneva: The Gold Standard Foundation.
Gold Standard Foundation (2012f). *The Gold Standard Requirements: Version 2.2*. Geneva: The Gold Standard Foundation.
Gold Standard Foundation (2012g). *The Gold Standard Toolkit: Version 2.2*. Geneva: The Gold Standard Foundation.
Gold Standard Foundation (2012h). *The Gold Standard: Carbon for Development*. Geneva: The Gold Standard Foundation.
Gold Standard Foundation (2012i). *Standalone Micro-Scale Scheme Rules*. Geneva: The Gold Standard Foundation.
Gold Standard Foundation (2013a). *The Gold Standard 'Technical Advisory Committee': Governance, Guidelines and Responsibilities*. Available at: www.cdmgoldstandard.org/wp-content/uploads/2011/09/TAC-ToRs.pdf Available at:
Gold Standard Foundation (2013b). *Governance*. Available at: www.cdmgoldstandard.org/about-us/governance (accessed July 1, 2013).
Gold Standard Foundation (2013c). *GS Methodologies*. Available at: www.cdmgoldstandard.org/project-certification/gs-methodologies (accessed September 27, 2013).
Gold Standard Foundation (2013d). *Land Use & Forests: Certification Process*. Available at: www.cdmgoldstandard.org/luf/luf_requirements (accessed September 20, 2013).

Gold Standard Foundation (2013e). *Project Pipeline*. Available at: www.cdmgoldstandard.org/our-activities/project-pipeline (accessed July 5, 2013).

Gold Standard Foundation (2013f). *Project Registry*. Available at: www.cdmgoldstandard.org/our-activities/project-registry (accessed September 27, 2013).

Gold Standard Foundation (2013g). *Who We Are*. Available at: www.cdmgoldstandard.org/about-us/who-we-are (accessed May 21, 2013).

Goodward, Jenna; Kelly, Alexia (2010). *The Bottom Line on Offsets*. Washington, DC: World Resources Institute.

Goswami, Urmi A. (2012). UN Climate Change Negotiations 2012: Carbon Credit Market May Collapse Soon. *The Economic Times*, December 1.

Green, Jessica F. (2013). Order out of Chaos: Public and Private Rules for Managing Carbon. *Global Environmental Politics* 13 (2): 1–25.

Gronewold, Nathanial (2009). Is the Clean Development Mechanism Slumping Toward Extinction? *The New York Times*, March 20.

Guigon, Pierre; Bellassen, Valentin; Ambrosi, Philippe (2009). *Voluntary Carbon Markets: What the Standards Say*... Paris: Caisse des Dépôts.

Gulbrandsen, Lars H. (2005). Mark of Sustainability? Challenges for Fishery and Forestry Eco-Labeling. *Environment* 47 (5): 8–23.

Hamilton, Katherine; Sjardin, Milo; Shapiro, Allison; Marcello, Thomas (2009). *Fortifying the Foundation: State of the Voluntary Carbon Markets 2009*. Washington, DC; New York: Ecosystem Market Place and New Carbon Finance.

Harris, Elizabeth (2007). *The Voluntary Carbon Offsets Market: An Analysis of Market Characteristics and Opportunities for Sustainable Development*. London: International Institute for Environment and Development.

Harvey, Fiona (2007). Beware the Carbon Offsetting Cowboys. *Financial Times*, April 26.

Harvey, Fiona (2012). Global Carbon Trading System Has 'Essentially Collapsed'. *The Guardian*, September 10.

Headon, Sam (2009). Whose Sustainable Development? Sustainable Development under the Kyoto Protocol, the 'Coldplay Effect', and the CDM Gold Standard. *Colorado Journal of International Environmental Law and Policy* 20 (2): 127–156.

Hoffmann, Matthew (2011). *Climate Governance at the Crossroads: Experimenting With a Global Response After Kyoto*. Oxford: Oxford University Press.

International Carbon Reduction and Offset Alliance (2013). *About Us*. Available at: www.icroa.org/25/about-us/ (accessed May 31, 2013).

IPCC (2007). *Climate Change 2007. Mitigation of Climate Change. Contribution of Working Group III to the Fourth Assessment Report of the Intergovernmental Panel on Climate Change*. Cambridge, UK: Cambridge University Press.

Karakosta, Charikleia; Marinakis, Vangelis; Letsou, Panagiota; Psarras, John (2013). Does the CDM Offer Sustainable Development Benefits or Not? *International Journal of Sustainable Development and World Ecology* 20 (1): 1–8.

Kollmuss, Anja; Lazarus, Michael; Lee, Carrie; Le Franc, Maurice; Polycarp, Clifford (2010). *Handbook of Carbon Offset Programs: Trading Systems, Funds, Protocols and Standards*. London: Earthscan.

Kollmuss, Anja; Zink, Helge; Polycarp, Clifford (2008). *Making Sense of the Voluntary Carbon Market: A Comparison of Carbon Offset Standards*. Stockholm: Stockholm Environment Institute and Tricorona.

Lederer, Markus (2010). Evaluating Carbon Governance: The Clean Development Mechanism From an Emerging Economy Perspective. *Journal of Energy Markets* 3 (2): 3–25.

Lederer, Markus (2012). Market Making Via Regulation: The Role of the State in Carbon Markets. *Regulation and Governance* 6 (4): 524–544.

Leonard, Kathleen (2009). *Quality Enhancement in Voluntary Carbon Markets: Opening Up for Mainstream*. Hamburg: Diplomica.

Levin, Kelly; Cashore, Benjamin; Koppel, Jonathan (2009). Can Non-State Certification Systems Bolster State-Centered Efforts to Promote Sustainable Development Through the Clean Development Mechanism? *Wake Forest Law Review* 44 (3): 777–798.

Levin, Peter; Espeland, Wendy Nelson (2002). Pollution Futures: Commensuration, Commodification, and the Market for Air. In: Hoffman, Andrew; Ventresca, Marc. *Organizations, Policy, and the Natural Environment*. Stanford, CA: Stanford University Press, 119–150.

Lipschutz, Ronnie D.; Fogel, Cathleen (2002). 'Regulation for the Rest of Us?' Global Civil Society and the Privatization of Transnational Regluation. In: Hall, Rodney Bruce; Biersteker, Thomas J. *The Emergence of Private Authority in Global Governance*. Cambridge, UK: Cambridge University Press, 115–140.

Liverman, Diana M. (2010). Carbon Offsets, the CDM, and Sustainable Development. In: Schellnhuber, Hans Joachim; Molina, Mario; Stern, Nicholas H.; Huber, Veronika; Kadner, Susanne. *Global Sustainability: A Nobel Cause*. Cambridge, UK: Cambridge University Press.

Lövbrand, Eva; Rindefjäll, Teresia; Nordqvist, Joakim (2009). Closing the Legitimacy Gap in Global Environmental Governance? Lessons From the Emerging CDM Market. *Global Environmental Politics* 9 (2): 74–100.

Lovell, Heather C. (2010). Governing the Carbon Offset Market. *Wiley Interdisciplinary Reviews: Climate Change* 1 (3): 353–362.

Lund, Emma (2010). Dysfunctional Delegation: Why the Design of the Clean Development Mechanism's Supervisory System is Fundamentally Flawed. *Climate Policy* 10 (3): 277–288.

Ma'anit, Adam (2006). CO_2NNED: Carbon Offsets Stripped Bare. *The Internationalist* 391.

MacKenzie, Donald (2009). Making Things the Same: Gases, Emission Rights and the Politics of Carbon Markets. *Accounting Organizations and Society* 34 (3–4): 440–455.

Marcu, Andrei (2012). *The Future of the Clean Development Mechanism: Note on the Report "A Call to Action" of the High-Level Panel on CDM Policy Dialogue*. *CEPS Special Report 71*. Brussels: Center for European Policy Studies.

Marx, Axel; Cuypers, Dieter (2010). Forest Certification as a Global Environmental Governance Tool: What Is the Macro-Effectiveness of the Forest Stewardship Council? *Regulation & Governance* 4 (4): 408–434.

Mayer, Frederick; Gereffi, Gary (2010). Regulation and Economic Globalization: Prospects and Limits of Private Governance. *Business and Politics* 12 (3): 1–25.

Muller, Adrian (2008). Risk Management in the Clean Development Mechanism (CDM): The Potential of Sustainability Labels. In: Hansjürgens, Bernd; Antes, Ralf. Economics and Management of Climate Change: Risk, Mitigation and Adaptation. New York: Springer, 193–207.

Murray, James (2009). Government to Boost Demand for CDM Gold Standard Offsets. *BusinessGreen*, April 17.

Newell, Peter (2012). The Political Economy of Carbon Markets: The CDM and Other Stories. *Climate Policy* 12 (1): 135–139.

Newell, Peter; Paterson, Matthew (2010). *Climate Capitalism: Global Warming and the Transformation of the Global Economy*. Cambridge, UK: Cambridge University Press.

Nussbaumer, Patrick (2009). On the Contribution of Labelled Certified Emission Reductions to Sustainable Development: A Multi-Criteria Evaluation of CDM Projects. *Energy Policy* 37 (1): 91–101.

O'Neill, Kate (2009). *The Environment and International Relations*. Cambridge, UK: Cambridge University Press.

Offset Quality Initiative (2013). *OQI Objectives*. Available at: www.offsetqualityinitiative.org/about.html (accessed May 31, 2013).

Olsen, Karen Holm (2007). The Clean Development Mechanism's Contribution to Sustainable Development: A Review of the Literature. *Climatic Change* 84 (1): 59–73.

Olsen, Karen Holm; Fenhann, Jørgen (2008). Sustainable Development Benefits of Clean Development Mechanism Projects: A New Methodology for Sustainability Assessment Based on Text Analysis of the Project Design Documents Submitted for Validation. *Energy Policy* 36 (8): 2819–2830.

Paterson, Matthew (2010). Legitimation and Accumulation in Climate Change Governance. *New Political Economy* 15 (3): 345–368.

Pattberg, Philipp; Stripple, Johannes (2008). Beyond the Public and Private Divide: Remapping Transnational Climate Governance in the 21st Century. *International Environmental Agreements* 8 (4): 367–388.

Paulsson, Emma (2009). A Review of the CDM Literature: From Fine-Tuning to Critical Scrutiny? *International Environmental Agreements* 9 (1): 63–80.

Pearson, Ben (2007). Market Failure: Why the Clean Development Mechanism Won't Promote Clean Development. *Journal of Cleaner Production* 15 (2): 247–252.

Pérez-Lombard, Luis; Ortiz, José; González, Rocío; Maestre, Ismael R. (2009). A Review of Benchmarking, Rating and Labelling Concepts Within the Framework of Building Energy Certification Schemes. *Energy and Buildings* 41 (3): 272–278.

Peskett, Leo; Luttrell, Cecilia; Iwata, Mari (2007). *Can Standards for Voluntary Carbon Offsets Ensure Development Benefits? Forestry Briefing 13*. London: Overseas Development Institute.

Peters-Stanley, Molly; Hamilton, Katherine (2012). *Developing Dimension: State of the Voluntary Carbon Markets 2012*. Washington, DC; New York: Ecosystem Marketplace and Bloomberg New Energy Finance.

Peters-Stanley, Molly; Yin, Daphne (2013). *Maneuvering the Mosaic: State of the Voluntary Carbon Markets 2013*. Washington, DC; New York: Ecosystem Marketplace and Bloomberg New Energy Finance.

Peters, Anne; Koechlin, Lucy; Fenner Zinkernagel, Gretta (2009). Non-State Actors as Standard-Setters: Framing the Issue as an Interdisciplinary Fashion. In: Peters, Anne; Koechlin, Lucy; Förster, Till; Fenner Zinkernagel, Gretta. *Non-State Actors as Standard-Setters*. Cambridge, UK: Cambridge University Press, 1–32.

Raynolds, Laura T.; Murray, Douglas L.; Heller, Andrew (2007). Regulating Sustainability in the Coffee Sector: A Comparative Analysis of Third-Party Environmental and Social Certification Initiatives. *Agriculture and Human Values* 24 (2): 147–163.

Revkin, Andrew (2007). Carbon-Neutral Is Hip, But Is It Green? *New York Times*, April 29.

Schiermeier, Quirin (2006). Climate Credits. *Nature* 444 (7122): 976–977.

Schneider, Lambert (2007). *Is the CDM Fulfilling Its Environmental and Sustainable Objectives? An Evaluation of the CDM and Options for Improvement*. Berlin: Ökoinstitut.

Smith, Kevin (2007). *The Carbon Neutral Myth: Offset Indulgences for Your Climate Sins*. Amsterdam: Carbon Trade Watch.

Stephan, Benjamin; Paterson, Matthew (2012). The Politics of Carbon Markets: An Introduction. *Environmental Politics* 21 (4): 545–562.

Sterk, Wolfgang; Wittneben, Bettina (2009). Enhancing the Clean Development Mechanism Through Sectoral Approaches: Definitions, Applications and Ways Forward. *International Environmental Agreements* 6 (3): 271–287.

Sterk, Wolfgang; Rudolph, Frederic; Arens, Christof; Eichhorst, Urda; Kiyar, Dagmar; Wang-Helmreich, Hanna; Swiderski, Magdalene (2009). *Further Development of the Project-Based Mechanisms in a Post-2012 Regime*. Berlin: German Environment Ministry.

Stern, Nicholas H. (2007). *The Economics of Climate Change: The Stern Review*. Cambridge, UK: Cambridge University Press.

Streck, Charlotte (2007). The Governance of the CDM: The Case for Strength and Stability. *Environmental Liability* 15 (2): 91–100.

Streck, Charlotte (2010). *The Concept of Additionality Under the UNFCCC and the Kyoto Protocol: Implications for Environmental Integrity and Equity*. London: University College London.

Streck, Charlotte; Lin, Jolene (2008). Making Markets Work: A Review of CDM Performance and the Need for Reform. *European Journal of International Law* 19 (2): 409–442.

Stripple, Johannes (2010). Weberian Climate Policy: Administrative Rationality Organized as a Market. In: Bäckstrand, Karin; Khan, Jamil; Kronsell, Annica; Lövbrand, Eva. *Environmental Politics and Deliberative Democracy: Examining the Promise of New Modes of Governance*. Cheltenham: Edward Elgar, 67–84.

Stripple, Johannes; Lövbrand, Eva (2010). Carbon Market Governance Beyond the Public-Private Divide. In: Biermann, Frank; Pattberg, Philipp; Zelli, Fariborz. *Global Climate Governance Beyond 2012*. Cambridge, UK: Cambridge University Press, 165–182.

Subbarao, Srikanth; Lloyd, Bob (2011). Can the Clean Development Mechanism (CDM) Deliver? *Energy Policy* 39 (3): 1600–1611.

Sutter, Christoph; Parreno, Juan Carlos (2007). Does the Current Clean Development Mechanism (CDM) Deliver Its Sustainable Development Claim? An Analysis of Officially Registered CDM Projects. *Climatic Change* 84 (1): 75–90.

Swiss Federal Office for the Environment (2013). *Fact Sheet: Emission Reductions Achieved Abroad: Quality, Quantity and Carry-Over*.

Taiyab, Nadaa (2006). *Exploring the Market for Voluntary Carbon Offsets*. London: International Institute for Environment and Development.

Taylor, Peter Leigh; Murray, Douglas L.; Raynolds, Laura T. (2005). Keeping Trade Fair: Governance Challenges in the Fair Trade Coffee Initiative. *Sustainable Development* 13 (3): 199–208.

The World Bank (2011). *State and Trends of the Carbon Market 2011*. Washington, DC: The World Bank.

Transparency International (2011). *Global Corruption Report: Climate Change*. London: Earthscan.

UNFCCC (1997). *Kyoto Protocol to the United Nations Framework Convention on Climate Change*. Bonn: UNFCCC Secretariat.

UNFCCC (2001). *Report of the Conference of the Parties on Its Seventh Session, held at Marrakesh from October 29 to November 10, 2001. Addendum: Part Two: Action Taken by the Conference of the Parties. Volume II: FCCC/CP/2001/13/Add.2*. Bonn: UNFCCC Secretariat.

UNFCCC (2004). *The Kyoto Protocol's Clean Development Mechanism Takes Off: First CDM Project Registered. Press Release, November 18*. Bonn: UNFCCC Secretariat.

UNFCCC (2007). *Admission of Observers: Intergovernmental and Non-Ggovernmental Organizations. FCCC/CP/2007/2*. Bonn: UNFCCC Secretariat.

UNFCCC (2009). *Proceedings of the Practitioners Workshop on AMS-I.E, AMS-II.G and AMS I.C: CDM Methodologies for Household Cooking Energy Supply*. Bonn: UNFCCC Secretariat.

UNFCCC (2010). *Clean Development Mechanism Small Scale Working Group. F-CDM-SSCwg ver 01 SSC_401*. Bonn: UNFCCC Secretariat.

UNFCCC (2011a). *Executive Board of the Clean Development Mechanism: 61st Meeting Report. CDM-EB-61*. Bonn: UNFCCC Secretariat.

UNFCCC (2011b). *Project Developer Forum: Letter to the Board. F-CDM-RtB*. Bonn: UNFCCC Secretariat.

UNFCCC (2012a). *Benefits of the Clean Development Mechanism*. Bonn: UNFCCC Secretariat.

UNFCCC (2012b). *Kyoto Protocol's Clean Development Mechanism Passes One Billionth Certified Emission Reduction Milestone. Press Release, September 7*. Bonn: UNFCCC Secretariat.

UNFCCC (2012c). *Methodological Tool: Tool for the Demonstration and Assessment of Additionality. Version 07.0.0*. Bonn: UNFCCC Secretariat.

UNFCCC (2013a). *CDM Insights: Project Activities*. Available at: http://cdm.unfccc.int/Statistics/Public/CDMinsights/index.html (accessed June 24, 2013).

UNFCCC (2013b). *Panels, Working Groups, Teams*. Available at: http://cdm.unfccc.int/Panels/index.html (accessed June 28, 2013).

United Nations Environment Programme Risø Centre (2013). *CDM/JI Pipeline Overview Page*. Available at: http://cdmpipeline.org/overview.htm (accessed June 24, 2013).

Verified Carbon Standard Association (2012). *VCS & CCB Join Forces to Streamline Project Approval and Credit Issuance. Press Release, November 28*. Washington, DC: Verified Carbon Standard Association.

Verified Carbon Standard Association (2013). *Who We Are: Our Mission*. Available at: http://v-c-s.org/who-we-are/mission-history (accessed May 22, 2013).

Vitelli, Allessandro (2013). *Carbon Offset Projects Look for Exit as UN Prices Crash 98%. June 12*. New York: Bloomberg.

Wara, Michael (2007). Is the Global Carbon Market Working? *Nature* 445 (7128): 595–596.

Werksman, Jacob (1998). The Clean Development Mechanism: Unwrapping the 'Kyoto Surprise'. *Review of European, Comparative and International Environmental Law* 7 (2): 147–158.

Werksman, Jacob; Cameron, James (2000). The Clean Development Mechanism: The Kyoto Surprise. In: Gómez-Echeverri, Luis. *Climate Change and Development: A Collaborative Project of the UNDP Regional Bureau for Latin America and Yale School of Forestry and Environmental Studies*. New Haven, CT: Yale School of Forestry and Environmental Studies, 249–270.

Wheatley, Steven (2009). Democratic Governance beyond the State: The Legitimacy of Non-State Actors as Standard Setters. In: Peters, Anne; Koechlin, Lucy; Förster, Till. *Non-State Actors as Standard-Setters*. Cambridge, UK: Cambridge University Press, 215–240.

Yamin, Farhana (2005). *Climate Change and Carbon Markets: A Handbook of Emission Reduction Mechanisms*. London: Earthscan.

Yamin, Farhana; Depledge, Joanna (2004). *The International Climate Change Regime: A Guide to Rules, Institutions and Procedures*. Cambridge, UK: Cambridge University Press.

Notes

1 The partnership initiating the Climate, Community and Biodiversity Standards comprised *British Petroleum*; the *Tropical Agriculture Research and Higher Education Center*; the *Center for International Forestry Research*; *Conservation International*; the *World Agroforestry Centre*; *Intel*; the *Hamburg Institute of International Economics*; *Nature Conservancy*; *SC Johnson*; *Weyerhaeuser*; and the *Wildlife Conservation Society* (Bayon, Hawn, and Hamilton 2007: 122).

2 The other two flexible mechanisms introduced with the Kyoto Protocol are *International Emissions Trading* and *Joint Implementation*. For a comprehensive discussion of these instruments, see the work by Yamin and Depledge (2004: 136–196).

3 The abbreviation CO_2e stands for carbon dioxide equivalents, which is the standard measurement unit used to compare different types of GHGs based on their global warming potential.

4 Most recently, the Gold Standard Foundation has started to expand its scope into land use and forestry. In collaboration with different partner organizations, the Gold Standard currently develops particular requirements for project activities in the areas of afforestation and reforestation, improved forest management, and climate-smart agriculture (Gold Standard Foundation 2013d).

5 The complete list of the various specific criteria for project eligibility developed by the Gold Standard can be found in Annex C of the Gold Standard rules and procedures (Gold Standard Foundation 2012a).

6 These principles include respect for internationally proclaimed human rights; preservation of settlements and cultural heritage; protection of employees' freedom of association and their right to collective bargaining; prohibition of forced or compulsory labor as well as child labor; a ban on any form of discrimination; safe and healthy work conditions; a precautionary approach to environmental challenges; conservation of critical natural habitats; and anti-corruption measures (Gold Standard Foundation 2012b).

7 Personal interview conducted on December 5, 2012 with Adrian Rimmer, *The Gold Standard Foundation's Chief Executive Officer*, during the 18th Conference of the Parties to the UNFCCC held in Doha from November 26 to December 8, 2012.

8 Personal interviews conducted on December 3, 2012 with Sven Braden, CARLO Foundation; René Estermann, MyClimate; and Simone Mori, Enel Foundation, during the 18th Conference of the Parties to the UNFCCC held in Doha from November 26 to December 8, 2012.

9 Projects will fall under the micro-scale scheme if the GHG emission reductions achieved through the project do not exceed the amount of 10,000 tCO_2e per year (Gold Standard Foundation 2012i).

10 Personal interview conducted on December 5, 2012 with Adrian Rimmer, *The Gold Standard Foundation's Chief Executive Officer*, during the 18th Conference of the Parties to the UNFCCC held in Doha from November 26 to December 8, 2012.

11 Personal interview confucted on December 5, 2012 with Tanya Petersen, *The Gold Standard Foundation's Director of Marketing and Communications*, during the 18th Conference of the Parties to the UNFCCC held in Doha from November 26 to December 8, 2012.

6 Business self-regulation

The Greenhouse Gas Protocol

Overview

The origin of business self-regulation as it is currently practiced date back to the 1960s. At that time, several multinational corporations began to adopt the term 'corporate social responsibility' in order to highlight their philanthropic activities and responsible business practices (e.g. Carroll 1999). While the concept of corporate social responsibility was initially discussed primarily in the United States, it has gradually become a global phenomenon in the past decades (Vogel 2005). Basically, the concept implies 'that business enterprises have some responsibility to society beyond that of making profits for their shareholders' (Carroll and Shabana 2010: 85). To underline their commitment to responsible business behavior, numerous corporations have developed or subscribed to so-called voluntary codes of conduct in the past few years. In general, these codes of conduct consist of more or less broadly defined guidelines for socially and ethically responsible business performance. Today, almost every multinational corporation and many smaller enterprises have committed themselves to a certain code of conduct and published the respective guidelines on their websites. The issues addressed in these codes embrace human rights, labor standards, non-discrimination rules, anti-corruption measures, and environmental protection.

One of the most prominent business codes is the *United Nations Global Compact*, which was initiated by the former United Nations Secretary-General Kofi Annan at the World Economic Forum held in Davos in 1999 (United Nations Global Compact 2013). It consists of ten principles that aim to hold businesses accountable for their operations and urge them to benefit economies and societies throughout the world. Moreover, the Global Compact encourages civil society organizations to scrutinize the responsibilities of corporations and thereby 'forms a governance framework without necessarily applying a legal framework' (Sahlin-Andersson 2006: 599). Other well-known examples of business codes of conduct include the *Business Charter for Sustainable Development*, the *ISO 14000 Environmental Management Standards*, the *OECD Guidelines for Multinational Enterprises*, the *Chemical Manufacturers Association's Responsible Care Program*, and the principles of the *Coalition for Environmentally Responsible Economies*. Although these codes of conduct differ in a number of ways, they all have in common that they are not legally binding and that individual corporations voluntarily accept their provisions for social and ethical responsibilities. Hence, they are clearly distinct from conventional 'command-and-control' regulatory approaches (e.g. Kolk and Tulder 2005).

Several factors have been proposed to explain the recent growth of voluntary business regulation in world politics. First and foremost, due to the expansion of economic globalization, nation-states and international institutions have apparently lost some of their control over certain regulatory functions, particularly pertaining to the activities of globally operating corporations (e.g. Strange 1996). This has raised the question of how multinational corporations can be held accountable for their activities, and increased the public pressure on corporations through activist campaigns and critical media reports (e.g. Newell 2000; Koenig-Archibugi 2004; Porter and Kramer 2006). As a result, many corporations now engage in dialogues with activist groups and seek to avoid becoming a target of critical campaigns by adopting a specific code of corporate conduct. Second, and related to the previous point, in such a politicized environment, corporations are increasingly concerned about their reputation. Various authors have shown that particularly large companies with a strong and visible brand are highly vulnerable to negative publicity and therefore aim at enhancing their reputation through high-quality production standards (Bennett and Lagos 2007; Conroy 2007; Deitelhoff and Wolf 2013). Third, according to a number of authors, corporations undertake self-regulatory efforts to forestall or slow down the development of more stringent national or international regulations (Braithwaite and Fisse 1993: 222–224; Gereffi, Garcia-Johnson, and Sasser 2001: 59; Vogel 2010: 77). These scholars point out that many corporations favor self-regulatory measures, as they allow them to develop and formulate provisions that are in line with their own corporate interests. In addition, authors emphasize that business leaders might undergo individual learning processes and suggest that certain industry sectors have disseminated knowledge and information on the benefits of voluntary business regulation (Ruggie 2003; Pattberg 2006). This has led to several sector-specific rules and procedures and a number of widely accepted best or good practices for responsible corporate behavior within the business community (Haufler 2001: 111).

Not surprisingly, adherents of classical approaches to international politics have not paid much attention to the role of private corporations in world politics. Only in the past few years have an increasing number of authors recognized business actors 'as being able to provide knowledge, expertise, material resources and strategic advantages to institutions of global governance' (Rittberger *et al.* 2008: 7). Scholars concerned with the changing role of the corporate sector in world politics have focused on a number of specific aspects regarding voluntary global business regulation. Examples of the issues addressed in their studies include the emerging partnerships between corporations and non-governmental organizations (e.g. Arts 2002; Kourula and Halme 2008; Utting 2012), the interaction of business self-regulatory initiatives and governmental intervention (e.g. King and Lenox 2000; Gond, Kang, and Moon 2011), and the general effectiveness of business self-regulation (e.g. Kolk and Tulder 2002; Fuchs 2007; Borck and

Coglianese 2009). Overall, the emergence of voluntary business regulation in global affairs has generated a controversial debate among scholars and policy-makers concerned with world politics. For proponents, the advantages of global business self-regulation are clear. They contend that voluntary corporate standards are marked by greater flexibility and can be implemented more easily than traditional forms of governmental regulation. Moreover, they may have a long-lasting positive impact on the behavior of corporations (Sahlin-Andersson 2004; Ruggie 2007; Brammer, Jackson, and Matten 2012). Critics, on the other hand, hold that business self-regulatory initiatives often constitute little more than 'window-dressing' activities without real enforcement mechanisms and are, in fact, inherently incapable of eliminating the negative social effects of globalized capitalism (Lipschutz and Rowe 2005: 4). While these two perspectives represent two of the most contrasting views in the scholarly discussion, recent studies imply that the success of voluntary business regulation in driving corporations towards more socially and environmentally responsible practices varies enormously across different industry sectors (e.g. Vogel 2010).

In the past few years, an increasing number of corporations have also started to engage in the voluntary management of their GHG emissions. Certainly, the different business self-regulatory initiatives aimed at tackling climate change did not appear out of nowhere. When concerns about the problem of climate change led to initial policy responses at the intergovernmental level in the late 1980s, the vast majority of corporations vehemently opposed any kind of standards that put limits on their activities. After the adoption of the Kyoto Protocol, however, many business actors changed their strategy and began to adopt a proactive stance towards the problem of climate change (Pinkse and Kolk 2009: 3). Since then, companies have not only complied with existing regulations established by nation-states and international institutions, but have also taken voluntary steps to tackle climate change. Most obviously, corporations voluntarily calculate the GHG emissions associated with their operations and publish reports on their social and environmental performance (Association of Chartered Certified Accountants and Global Reporting Initiative 2009). Beyond that, enterprises are gradually reducing their GHG emissions on a voluntary basis through the introduction of energy efficiency programs and low-carbon technologies. Against this backdrop, many authors have recently pointed to the growing importance of business self-regulatory initiatives for adjusting the regulatory deficit in the policy domain of climate change (e.g. Begg, van der Woerd, and Levy 2005; Levy and Newell 2005a; Sullivan 2008a; Strasser 2011; Stoner and Wankel 2012). These authors argue that voluntary global business regulation can help close the gap in the implementation of international climate agreements. According to Philipp Pattberg and Johannes Stripple, business self-regulatory initiatives have consequently attained authority in global climate governance because they establish the norm of corporate disclosure of GHG emissions and voluntary GHG emission reductions (Pattberg and Stripple 2008: 383).

Thus, in sum, business self-regulation has become increasingly prominent in global policy-making and attracted the interest of numerous scholars of world politics. In the past few years, several authors have also dedicated growing attention to voluntary efforts of the corporate sector to address climate change. Using again the same structure as in the previous two case studies, this chapter continues with a review of the emergence of business self-regulatory initiatives concerned with the issue of climate change. Thereafter, I examine how voluntary corporate climate initiatives operate, summarize why they are considered important in global climate governance, and connect the discussion to the theoretical background presented in the third chapter of this study. Then, I focus on one business self-regulatory initiative and explore its interplay with the intergovernmental level. By employing the analytical framework outlined above, I investigate in particular how the different areas of operation of the *Greenhouse Gas Protocol* relate to the international climate regime. In the final sections, I sum up the main findings from the empirical analysis and formulate conclusions for the theoretical debate on the concept of authority in global climate governance.

The emergence of business self-regulation in global climate governance

Business and industrial activities account for the lion's share of human-induced GHG emissions. Consequently, the introduction of emission controls for GHGs poses a difficult challenge for most globally operating corporations. In general terms, corporate actors are confronted with the risk of higher costs for energy and lower demands for energy-intensive products. The industry sectors most heavily affected by political measures addressing climate change through the adoption of national GHG emission reduction targets are the fossil fuel and automobile industries, as well as several other industry sectors that depend on low energy prices, particularly the aluminum, cement, and paper industries. For that reason, the initial business response to the issue of climate change was, in large parts of the business community, marked by great skepticism and at times even hostility (Newell and Paterson 1998: 682–688; Pinkse and Kolk 2009: 3–7; Bulkeley and Newell 2010: 88–92). Especially in the United States, several large companies from the oil and automobile industries made great efforts to question the scientific basis of the problem of climate change and highlighted the economic costs associated with GHG emission controls (e.g. Jones and Levy 2009). To coordinate their lobbying strategies, companies from the United States and other industrialized countries formed different so-called umbrella groups. The two most notable examples in this regard constitute the *Global Climate Coalition* and the *Climate Council*. These organizations have, in the early stages of the international climate regime, strongly lobbied against the introduction of regulatory measures to mitigate climate change (Newell and Paterson 1998: 683). In subsequent years, however, the picture changed step-by-step and a number of companies have now started to perceive the issue of climate change increasingly as a business opportunity rather than a threat to their profit margins (e.g. Lash and Wellington 2007). According to various authors, the emergence of a positive approach towards addressing climate change among a certain segment of the business community has mainly been caused by the outcome of the international climate negotiations. As Jonatan Pinkse and Ans Kolk acknowledge, the key factor for corporate strategic change was the introduction of legally binding obligations for industrialized countries to reduce their GHG emissions through the Kyoto Protocol. These two scholars state that '[t]his event spurred the development of regulation and increased the pressure from non-governmental organisations (NGOs) on governments to ensure ratification of the Protocol, and on companies, which were urged to take appropriate steps to address global warming' (Pinkse and Kolk 2009: 3). They further hold that in the years following the adoption of the Kyoto Protocol corporations did not only take measures to achieve compliance with the emerging regulations under national legislation. In fact, several corporations went beyond compliance and decided to voluntarily address the problem of climate change, and moved towards a more environmentally sound production.

Basically, two broad dimensions of voluntary business regulation can be distinguished in global climate governance. The first dimension is the strategic choice by several companies to understand climate change as a management improvement opportunity. Some firms have played a particularly active role in this regard. Examples include the oil and gas companies *BP* and *Shell*, the chemical enterprise *DuPont*, the technology and consulting corporation *IBM*, and the industrial conglomerate *General Electric*. All of these well-known multinational corporations have undertaken voluntary efforts to invest in low-carbon products and technologies, and communicated their particular climate change commitment to their clients and shareholders (Kolk and Levy 2001: 501–502; Vogel 2005: 123–126; Bulkeley and Newell 2010: 92–93). The formation of this accommodative stance towards climate change in some parts of the corporate sector has been supported by different business-oriented organizations, such as the *Pew Center on Global Climate Change* or the *Climate Group*. These organizations contributed to the spread of a certain 'win-win' rhetoric of ecological modernization, 'which puts faith in technology, entrepreneurship, voluntary partnerships, and flexible market-based measures' (Jones and Levy 2009: 223). The 'win-win' concept of voluntary corporate action is based on the premise that internal corporate solutions for the respective environmental problem are available and that these improvements are also profitable for the corporation (Auld, Bernstein, and Cashore 2008: 415). In other words, the concept presupposes that voluntary business activities to control GHG emissions produce cost savings and new market opportunities for companies (e.g. Porter and van der Linde 1995; Mol 2001; Jänicke and Jacob 2004). According to Harriet Bulkeley and Peter Newell, this type of business self-regulation reflects 'the rise of climate change as a corporate social responsibility (CSR) issue as well as growing recognition of the economic possibilities heralded by low carbon technologies and new carbon markets' (Bulkeley and Newell 2010: 92). In the past few years, this type of business self-regulation has come under critical scrutiny. Several authors have pointed out that despite all the media reports on considerable investments by a certain branch of the corporate sector in low-carbon technologies and GHG emission reduction activities, overall emissions continue to increase globally (York and Rosa 2003;

Jones and Levy 2009; Foster 2012). These scholars argue that energy-efficiency improvements and the growth of renewable energies cannot adequately solve the problem of climate change given the tremendous economic growth rates and energy demands of emerging economies and some developing countries.

The second dimension of global business self-regulation is the recent growth of voluntary corporate GHG accounting and reporting instruments. This type of voluntary business regulation has lately gained prominence and can be regarded as the most common form of voluntary business action against climate change (Kolk 2008: 228). According to several authors, companies have begun to voluntarily measure and manage their GHG emissions because they expect the introduction of future mandatory GHG emission controls (e.g. Jones and Levy 2009: 229). More specifically, by creating GHG emission inventories for their operations, companies seek to prepare for the participation in emission trading schemes or other market-based instruments. As Kolk, Levy, and Pinkse point out, 'business has intensified its development of GHG accounting and management capabilities in order to establish baselines, measure actual emissions and budget for the future purchase (or sale) of emission credits' (Kolk, Levy, and Pinkse 2008: 720). Since the participation in GHG accounting and management instruments entails considerable costs for corporations, this type of business self-regulation can be perceived as a 'win-lose' situation viewed from the individual firm's perspective. In contrast to the 'win-win' concept stated above, in 'win-lose' situations, internal corporate solutions for the environmental problem appear to be largely unprofitable for the corporation. Therefore, they have been conceptualized by Graeme Auld, Steven Bernstein, and Benjamin Cashore as 'The New Corporate Social Responsibility' (Auld, Bernstein, and Cashore 2008). These scholars contend that 'win-lose' situations 'require the creation of some external economic benefit or change in the competitive environment to offset the environmental and social costs of new or altered practices' (Auld, Bernstein, and Cashore 2008: 415). Two prominent examples of this type of business self-regulation are the *Carbon Disclosure Project* and the *Greenhouse Gas Protocol*.

The Carbon Disclosure Project was launched in 2000 by a group of global institutional investors with the aim of gaining insight into the climate risk profiles of the world's largest corporations. By sending standardized questionnaires to corporations, the Carbon Disclosure Project seeks to motivate the business sector to measure its GHG emissions and report on its efforts to mitigate climate change (Kolk, Levy, and Pinkse 2008). Since its introduction, the number of corporations using the survey and the procedures offered by the Carbon Disclosure Project to self-report their climate-related activities has considerably increased from 235 in 2003 to over 4,100 in 2012 (Carbon Disclosure Project 2013b). Once a year, the Carbon Disclosure Project publishes a report with the results of the corporate responses to the survey and lists the companies with the most progressive performances with regard to climate change. While the Carbon Disclosure Project is widely conceived as a prime example of global business self-regulation, a number of authors have more recently questioned the quality of the information provided by the participating firms. Pointing to the lack of uniform methodologies for GHG measurement and reliability checks, they maintain that it remains rather unclear whether the disclosed information is in any way used by internal and external decision-makers (Kolk, Levy, and Pinkse 2008: 741; see also Harmes 2011; Knox-Hayes and Levy 2011).

A similar business self-regulatory initiative is the Greenhouse Gas Protocol that was jointly established by the *World Business Council for Sustainable Development* and the World Resources Institute in 1998. In general, the Greenhouse Gas Protocol constitutes an international corporate standard for GHG accounting and reporting, which was first launched in 2001 and later revised in 2004 (Greenhouse Gas Protocol 2004). The original aim of the Protocol was to harmonize the various emerging practices for measuring and reporting GHG emissions and to ensure that different emission trading schemes and other market-based instruments adopt consistent approaches to GHG accounting (Bayon, Hawn, and Hamilton 2007: 118). According to its own website, the Greenhouse Gas Protocol is 'the most widely used international accounting tool for government and business leaders to understand, quantify, and manage greenhouse gas emissions' (Greenhouse Gas Protocol 2013a). Within the last few years, the Greenhouse Gas Protocol has developed a number of specific rules and procedures to assist corporations in measuring their GHG emissions and calculating their individual carbon footprint. Obviously, the activities undertaken by the Carbon Disclosure Project and the Greenhouse Gas Protocol complement each other. While the Carbon Disclosure Project seeks to encourage businesses to measure and report their GHG emissions, the Greenhouse Gas Protocol constitutes a standardized instrument for corporate-level emission measurement and management.

As noted above, until the early 1990s, most corporations still opposed any kind of measures to address the problem of climate change. Only with the introduction of legally binding GHG emission reduction targets through the Kyoto Protocol in 1997 has the picture changed and business actors have now begun to undertake voluntary efforts to tackle climate change. Thereafter, different business advocacy groups highlighted the advantages of businesses' self-regulatory efforts over external regulations at various international environmental conferences. Most remarkably in this regard was the 2002 World Summit on Sustainable Development in Johannesburg organized under the auspices of the United Nations. According to Jennifer Clapp, at this event business actors were able to strengthen the faith in business self-regulation by promoting examples of industry partnerships for sustainable development and voluntary initiatives (Clapp 2005). In the years following this conference, corporations have tried to exert a similar impact on the outcomes of international climate negotiations. The intention of most parts of the business community is thereby to escape calls for stringent mandatory regulation and to prevent strengthened GHG emission controls. This underscores the close relationship between global business self-regulation and the international climate regime, which will be further examined in this chapter by focusing on the interplay between one voluntary business initiative (i.e. the Greenhouse Gas Protocol) and the intergovernmental level.

Business self-regulation and climate change

The previous sections have indicated that in the past few years, we have been witnessing the emergence of a great variety of business self-regulatory initiatives in global climate governance. While there are many different categorizations, scholars usually distinguish between three types of voluntary business regulation in global environmental governance: (i) voluntary agreements between business actors and governmental agencies, (ii) partnerships for sustainable development, and (iii) corporate self-commitments to engage in the mitigation of environmental problems (cf. Mazurkiewicz 2005). The following sections describe these types of voluntary business regulation and provide examples of each particular type to illustrate how business self-regulatory initiatives operate in the policy domain of climate change.

Voluntary agreements

A first type of voluntary business regulation is the development of voluntary agreements between business actors and governmental agencies. Voluntary agreements can be defined as policy instruments established by nation-states aimed at motivating companies to take voluntary steps to tackle environmental problems (Delmas and Terlaak 2001). Generally, voluntary agreements can take two forms: *negotiated agreements* and *public voluntary programs* (OECD 1999). *Negotiated agreements*, on the one hand, are specific contracts between the private sector and the public regulator. These contracts are often negotiated between a certain industry and a national government department and involve a certain emission reduction target with a timetable (Thalmann and Baranzini 2004: 5). Typically, negotiated agreements are adopted instead of implementing more stringent regulations, such as an environmental tax or similar measures. The regulating body, on the other hand, primarily designs *public voluntary programs*. In most instances, these programs consist of a set of guidelines and a number of requirements, which corporations can choose to accept or decline. If the companies take part in these programs and adhere to the provisions, they will normally be rewarded by the government through subsidies, technical assistance, or an environmental logo that enhances the participating firms' reputation (Carraro and Lévêque 1999: 2). Hence, both forms of voluntary agreements are characterized by a high degree of government involvement. Due to the uncertainty surrounding the issue of climate change and the relative flexibility of voluntary agreements, this instrument has been widely used by national governments to start addressing the problem of climate change (Pinkse and Kolk 2009: 46). Among the various examples are Australia's *Greenhouse Challenge Plus*, the German *Agreement on Climate Protection*, the Japanese *Keidanren Voluntary Action Plan for the Environment*, Sweden's *Program for Improving Energy Efficiency*, and the *Climate Leaders Initiative* launched by the government of the United States. While some of these voluntary agreements have been introduced as an alternative to legally binding regulations, in many European countries, they are part of a broader strategy, which also comprises mandatory policy instruments (Morgenstern and Pizer 2007).

Multi-stakeholder initiatives

A second type of voluntary business regulation is the development of multi-stakeholder partnerships for sustainable development. As noted earlier, this policy instrument was particularly promoted at the 2002 World Summit on Sustainable Development and is considered by many scholars and policy-makers as a promising alternative to the many deadlocked intergovernmental negotiations on environmental issues (Pattberg *et al.* 2012). Basically, multi-stakeholder partnerships for sustainability can be understood as 'collaborative arrangements in which actors from two or more spheres of society (state, market and civil society) are involved in a non-hierarchical process through which these actors strive for sustainability' (Glasbergen 2007: 2). While their overall number has increased considerably in the past few years, these partnerships do not play a large role in engaging the business sector in the promotion of sustainable development. In fact, most partnerships are carried out by United Nations agencies, non-governmental environmental organizations, and national governments (e.g. Andonova 2010). One example of a climate-related partnership involving business actors is the Global Methane Initiative, formerly known as the Methane to Markets Partnership. This initiative was launched in 2004 by a coalition of corporations, non-governmental organizations, and research institutes to reduce global methane emissions and to promote the abatement, recovery, and use of methane as a clean energy source (Global Methane Initiative 2013). Although there are some other instances of multi-stakeholder partnerships that include corporations and seek to tackle the climate change problem (Bäckstrand 2008; Andonova, Betsill, and Bulkeley 2009; van Asselt and Zelli 2014), in general the involvement of business actors in multi-stakeholder partnerships to address climate change is, according to Pinkse and Kolk, rather limited (Pinkse and Kolk 2009: 56).

Company self-commitments

A third type of voluntary business regulation is the development of self-commitments by companies to engage in the mitigation of environmental problems. Under this headline fall a number of self-regulatory programs launched by individual firms and groups of firms to improve their environmental performance. In contrast to the two other types of business self-regulation depicted above, company self-commitments are established by the companies without a regulatory counterpart (Croci 2005). Concerning the matter of climate change, company self-commitments 'aim to effectively manage greenhouse gas (GHG) emissions internally, and to disclose information on the risks and opportunities of climate change to investors and other external stakeholders' (Pinkse and Kolk 2009: 63). In recent years, these activities have also included efforts made by companies to track and report their individual carbon footprints (Peters 2010). As noted above, this form of voluntary business regulation has matured considerably in the past few years and represents the most common action on climate change undertaken by multinational corporations (Kolk 2008: 228).

These unilateral corporate activities aimed at addressing the problem of climate change can be divided into three sub-categories (cf. Pinkse and Kolk 2009). First, corporations conduct GHG emission inventories to gain an overview of their strategic opportunities and challenges with regard to climate change. This is the most basic step of corporate action on climate change. As Adair Turner, former chairman of the United Kingdom's *Financial Service Authority*, put it: 'The first step towards managing carbon emissions is to measure them because in business what gets measured gets managed' (Turner cited in Southworth 2009: 334). While in Europe, several industry sectors are required by law to track their GHG emissions, mostly in order to participate in the *European Union Emissions Trading System*, many corporations based in other countries are not under such an obligation. Nonetheless, numerous companies from industrialized and developing countries that are not subject to mandatory GHG accounting and reporting have begun to measure and track their GHG emissions on a voluntary basis. Since the accurate calculation of GHG emissions from corporate operations is rather difficult, a number of different standards have emerged in the past few years to facilitate the measurement and tracking of GHG emissions. As noted above, among these, the Greenhouse Gas Protocol is the most widely used instrument (Green 2010).

Second, on the basis of their individual GHG emission inventories, corporations set specific internal targets to reduce or stabilize their emissions. A number of different considerations play a role when companies commit themselves to a voluntary emission control target. By setting a target, companies seek to show leadership, improve their reputation and, perhaps most important, become early movers on the issue of climate change since this provides them with considerable strategic advantages over their competitors (Hoffman 2005). Thereby, the shadow of future mandatory regulations is often the key driving force behind corporate initiatives to adopt GHG emission control targets (Pinkse and Kolk 2009: 73–74). Compared to the great number of corporations having conducted a GHG emission inventory, relatively few companies have decided thus far to commit themselves to a specific target to control the GHG emissions associated with their operations (Cogan 2008). This can largely be attributed to regulatory uncertainty and the unclear future of the international climate regime.

Third, a number of corporations have also started to voluntarily report their climate-related activities. While corporate self-reporting in the policy domain of climate change is still in its infancy, the number of companies that disclose information on corporate GHG emissions and their climate change mitigation efforts has considerably grown in the last few years. As shown by the most recent survey of the Carbon Disclosure Project, especially large multinational corporations have strengthened their capacities to report on their activities to tackle climate change in the last decade (Carbon Disclosure Project 2013a). Thereby, it is apparent that there are significant differences between countries. Generally speaking, companies from the United States remain far behind European companies, whereas Japanese corporations take an intermediate position when it comes to corporate climate reporting. This variation reflects the different positions of these countries in the international climate regime, which indicates that companies relate their GHG accounting and reporting activities to the respective regulatory environment that they are operating in (Pinkse and Kolk 2009: 86). This point is crucial for the analysis in this chapter and will be further elaborated below.

To sum up, a number of different business self-regulatory initiatives can be distinguished, which are concerned with the issue of climate change. These initiatives range from voluntary agreements characterized by a high degree of governmental intervention and a number of climate-related multi-stakeholder partnerships, to different kinds of company self-commitments to engage in the mitigation of climate change. While these types of voluntary business regulation differ in several aspects and function according to slightly varying procedures, they all belong to the same category of policy instruments that have emerged beyond traditional regulatory approaches and market-based instruments in global environmental governance (Mazurkiewicz 2005: 33). In practice, the distinction between the three ideal types of business self-regulatory initiatives is often not clear-cut since a number of hybrid forms exist. In the following sections of this chapter, the analysis concentrates on a business self-regulatory initiative that can be conceived as a combination of a multi-stakeholder partnership and individual company self-commitments to measure and manage GHG emissions.

The relevance of business self-regulation

Over the last decades, scholars and policy-makers alike have acknowledged that corporations have become increasingly important actors in world politics. As David Levy and Peter Newell put it, 'firms are now key political players, engaging with and shaping global processes in direct and indirect ways' (Levy and Newell 2005b: 3). To illustrate this point, scholars refer to figures indicating that the individual turnover generated by several multinational corporations clearly exceeds the gross national product of many countries (Jenkins 1987; Engwall 2006; Ietto-Gillies 2012). They also point to the significant rates of growth in the amount of foreign direct investments made by multinational corporations (Dunning 1981; Clapp 2005). And they note that multinational corporations control essentially every stage of today's global value and production chains (Dauvergne and Lister 2010). This demonstrates that the activities of globally operating corporations have an enormous impact on the daily lives of practically the entire world's population.

The increasing significance of the corporate sector in world politics has recently also become evident in global climate governance. As a matter of course, corporations are viewed as a main driver of the problem of climate change. Industry accounts for about one-third of global energy consumption and nearly 40 percent of worldwide GHG emissions (International Energy Agency 2009). The major part of these emissions is attributable to the manufacturing sector, especially the large primary material industries, such as aluminum, cement, chemicals, iron, paper, and steel. According to the IPCC, only if the industrial sector successfully transforms its energy usage and drastically reduces its GHG emissions can the increase in global mean temperature be constrained to about 2 degrees Celsius above pre-industrial levels (IPCC 2014). In fact, as various scholars have pointed out, corporations can serve as engines of global change and redirect their operational activities towards addressing environmental problems (e.g. Levy and Newell 2005b: 1). The corporate sector develops and disseminates renewable energy, energy-efficiency systems, and other abatement technologies to reduce global GHG emissions. Beyond that, in the past few years, it has become increasingly clear that the business sector has to provide most of the global investments and financial flows needed to implement large-scale climate change mitigation and adaptation projects (UNFCCC 2008; International Finance Corporation 2011; Global Environment Facility 2012). As a result, corporations are no longer solely perceived as subjects of regulation, but have now adopted an influential political role in the global response to climate change (Levy and Newell 2005b; Clapp and Meckling 2013). This is the context in which voluntary global business initiatives have emerged to tackle the problem of climate change. Despite the various efforts made by the corporate sector to voluntarily manage their GHG emissions, however, it remains open to debate in what way global business self-regulation contributes to global climate governance.

Link to the theoretical background

The discussion so far has underlined that various scholars regard voluntary corporate efforts as central components in the global response to climate change. They argue that business self-regulatory initiatives concerned with the issue of climate change have attained an authoritative role in global climate policy-making (e.g. Levy and Newell 2005b; Pattberg and Stripple 2008; Bulkeley and Newell 2010). These authors assert that the emergence of voluntary business regulation in the policy domain of climate change causes a shift of authority from nation-states and international institutions towards climate initiatives launched by actors other than the nation-state. More specifically, they maintain that state-based forms of governance have been joined by new modes of governance propelled by business actors that cope with the problem of climate change largely independently of the decisions made by nation-states and international institutions. Accordingly, they contend that the intergovernmental level has lost its dominant position in the global response to climate change due to the development of alternative climate governance arrangements. Nonetheless, I argue that the different facets of the relationship between voluntary corporate climate change strategies and the international climate regime have not been analyzed adequately thus far. Despite widespread scholarly recognition of the growing importance of multinational corporations and business self-regulatory initiatives in global climate governance, a systematic understanding of their interplay with existing modes of inter-state cooperation is still lacking. For that reason, the present case study goes one step further than many previous studies of individual voluntary corporate climate initiatives and analyzes the wider implications associated with their emergence for global climate governance. Based on the theoretical background and analytical framework depicted in the third chapter of this book, the present chapter particularly explores the relationship between the Greenhouse Gas Protocol and the international climate regime. In this endeavor, the Greenhouse Gas Protocol is considered an illustrative instance of a *business* climate governance arrangement. As in the two preceding chapters, the case study starts with an overview of the Greenhouse Gas Protocol and a brief description of its main areas of application, organizational structure, and perception in the literature. After that, I recapitulate the three conceptual assumptions about the relation between transnational governance arrangements and the intergovernmental level and explore how the Greenhouse Gas Protocol's different areas of operation relate to the international climate regime.

The Greenhouse Gas Protocol and the international climate regime

Overview of the Greenhouse Gas Protocol

The initiative to develop the Greenhouse Gas Protocol was jointly launched by the World Business Council for Sustainable Development and the World Resources Institute in 1998. Recognizing the need for an international GHG accounting and reporting standard, these two organizations started a multi-stakeholder process involving business actors such as *Norsk Hydro*, *Tokyo Electric*, and *Shell*, as well as a number of business-oriented non-governmental environmental organizations like the *Energy Research Institute*, the Pew Center on Global Climate Change, and the World Wide Fund for Nature (Greenhouse Gas Protocol 2013a). After three years of intense consultations between these organizations and broad external input by hundreds of experts, the first version of the Greenhouse Gas Protocol was released in 2001. Since then, the Greenhouse Gas Protocol has produced several calculation tools and additional guidelines to assist companies in measuring and reporting their GHG emissions. Essentially, the Greenhouse Gas Protocol's objective is to form a reliable accounting and reporting platform which enables businesses to make informed decisions on the GHG risks and reduction opportunities of their operations (Sundin and Ranganathan 2002: 138). In the past few years, the Greenhouse Gas Protocol's two founding organizations have undertaken various efforts to promote the adoption of the Greenhouse Gas Protocol guidelines as a basic instrument for corporate responses to climate change. In this context, the representatives of the Greenhouse Gas Protocol were also actively involved in the international climate change conferences.

Main areas of application

First and foremost, the Greenhouse Gas Protocol represents an accounting and reporting instrument for the measurement and management of corporate GHG emissions. The main element of the Greenhouse Gas Protocol is the *Corporate Accounting and Reporting Standard*. Since its initial release in 2001, hundreds of companies have used this standard for calculating and disclosing the amount of GHG emissions associated with their operations. In 2004, the World Business Council for Sustainable Development and the World Resources Institute published a revised version of the Corporate Accounting and Reporting Standard providing further guidance for companies, as well as a number of case studies on voluntary business action towards tackling climate change (Greenhouse Gas Protocol 2004). The standard has been widely adopted by emission reporting schemes around the world and lays the foundation for practically every existing or emerging GHG accounting program. Most notably, in 2006 the *International Organization for Standardization* adopted the Corporate Accounting and Reporting Standard of the Greenhouse Gas Protocol as the basis for the *ISO 14064-1 Specification with Guidance at the Organization Level for Quantification and Reporting of Greenhouse Gas Emissions and Removals* (International Organization for Standardization 2006). According to the Greenhouse Gas Protocol's website, '[t]his milestone highlighted the role of the GHG Protocol's Corporate Standard as the international standard for corporate and organizational GHG accounting and reporting' (Greenhouse Gas Protocol 2013a). Other prominent examples of organizations or programs that are built on the Greenhouse Gas Protocol include the *Business Leaders Initiative on Climate Change*, the *Carbon Disclosure Project*, the *Climate Leaders Initiative*, the *Climate Neutral Network*, and the *Climate Registry*.

The wide adoption of the Greenhouse Gas Protocol was strongly propelled by its two founding organizations, the World Business Council for Sustainable Development and the World Resources Institute. In the early stages of the initiative, the leaders of the business self-regulatory initiative devoted much effort to persuade other organizations to use their methodology and considerably shaped the discussion on the emerging practices of GHG measurement and reporting (Green 2010). In subsequent years, the Greenhouse Gas Protocol strongly advocated the promotion of the application and implementation of its guidelines. In particular, the Greenhouse Gas Protocol partnered with business groups from carbon-intensive industries, published numerous calculation tools and additional guidelines for GHG accounting and reporting, and developed specific training courses and capacity building programs. In recent years, the representatives of the Greenhouse Gas Protocol have also increasingly used the Conferences of the Parties to the UNFCCC as a platform for their outreach strategy and for exerting influence on relevant stakeholders, national governments, and international organizations.

Organizational structure

The Greenhouse Gas Protocol is jointly convened by the World Business Council for Sustainable Development and the World Resources Institute. Both organizations employ staff members for the management of the Greenhouse Gas Protocol who together form the *Greenhouse Gas Protocol Team* led by the *Greenhouse Gas Protocol Director*. This team has grown steadily in the past few years and currently comprises 17 carbon accounting professionals (Greenhouse Gas Protocol 2013f). They each have different responsibilities, ranging from the further development of the various guidelines (i.e. the *Corporate Value Chain Standard*, the *Global Protocol for Community-Scale Emissions*, and the *Product Life Cycle Standard*) to public relations and outreach activities for the promotion of the wide adoption of the Greenhouse Gas Protocol. In addition, staff members of the Greenhouse Gas Protocol Team conduct workshops, provide technical assistance to corporations in various emerging economies and developing countries, and design special training courses for GHG accounting and reporting. These training courses take place in different world regions and are conducted by certified trainers.

Perception in the literature

Notwithstanding its prevalence in the field of GHG measurement and management, the Greenhouse Gas Protocol has only recently attracted wider attention among scholars of global environmental politics. Most of these authors consider the Greenhouse Gas Protocol to be a remarkably successful business self-regulatory initiative (e.g. Sundin and Ranganathan 2002; Bayon, Hawn, and Hamilton 2007; Grover 2008; Bulkeley and Newell 2010; Green 2010). In particular, they argue that the Greenhouse Gas Protocol can be regarded as a highly credible instrument for GHG accounting and reporting due to its inclusive and transparent development process involving hundreds of different stakeholders and a public database with all relevant working documents (Sundin and Ranganathan 2002: 138). They emphasize the evolution of the Greenhouse Gas Protocol from a relatively small private initiative to the most widely used international accounting and reporting instrument for the measurement and management of corporate GHG emissions (Grover 2008: 5). And they point out that the Greenhouse Gas Protocol has exerted significant influence on the emerging practice of GHG accounting around the world. Adding to that, Jessica Green contends that the Greenhouse Gas Protocol can consequently be regarded as an illustrative instance of 'private entrepreneurial authority' (Green 2010: 2). Above all, these authors refer to the Greenhouse Gas Protocol as a high-quality standard for corporate GHG measurement and management, which has considerably shaped the way different actors, including businesses, environmental groups, national and sub-national governments, as well as international organizations, carry out GHG accounting and reporting.

However, there are also a number of critical voices. Some authors have questioned whether the standards developed by the Greenhouse Gas Protocol Team are rigorously applied by the corporate sector. For instance, Rory Sullivan, Rachel Crossley and Jennifer Kozak reveal that companies are not strictly deploying the provisions as specified in the Corporate Accounting and Reporting Standard of the Greenhouse Gas Protocol, particularly with regard to the accounting and reporting of GHG emissions that are not directly linked to their operations (Sullivan, Crossley, and Kozak 2008: 13). In a similar vein, Pinkse and Kolk state that companies have generally not made much progress in corporate GHG accounting and reporting in the past few years, leading to low-quality data on the GHG emissions of individual companies (Pinkse and Kolk 2009: 70–71). Taking these findings into account, I contend that the function of the Greenhouse

Gas Protocol in global climate governance can only be assessed appropriately by analyzing its relationship to the international climate regime. Therefore, the remainder of this chapter explores the Greenhouse Gas Protocol's interplay with the intergovernmental level.

Conceptual assumptions and theoretical expectations

After I provided an overview of the Greenhouse Gas Protocol's main areas of application, organizational structure, and perception in the literature, in the following sections I link the case study to the analytical framework of this book. Drawing on the three conceptual assumptions presented in the research design, I now study the relationship between the Greenhouse Gas Protocol and the intergovernmental level. The first conceptual assumption portrays a *conflictive relationship* between transnational climate initiatives and the international climate regime. It suggests that transnational governance arrangements depart from the ultimate objective and basic principles of the UNFCCC and weaken the norms and rules stipulated in international climate agreements. Consequently, in the present case study, I would expect that the Greenhouse Gas Protocol seeks to prevent mandatory GHG emission controls and to establish the practice of business self-regulation as an alternative mode of governance to the intergovernmental level. The second conceptual assumption portrays a *complementary relationship* between transnational climate initiatives and the international climate regime. It implies that the emergence of transnational governance arrangements leads to a division of responsibilities between sub- and non-state actors and the UNFCCC, thereby strengthening the norms and rules set out in international climate agreements. Hence, in the case study in this chapter, I would expect that the Greenhouse Gas Protocol contributes to closing the implementation gap in the international climate regime by providing adequate means for corporate GHG accounting and reporting. And the third conceptual assumption portrays a *dependency relationship* between transnational climate initiatives and the international climate regime. It supposes that transnational governance arrangements are a side issue to the UNFCCC process and rely on the norms and rules anchored in international climate agreements. Accordingly, in the case analyzed here, I would expect that the Greenhouse Gas Protocol remains largely dependent on the international regulatory framework, which incentivizes private companies to measure and manage their GHG emissions. Naturally, these conceptual assumptions and theoretical expectations will again guide the following analysis and help identify relevant empirical findings (see Table 6.1). At the end of the case study, I return to this analytical framework and formulate conclusions for the debate on the concept of authority in global climate governance.

The Greenhouse Gas Protocol's central areas of operation

The investigation of the relationship between the Greenhouse Gas Protocol and the international climate regime is structured around three central areas of

Table 6.1 Conceptual assumptions and theoretical expectations for the empirical analysis of the relationship between the Greenhouse Gas Protocol and the international climate regime

Conceptual assumptions	*The Greenhouse Gas Protocol: Theoretical expectations*
Conflictive relationship	The Greenhouse Gas Protocol seeks to prevent mandatory GHG emission controls and to establish the practice of business self-regulation as an alternative mode of governance to the intergovernmental level
Complementary relationship	The Greenhouse Gas Protocol contributes to closing the implementation gap in the international climate regime by providing adequate means for corporate GHG accounting and reporting
Dependency relationship	The Greenhouse Gas Protocol remains to a large extent dependent on the international regulatory framework that incentivizes private companies to measure and manage their GHG emissions

operation of the Greenhouse Gas Protocol. As the next step, I study the main element of the Greenhouse Gas Protocol, which is the Corporate Accounting and Reporting Standard. Then, I look at the various efforts undertaken by the Greenhouse Gas Protocol's founding organizations to promote the worldwide adoption of their guidelines. Finally, I focus the analysis on the involvement of the Greenhouse Gas Protocol in the UNFCCC conferences.

The Greenhouse Gas Protocol's corporate standard

As already stated above, the first version of the Corporate Accounting and Reporting Standard was published in 2001 after an extensive multi-stakeholder dialogue lasting for more than three and a half years. After its initial publication, the standard was tested by about 30 companies in nine countries to identify shortcomings and improvement opportunities (Greenhouse Gas Protocol 2013c). Thereupon, a second consultation process was started, resulting in the release of the revised edition of the Corporate Accounting and Reporting Standard in 2004 (Greenhouse Gas Protocol 2004). This standard constitutes the core element of the Greenhouse Gas Protocol and is widely perceived as a high-quality guidance document for conducting corporate GHG emission inventories. In the following paragraphs, I discuss the main aspects of this document.

PRIMARY OBJECTIVE AND GUIDING PRINCIPLES

The primary objective of the Corporate Accounting and Reporting Standard is to establish 'generally accepted GHG accounting principles (…) intended to underpin and guide GHG accounting and reporting to ensure that the reported information represents a faithful, true, and fair account of a company's GHG emissions' (Greenhouse Gas Protocol 2004: 6). The different principles stipulated by the Greenhouse Gas Protocol are largely based on established financial accounting practices. In particular, they propose (i) that corporate GHG emission inventories contain all relevant information needed by internal and external users for decision-making, (ii) that all significant sources of GHG emissions are accounted for, (iii) that consistent methodologies are used to allow for meaningful comparisons of emissions over time, (iv) that all information is disclosed in a transparent manner based on clear documentation and archives, and (v) that the provided data are sufficiently precise and uncertainties are reduced as far as practicable (Greenhouse Gas Protocol 2004: 7–9). To assist companies in complying with these principles, the Corporate Accounting and Reporting Standard offers detailed practical advice and provides a number of case studies on voluntary business actions addressing climate change. Most important for the focus of this chapter, the standard covers the accounting and reporting of exactly the six GHGs that are regulated by the Kyoto Protocol. Furthermore, when nation-states recently agreed to add *nitrogen trifluoride* (hereafter NF_3) to the basket of regulated GHGs in the second commitment period of the Kyoto Protocol (UNFCCC 2012), the Greenhouse Gas Protocol Team released shortly thereafter an amendment to the Corporate Accounting and Reporting Standard, which requires companies from this time forth to measure and report their NF_3 emissions (Greenhouse Gas Protocol 2013g).[1] This is the first clear indication that the guidelines developed by the Greenhouse Gas Protocol Team are closely aligned with the norms and rules established by nation-states at the intergovernmental level.

SETTING ORGANIZATIONAL AND OPERATIONAL BOUNDARIES

At the outset of every GHG emission inventory, companies have to draw a measurement line and determine for which GHG emissions they will take responsibility. The Greenhouse Gas Protocol recommends companies set clear organizational as well as operational boundaries for GHG measurement and management. At first, companies need to address the question of how to account for emissions from joint ventures, subsidiaries, and other partially owned facilities (i.e. *setting organizational boundaries*). The Corporate Accounting and Reporting Standard offers two different approaches for companies to consolidate their GHG emissions: the *equity share approach* and the *control approach* (Greenhouse Gas Protocol 2004: 17–23). Under the equity share approach, a company accounts for GHG emissions according to its share of equity (reflecting its economic interest) in the respective facility, whereas under the control approach, a company accounts for 100 percent of the GHGs emitted by those facilities over which it has control (defined as either financial or operational control). The choice of a company as to how to account for GHG emissions from partially owned facilities of course has substantial consequences on the outcome of the GHG emission inventory (Pinkse and Kolk 2009: 69). After having determined its organizational boundaries, a company needs to identify the different sources of the emissions that can be associated with its operations and categorize them as direct or indirect emissions (i.e. *setting operational boundaries*). The Corporate Accounting and Reporting Standard distinguishes between three so-called *emission scopes*, representing different kinds of sources of corporate GHG emissions (Greenhouse Gas Protocol 2004: 25-33). *Scope 1* emissions occur from sources that are owned or controlled by the company, as, for instance, emissions from fossil fuel combustion in company-owned boilers, industrial processing, and fugitive emissions (direct GHG emissions). *Scope 2* accounts for all emissions from the generation of purchased electricity consumed by the company (electricity indirect GHG emissions). And *scope 3* subsumes all other sources, including emissions from the extraction and production of purchased materials, transport in vehicles not owned or controlled by the company, or the use of sold products and services (all other indirect GHG emissions). This is clearly the broadest category and constitutes in the vast majority of cases the largest part of a company's GHG emissions.

The depiction of the different approaches and concepts that companies have to deal with when compiling their GHG emission inventories illustrates that the measurement and management of GHG emissions is a highly complex process. Prior to the publication of the Corporate Accounting and Reporting Standard, no globally applicable rules and procedures existed for the measurement of GHG emissions at the corporate level. Today, the guidelines developed by the Greenhouse Gas Protocol Team, especially the equity share and control approaches as well as the distinction between the three emission scopes, can be considered the common language and practice of corporate GHG accounting (Sullivan, Crossley, and Kozak 2008; Green 2010). This shows that the Greenhouse Gas Protocol has filled a regulatory gap in global climate governance by providing the means for individual companies to comprehensively account and report their GHG emissions. Every country that seeks to implement GHG emission controls needs to structure its GHG emissions on an absolute basis or at least at the sector level where the greatest potential for GHG emission reductions lies. Hence, the GHG measurement data provided by the corporate sector constitute the first step for all national GHG emission inventories and climate change mitigation policies. Therefore, it can be argued that the Corporate Accounting and Reporting Standard of the Greenhouse Gas Protocol contributes to promoting the norms and rules set out in international climate agreements.

UTILIZATION OF THE STANDARD BY THE CORPORATE SECTOR

The number of corporations using the Corporate Accounting and Reporting Standard to calculate and communicate their climate impact has steadily increased in the past decade. According to the *Corporate Climate Communications Report* released in 2008 by one of the world's leading online directories of corporate social responsibility reports, about 60 percent of the climate reports published by the *Fortune Global 500* are based on the Greenhouse Gas Protocol's rules and procedures for measuring and reporting GHG emissions (CorporateRegister.com 2008: 7).[2] On its own website, the Greenhouse Gas Protocol states that more than

1,000 businesses and organizations worldwide have utilized the Corporate Accounting and Reporting Standard to conduct their GHG emission inventories (Greenhouse Gas Protocol 2013a). Although these figures provide only a rough measure of the adoption of the Corporate Accounting and Reporting Standard by the corporate sector, they underline 'that the Greenhouse Gas Protocol is *the* standard for corporate-level measurement' (Green 2010: 14, emphasis in original). This is further evidence that the Greenhouse Gas Protocol helps implement the norms and rules established by nation-states in international climate negotiations. Interestingly, the Corporate Accounting and Reporting Standard is not only widely used by companies from industrialized countries as the basis for their climate change strategies, but the guidelines of the Greenhouse Gas Protocol are to a growing extent also employed by large companies from emerging economies and developing countries (Ozawa-Meida, Fransen, and Jiménez-Ambriz 2008; Pinkse and Kolk 2009: 83–85; Green 2010: 23). These corporations have begun to apply the Greenhouse Gas Protocol's tools and methodology to conduct their GHG emission inventories. Thereby, the Greenhouse Gas Protocol Team provides them with technical and administrative assistance (Greenhouse Gas Protocol 2007; 2009; 2011a). Emerging economies and developing countries have generally resisted monitoring their GHG emissions and are so far under no explicit GHG emission reduction obligations in the international climate regime. The efforts made by companies from these countries might therefore motivate their national governments to agree to GHG emission controls in a future commitment period. From this perspective, the Greenhouse Gas Protocol can be seen as a pioneer initiative in the global response to climate change.

GUIDELINES FOR GHG ACCOUNTING FROM VALUE CHAIN ACTIVITIES

In the past few years, the Greenhouse Gas Protocol Team has expended considerable efforts to establish guidelines for the measurement and management of indirect GHG emissions resulting from value chain activities (scope 3 emissions). As noted above, these emissions usually represent the largest part of the overall amount of GHGs emitted by an individual company, since they comprise emissions from *upstream activities* (i.e. products and services purchased by the company) and *downstream activities* (i.e. use and disposal of products and services sold by the company). In certain industry sectors, more than 75 percent of a company's total GHG emissions can be attributed to scope 3 emission sources (Huang, Weber, and Matthews 2009). Compared with scope 1 (direct GHG emissions) and scope 2 emissions (electricity indirect GHG emissions), the emissions from value chain activities are relatively difficult to quantify due to the broad range of emission sources falling into this category. Nevertheless, to obtain a credible and complete picture of a company's GHG emissions, they must be calculated and taken into account (Pinkse and Kolk 2009: 69–70). Accordingly, in 2008, the World Business Council for Sustainable Development and the World Resources Institute started a multi-stakeholder dialogue, which led to the publication of a comprehensive guide supplementing the Corporate Accounting and Reporting Standard in 2011

(Greenhouse Gas Protocol 2011b). After this publication, the Greenhouse Gas Protocol Team organized numerous events and training courses in several countries to promote the adoption of this additional guideline (Greenhouse Gas Protocol 2012b; 2013h). As various authors have stated, however, many companies are still largely reluctant to account for and report the GHG emissions resulting from their supply chains (Sullivan, Crossley, and Kozak 2008; Jackson and Knight 2011; Downie and Stubbs 2012). These scholars contend that as soon as GHG accounting involves significant costs for corporations, the quality of the disclosed information leaves much to be desired. This is underlined by a recent report of the Carbon Disclosure Project, which states that 'current scope 3 reporting does not reflect the full impact of companies' activities, and may mislead as to the full carbon impact of a company' (Carbon Disclosure Project 2013a: 9). In other words, the quality of corporate GHG emission inventories with regard to the incorporation of indirect GHG emissions beyond those from purchased electricity remains questionable. Obviously, one of the main causes for the reluctance of many firms to conduct credible and complete GHG emission inventories is the absence of a wide-ranging international policy framework. As a Senior Associate at the World Resources Institute acknowledged in a personal interview, 'because of the uncertainty about the introduction of more stringent international greenhouse gas regulations, corporations put only limited resources into the calculation of their emissions.'[3] Furthermore, he noted that only a clear political signal that strong mandatory GHG emission controls are about to be adopted will impel companies to measure their entire value chain emissions, since this would suddenly increase the global carbon price and the costs of goods purchased by companies.

BARRIERS TO THE APPLICATION OF THE CORPORATE STANDARD

Businesses measure their GHG emissions for various reasons. In general, they seek to manage the risks associated with unstable resource and energy costs, react to changing consumer behavior, and address the demands from investors, shareholders, and other stakeholders. As indicated above, the key driver of voluntary business action on climate change is the threat of future GHG emission controls (Hoffman 2005: 39; Pinkse and Kolk 2009: 73; Southworth 2009: 342). In particular, several authors have pointed out that companies comply with the rules and procedures of the Greenhouse Gas Protocol in order to prepare for the introduction of international GHG regulations and, perhaps more importantly, the participation in market-based instruments (e.g. Pinkse and Kolk 2009: 87; Hoffmann 2011: 132). The concrete rationale of corporations is that a GHG inventory compiled in conformance with the Greenhouse Gas Protocol's Corporate Accounting and Reporting Standard will most likely be compatible with future mandatory controls and emission trading systems. In this regard, Jessica Green argues that corporations strive for pre-compliance action and intend to obtain first-mover advantages over their competitors (Green 2010: 2). However, this logic will only hold if the likelihood of stringent regulations is reasonably high. In the United States, for instance, companies have faced only modest political and economic incentives for action on climate change because of the government's withdrawal from the Kyoto process. Consequently, corporate accounting and reporting practices in the United States remain largely behind those of European businesses (Kolk, Levy, and Pinkse 2008; Jones and Levy 2009; Southworth 2009).

Against this backdrop, it can be argued that the absence of ambitious national GHG emission reduction targets and the general lack of clarity regarding the adoption of a new market-based instrument (or the reform of the Clean Development Mechanism) constitute the main barriers towards the application of comprehensive corporate GHG accounting and reporting standards. As stated earlier, the adoption of the Kyoto Protocol in 1997 and its entry into force in 2005 have prompted many firms to place climate strategy within the realm of risk management. In consequence, several companies have invested substantial resources in the establishment of corporate GHG emission inventories. But due to the slow evolution of the international climate regime in the last decade, many executives of multinational corporations have come to the decision not to further develop their voluntary programs for tackling climate change. In fact, as some scholars have put it, numerous companies have taken a *wait-and-see stance* on climate change, while they continue to observe the international regulatory landscape so as to not lose track of new developments (Dunn 2005: 45; Sullivan, Crossley, and Kozak 2008: 24; Okereke and Küng 2013: 299–300). Put differently, the continued uncertainty regarding the nature and timing of future international climate agreements makes business actors reluctant to undertake tangible mitigation efforts. Concerning this matter, Thierry Berthoud, the *Managing Director for Energy and Climate* of the World Business Council for Sustainable Development stated: 'What businesses are looking for is a long-term and stable framework. (…) As soon as such a framework could be established giving certainty for action, businesses will start delivering a significant contribution to solving the problem.'[4] This implies that nation-states have to maintain a credible shadow of hierarchy to facilitate and encourage the development of effective business action on climate change.

The Greenhouse Gas Protocol's outreach strategy

In the past decade, the World Business Council for Sustainable Development and the World Resources Institute made great endeavors to promote the wide adoption of the Greenhouse Gas Protocol. In particular, the two organizations collaborated closely with different industry groups, published numerous calculation tools as well as additional guidelines, and developed specific training courses and capacity building programs for companies from emerging economies and developing countries. This section examines these activities aimed at supporting the broad application of the Greenhouse Gas Protocol's rules and procedures.

COLLABORATION WITH CARBON-INTENSIVE INDUSTRIES

Shortly after the inception of the Greenhouse Gas Protocol initiative in 1998, the World Business Council for Sustainable Development and the World Resources

Institute partnered with different industry associations. The idea of these partnerships was to disseminate the Greenhouse Gas Protocol guidelines among companies from carbon-intensive industry sectors. The earliest and most prominent examples in this regard are the *Cement Sustainability Initiative*, the *International Aluminum Institute*, and the *International Council of Forest and Paper Associations* (Greenhouse Gas Protocol 2004: 3). Initially, the collaboration between the Greenhouse Gas Protocol and these industry groups worked well and led to a number of achievements, such as the release of the *Calculation Tools for Estimating Greenhouse Gas Emissions from Pulp and Paper Mills*, the *Cement CO_2 Protocol*, and the *Aluminum Sector Greenhouse Gas Protocol*. All these instruments were developed by leading corporations from the respective industries in line with the Greenhouse Gas Protocol's principles to establish sector-specific guidelines for the calculation and communication of GHG emissions. In the past few years, however, these initiatives have apparently lost much of their appeal. Especially since the widely perceived failure of the Copenhagen Climate Summit in 2009, corporate interest in collaboration with the Greenhouse Gas Protocol has significantly diminished and companies from many carbon-intensive industries have become hesitant to put forth great effort into the accounting and reporting of their GHG emissions (e.g. Sullivan 2008b; Okereke and Küng 2013; Talbot and Boiral 2013). Although industry representatives recognize that stronger GHG emission controls are inescapable in the long run, they still avoid the high costs associated with the rigorous measurement of their GHG emissions. This is reflected in another statement by Thierry Berthoud, who noted: 'In the absence of a long-term policy framework and clear price signals, many corporations will not take on the difficult task to carefully measure and manage their emissions, but see the short-term profit and save their expenditures for participating in the program.'[5]

In this context, various authors have raised concerns that the Greenhouse Gas Protocol and similar voluntary business initiatives might principally undermine the norms and rules set out in international climate agreements (e.g. Andrews 1998; Levy and Egan 2003; Okereke, Wittneben, and Bowen 2012). Pointing to the involvement of corporations in the creation of GHG accounting and reporting standards, these scholars contend that companies 'hold a privileged position in the field of carbon governance, and enjoy increasing influence in structuring carbon reporting standards and information systems' (Knox-Hayes and Levy 2011: 6). They further claim that the private sector might exploit the regulatory vacuum in the field of corporate-level accounting and reporting and seek to position the guidelines of the Greenhouse Gas Protocol as alternatives to more stringent GHG emission controls established by nation-states at the intergovernmental level (Andrew and Cortese 2011). While the analysis in this chapter has pointed out that managers of corporations have indeed been involved in the development of Greenhouse Gas Protocol rules and procedures and sector-specific GHG measurement instruments, no evidence was found in the case study in support of this proposition with regard to the Greenhouse Gas Protocol.

PUBLICATION OF CALCULATION TOOLS AND ADDITIONAL GUIDELINES

The second element of the Greenhouse Gas Protocol's strategy to promote the broad application of its rules and procedures was to publish several cross-sector calculation tools and additional guidelines for certain business branches. In particular, the Greenhouse Gas Protocol Team has developed ten calculation tools that can be generally applied by companies for GHG measurement and management (Greenhouse Gas Protocol 2013b). Beyond that, it provided additional guidelines for small office-based organizations, service sector companies, and the information technology and communications sector (World Resources Institute 2002; 2006; Greenhouse Gas Protocol 2011c). These calculation tools and additional guidelines offer step-by-step advice and are accompanied by electronic worksheets to help companies conduct comprehensive inventories of their GHG emissions. They reflect the best practice of corporate GHG accounting and, most relevant for the analysis in this chapter, are created in conformance with the methodologies proposed by the IPCC for the compilation of GHG emission inventories at the national level (Greenhouse Gas Protocol 2004: 4). Hence, the tools and guidelines developed by the Greenhouse Gas Protocol Team lay the foundation for national GHG accounting and reporting in the international climate regime. This is further proof that the Greenhouse Gas Protocol can be seen as a complement to the norms and rules set out in international climate agreements.

Most important for this case study, however, David Rich from the World Resources Institute, who was involved in the design of several documents published by the Greenhouse Gas Protocol, stated in a personal interview that it does not matter how precise the guidelines are – they will not be used by the majority of firms if there is no stimulus from the intergovernmental level. Referring to the close connection between the operational activities of the Greenhouse Gas Protocol and the international climate negotiations, he particularly noticed that 'the success of our work largely depends on the continued UNFCCC process.'[6] Obviously, most companies will only rigorously account and report their GHG emissions if they are required to do so. This is also supported by a statement of the World Business Council for Sustainable Development released after the 2012 Conference of the Parties to the UNFCCC held in Doha:

> For business the absence of ambitious targets in the short-term and the lack of clarity on the tools to assist scale-up of private investment in low-carbon technologies in both developed and also major emerging economies hinders progressive investment plans and increases the possibility of lock-in for long-term projects.
>
> (World Business Council for Sustainable Development 2012: 2)

TRAINING COURSES AND CAPACITY BUILDING PROGRAMS

A third element of the outreach strategy pursued by the Greenhouse Gas Protocol is the development of specific training courses and capacity building programs for companies and other types of organizations willing to measure and report their

GHG emissions. In this engagement, the Greenhouse Gas Protocol has been particularly active in various countries from different regions, such as Brazil, China, India, Mexico, and the Philippines (Greenhouse Gas Protocol 2006; 2007; 2008; 2011a; 2012a). In these countries, the Greenhouse Gas Protocol Team has established national programs that operate in partnership with local business associations and national government agencies (Green 2010: 23). Thereby, the underlying intention of the Greenhouse Gas Protocol is to enhance the corporate GHG accounting and reporting capacities and to 'build a pool of trained GHG practitioners and GHG measurement and management professionals' (Greenhouse Gas Protocol 2013e). This again underscores the pioneer character of the Greenhouse Gas Protocol already mentioned above. In recent years, the Greenhouse Gas Protocol has started a number of new initiatives to support companies from less developed countries in their efforts to address climate change (Greenhouse Gas Protocol 2013d). For instance, the Greenhouse Gas Protocol Team has designed various courses to educate qualified instructors to be able to provide training for corporate GHG accounting, reporting, and inventory development. It has also established a certificate program for GHG accounting trainers to ensure that the course leaders have the necessary expertise to conduct high-quality workshops. In addition, it has created a program design course for organizations interested in developing and conducting similar programs in order to catalyze the establishment of new GHG accounting and reporting programs. These measures illustrate the great deal of effort devoted by the Greenhouse Gas Protocol to strengthen GHG emission accounting and reporting capacities in emerging economies and developing countries.

But despite all these activities to promote the rules and procedures of the Greenhouse Gas Protocol in other parts of the world, different Greenhouse Gas Protocol Trainers acknowledged in personal conversations that the current stalemate in the international climate negotiations considerably hampers their work. In particular, they noted that 'one of the main reasons why corporations use the Greenhouse Gas Protocol methodology is to prepare for the participation in emission markets.'[7] In addition, they pointed out that only the creation of a global market mechanism, which enables carbon trading between nations, industry sectors, and climate change mitigation projects, could motivate companies to undertake real efforts to tackle climate change. Similarly, Kolk, Levy, and Pinkse argue that the necessary enhancement of current business practices of disclosure, management, and accounting related to climate change 'require a global regime and/or more widespread carbon trading' (Kolk, Levy, and Pinkse 2008: 742). This suggests that only if legally binding GHG emission controls are introduced and accompanied by a large-scale market-based instrument will corporations take action on climate change in order to play their part in a carbon-constrained economy.

The Greenhouse Gas Protocol at the UNFCCC conferences

It was mentioned above that business groups that sought to prevent the adoption of legally binding GHG emission regulations dominated the early business participation in the international climate negotiations. In the 2000s, these groups lost much of their influence and at the same time more proactive corporate organizations gained prominence at the intergovernmental level (Pulver 2005; Lash and Wellington 2007; Falkner 2010). Among these organizations is the World Business Council for Sustainable Development, which together with the World Resources Institute organized several side events, workshops, and other social activities taking place in conjunction with the annual Conferences of the Parties to the UNFCCC (Grover 2008). On these occasions, the organizations tried to induce business representatives and other relevant stakeholders to adopt and implement the Greenhouse Gas Protocol guidelines for their corporate climate change strategies. For instance, shortly after the release of the first version of the Corporate Accounting and Reporting Standard, the World Business Council for Sustainable Development and the World Resources Institute hosted a joint side event at the 2002 Conference of the Parties to the UNFCCC held in Delhi to direct attention to the Greenhouse Gas Protocol. In addition, staff members of the Greenhouse Gas Protocol Team participated in numerous panel discussions on corporate GHG measurement and management practices to promulgate the rules and procedures of the Greenhouse Gas Protocol (Greenhouse Gas Protocol 2002; 2003). At subsequent Conferences of the Parties in Buenos Aires in 2004 and in Montreal in 2005, the Greenhouse Gas Protocol Team celebrated the launch of Mexico's pilot program for corporate GHG accounting and reporting as an innovative joint endeavor between the Greenhouse Gas Protocol, local business associations, and the Mexican government (Greenhouse Gas Protocol 2005a; 2005b). More recently, the World Resources Institute has also used the Conferences of the Parties as a platform to carry out technical workshops on new GHG accounting and reporting approaches and concepts (World Resources Institute 2013). Most relevant for the present case study, representatives of the Greenhouse Gas Protocol have at these and other events repeatedly called for a clear and stable international policy framework (e.g. Berthoud 2011; 2012; International Institute for Sustainable Development 2012). Moreover, the Greenhouse Gas Protocol's two founding organizations have also urged national delegates at the international climate change conferences to adopt more stringent GHG emission reduction targets and to set up a coherent UNFCCC-led cap and trade system (United Nations Environment Programme and World Resources Institute 2012; World Business Council for Sustainable Development 2013). This underscores once again the fact that the intergovernmental level is of utmost importance for the work of business self-regulatory initiatives.

Summary

In this chapter, I analyzed the interrelationship between a business self-regulatory initiative and the existing modes of inter-state cooperation in the issue area of climate change. In the remainder of the present chapter, I revert to the analytical framework and recapitulate the main findings from the case study. First, there are only weak theoretical indications that the Greenhouse Gas Protocol conflicts with the intergovernmental level. Some authors have emphasized the dominant position of the corporate sector in the creation of the Greenhouse Gas Protocol guidelines. They hold that individual companies might principally establish rules and procedures for corporate GHG accounting and reporting that are in line with their own corporate interests. These scholars further claim that the private sector might exploit the regulatory vacuum in the field of corporate-level accounting and reporting and seek to position the guidelines of the Greenhouse Gas Protocol as alternatives to more stringent GHG emission controls established by nation-states at the intergovernmental level. However, the analysis in this chapter did not yield any findings that consolidated this proposition with regard to the Greenhouse Gas Protocol.

Secondly, a number of findings suggest that the areas of operation of the Greenhouse Gas Protocol essentially complement existing modes of inter-state cooperation. The analysis has underlined that the Greenhouse Gas Protocol has filled a regulatory gap in global climate governance by providing the means for the corporate sector to conduct comprehensive GHG emission inventories. The Greenhouse Gas Protocol's various approaches and concepts of GHG accounting and reporting represent the common language and practice of corporate GHG measurement, and enable individual companies to take their first steps towards addressing climate change. In this way, the Greenhouse Gas Protocol provides the basis for all national GHG emission inventories and climate change mitigation policies. It can therefore be argued that the Greenhouse Gas Protocol contributes to the promotion of the norms and rules anchored in international climate agreements. Most interestingly in this regard is the fact that the guidelines provided by the Greenhouse Gas Protocol are to a growing extent also utilized by large companies from emerging economies and developing countries. These companies are supported by the Greenhouse Gas Protocol Team in their endeavor to comply with the rules and procedures for GHG measurement and management. Moreover, the Greenhouse Gas Protocol Team has undertaken various efforts to enhance the corporate GHG accounting and reporting capacities in various less-developed countries. While these countries have no explicit GHG emission reduction obligations under the current international climate regime, the voluntary steps taken by these companies lay the foundation for the adoption of future GHG emission controls. Consequently, business self-regulatory initiatives can be perceived as pioneers in the global response to climate change.

Third, the analysis in this chapter provides strong evidence that the adoption of the Greenhouse Gas Protocol greatly depends on the right incentive structure for the corporate sector to take action on climate change. In general terms, due to the lack of significant progress in the international climate negotiations, companies do not undertake costly efforts to measure and manage their GHG emissions. Although several corporations have started to account and report their GHG emissions, the quality of corporate GHG emission inventories remains questionable. In addition, numerous corporations have adopted a wait-and-see stance on the issue of climate change because of the absence of ambitious national GHG emission reduction targets and the general lack of clarity regarding the adoption of a new market-based instrument. In particular, several partnerships between the Greenhouse Gas Protocol and specific industry sectors have lost much of their appeal in the last decade, since corporate interest in the collaboration with the Greenhouse Gas Protocol has significantly diminished. This implies that many companies from carbon-intensive industries now go for the short-term benefit rather than invest in their GHG accounting and reporting capacities. As staff members of the Greenhouse Gas Protocol Team and Greenhouse Gas Protocol Certified Trainers commonly acknowledged, companies that measure and report their GHG emissions in line with the Greenhouse Gas Protocol guidelines are primarily interested in preparing for the effective participation in a global market mechanism or cap and trade systems. In the absence of such instruments that compel companies to take action on climate change, the guidelines and training courses developed by the Greenhouse Gas Protocol will arguably not encourage many companies to conduct reliable and complete inventories of their GHG emissions. All these examples illustrate that business action on climate change requires a coherent regulatory structure with mechanisms in place that allow for international trading between different countries, industries, and climate change mitigation projects. Accordingly, representatives of the Greenhouse Gas Protocol have recently urged national governments to establish a strong international climate agreement with a global market instrument in order to induce the corporate sector to increase its efforts to address climate change. This suggests that business self-regulatory initiatives have few operational capacities to tackle the problem of climate change without the establishment of an international regulatory framework and a clear stimulus for corporate action from the intergovernmental level (see Table 6.2).

Conclusions

This chapter has underscored the fact that the Greenhouse Gas Protocol plays a considerable role in global climate policy-making. The case study has demonstrated that the different areas of operation of the Greenhouse Gas Protocol facilitate the implementation of the norms and rules anchored in international climate agreements. The Greenhouse Gas Protocol can hence be seen as complementary to existing modes of inter-state cooperation. In particular, it can be argued that the business self-regulatory initiative provides important building blocks for future commitment periods adopted by nation-states in the international climate regime.

Nevertheless, similar to the two other case studies, the analysis in this chapter has revealed that the effective operation of the Greenhouse Gas Protocol to cope with the problem of climate change depends, to a large extent, on the existence of an international regulatory framework set up by nation-states at the intergovernmental level. The efforts undertaken by several companies to account and report their GHG emissions are primarily driven by corporate expectations of future GHG emission controls. Only if companies receive a clear political signal from the international climate change conferences that stringent GHG regulations

Table 6.2 Main findings from the analysis of the relationship between the Greenhouse Gas Protocol and the international climate regime

Conceptual assumptions	*The Greenhouse Gas Protocol: Main findings*
Conflictive relationship	Only weak theoretical indications
Complementary relationship	The Greenhouse Gas Protocol contributes to the implementation of the norms and rules of the international climate regime by providing the means for companies to comprehensively measure and manage their GHG emissions
	Several corporations from countries that do not have explicit GHG emission reduction obligations measure and report their emissions by using the guidelines, technical and administrative assistance, as well as training courses provided by the Greenhouse Gas Protocol
Dependency relationship	The adoption of the Greenhouse Gas Protocol greatly depends on the right incentive structure established by nation-states for the corporate sector to take action on climate change
	Due to the lack of significant progress in the international climate negotiations, the guidelines and training courses developed by the Greenhouse Gas Protocol will not encourage many companies to conduct reliable and complete inventories of their GHG emissions
	Representatives of the Greenhouse Gas Protocol have therefore recently urged national delegates to adopt more stringent GHG emission reduction targets and to set up a coherent UNFCCC-led cap and trade system

and a global market-based instrument are likely to be adopted in the near future will they put substantial efforts into the accurate calculation and communication of their GHG emissions. Therefore, it can be stated that business self-regulatory initiatives do not automatically lead to effective problem-solving, but need to be embedded in a coherent international policy framework. Voluntary business action on climate change can thus by no means be considered a substitute for multilateral treaty-making. Due to the absence of an adequate regulatory environment, there is presently no stimulus for companies to strive for pre-compliance action and first-mover advantages. As a consequence, the efforts of the corporate sector to measure and manage their GHG emissions remain dominated by short-term investment criteria and economic considerations. The analysis has shown that the corporate sector will only start taking action on climate change if companies have to prepare for future regulation. In other words, a stable international regulatory structure is crucial for encouraging corporate responses to climate change. Without the further evolution of the international climate regime, business self-regulatory initiatives will arguably make no tangible contribution to the global response to climate change. This does not imply that business self-regulatory initiatives are without effect in global politics. Yet, it has become apparent that such initiatives require an international umbrella with clear signals and incentives in order to become part of the solution for the problem of climate change.

Viewed from a theoretical perspective, it can be concluded that the Greenhouse Gas Protocol has attained authority in global climate governance. The rules and procedures created by the founding organizations of the Greenhouse Gas Protocol have closed a regulatory vacuum in the issue area of climate change and are widely accepted among relevant actors. In particular, the corporate GHG emission inventories compiled on the basis of the Greenhouse Gas Protocol can be incorporated into national GHG accounting and reporting systems. National governments might use these inventories to meet their (future) GHG emission reduction obligations under the international climate regime. This demonstrates that the Greenhouse Gas Protocol has acquired an authoritative function in the field of corporate-level GHG accounting and reporting. However, the emergence of business self-regulatory initiatives in the policy domain of climate change does not in any way render the norms and rules of the international climate regime obsolete. In fact, the case study in this chapter suggests that the principles, norms, rules, and decision-making procedures agreed upon by nation-states in international climate negotiations considerably shape individual and joint corporate commitments to address climate change. Based on this finding, it can be argued that there is no shift of authority from the intergovernmental level towards business self-regulatory initiatives concerned with climate change mitigation. Thus, the centrality of the international climate regime has not been challenged, but instead is further augmented by the expansion of voluntary business efforts for addressing the problem of climate change.

References

Andonova, Liliana B. (2010). Public-Private Partnerships for the Earth: Politics and Patterns of Hybrid Authority in the Multilateral System. *Global Environmental Politics* 10 (2): 25–53.

Andonova, Liliana B.; Betsill, Michele; Bulkeley, Harriet (2009). Transnational Climate Governance. *Global Environmental Politics* 9 (2): 52–73.

Andrew, Jane; Cortese, Corinne (2011). Accounting for Climate Change and the Self-Regulation of Carbon Disclosures. *Accounting Forum* 35 (3): 130–138.

Andrews, Richard N. (1998). Environmental Regulation and Business 'Self-Regulation'. *Policy Sciences* 31 (3): 177–197.

Arts, Bas (2002). 'Green Alliances' of Businesses and NGOs: New Styles of Self-Regulation or 'Dead-End Roads'? *Corporate Social Responsibility and Environmental Management* 9 (1): 26–36.

Association of Chartered Certified Accountants; Global Reporting Initiative (2009). *High-Impact Sectors: The Challenge of Reporting on Climate Change*. London: Certified Accountants Educational Trust.

Auld, Graeme; Bernstein, Steven; Cashore, Benjamin (2008). The New Corporate Social Responsibility. *Annual Review of Environment and Resources* 33: 413–435.

Bäckstrand, Karin (2008). Accountability of Networked Climate Governance: The Rise of Transnational Climate Partnerships. *Global Environmental Politics* 8 (3): 74–102.

Bayon, Ricardo; Hawn, Amanda; Hamilton, Katherine (2007). *Voluntary Carbon Markets: An International Business Guide to What They Are and How They Work*. London: Earthscan.

Begg, Kathryn; van der Woerd, Frans; Levy, David L., (eds). (2005). *The Business of Climate Change: Corporate Responses to Kyoto*. Sheffield: Greenleaf Publishing.

Bennett, W. Lance; Lagos, Taso (2007). Logo Logic: The Ups and Downs of Branded Political Communication. *The Annals of the American Academy of Political and Social Sciences* 611 (1): 193–206.

Berthoud, Thierry (2011). The Durban Dilemma: Where Do We Go From Here? *The Guardian*, December 1.

Berthoud, Thierry (2012). The Business Case for Progress in Doha. *Carbon Finance* Winter 2012: 4.

Borck, Jonathan C.; Coglianese, Cary (2009). Voluntary Environmental Programs: Assessing their Effectiveness. *Annual Review of Environment and Resources* 40: 305–324.

Braithwaite, John; Fisse, Brent (1993). Self-Regulation and the Control of Corporate Crime. In: Shearing, Clifford D.; Stenning, Philip C. *Private Policing*. Beverly Hills, CA: Sage, 221–246.

Brammer, Stephen; Jackson, Gregory; Matten, Dirk (2012). Corporate Social Responsibility and Institutional Theory: New Perspectives on Private Governance. *Socio-Economic Review* 10 (1): 3–28.

Bulkeley, Harriet; Newell, Peter (2010). *Governing Climate Change*. London: Routledge.

Carbon Disclosure Project (2013a). *Global 500 Climate Change Report 2013*. London: Carbon Disclosure Project.

Carbon Disclosure Project (2013b). *Reports & Data*. Available at: www.cdp.net/en-US/Results/Pages/overview.aspx (accessed October 28, 2013).

Carraro, Carlo; Lévêque, Francois (1999). Introduction: The Rationale and Potential of Voluntary Approaches. In: Carraro, Carlo; Lévêque, Francois. *Voluntary Approaches in Environmental Policy*. Dordrecht: Kluwer, 1–15.

Carroll, Archie B. (1999). Corporate Social Responsibility: Evolution of a Definitional Construct. *Business & Society* 38 (3): 269–295.

Carroll, Archie B.; Shabana, Kareem M. (2010). The Business Case for Corporate Social Responsibility: A Review of Concepts, Research and Practice. *International Journal of Management Studies* 12 (1): 85–105.

Clapp, Jennifer (2005). Transnational Corporations and Global Environmental Governance. In: Dauvergne, Peter. *Handbook of Global Environmental Politics*. Cheltenham: Edward Elgar, 284–297.

Clapp, Jennifer; Meckling, Jonas (2013). Business as a Global Actor. In: Falkner, Robert. *The Handbook of Global Climate and Environment Policy*. Chichester: Wiley-Blackwell, 286–303.

Cogan, Douglas C. (2008). Corporate Governance and Climate Change: Making the Connection. In: Clarke, Thomas; dela Rama, Marie. *The Fundamentals of Corporate Governance. Volume 4: Stakeholders and Sustainability*. London: Sage, 308–339.

Conroy, Michael E. (2007). *Branded! How the 'Certification Revolution' Is Transforming Global Corporations* Gabriola: New Society Publishers.

CorporateRegister.com (2008). *The Corporate Climate Communications Report 2007: A Study of Climate Change Disclosures by the Global FT500*. London: CorporateRegister.com.

Croci, Edoardo (2005). The Economics of Environmental Voluntary Agreements. In: Croci, Edoardo. *The Handbook of Environmental Voluntary Agreements: Design, Implementation and Evaluation Issues*. Dordrecht: Springer, 3–30.

Dauvergne, Peter; Lister, Jane (2010). The Power of Big Box Retail in Global Environmental Governance: Bringing Commodity Chains Back into IR. *Millennium: Journal of International Studies* 39 (1): 145–160.

Deitelhoff, Nicole; Wolf, Klaus Dieter (2013). Business and Human Rights. In: Risse, Thomas; Ropp, Stephen C.; Sikkink, Kathryn. *The Persistent Power of Human Rights: From Commitment to Compliance*. Cambridge, UK: Cambridge University Press, 222–238.

Delmas, Magali A.; Terlaak, Ann K. (2001). A Framework for Analyzing Environmental Voluntary Agreements. *California Management Review* 43 (3): 44–63.

Downie, John; Stubbs, Wendy (2012). Corporate Carbon Strategies and Greenhouse Gas Emission Assessments: The Implications of Scope 3 Emission Factor Selection. *Business Strategy and the Environment* 21 (6): 412–422.

Dunn, Seth (2005). Down to Business on Climate Change: An Overview of Corporate Strategies. In: Begg, Kathryn; Van der Woerd, Frans; Levy, David L. *The Business of Climate Change: Corporate Responses to Kyoto*. Sheffield: Greenleaf Publishing, 31–46.

Dunning, John H. (1981). *International Production and the Multinational Enterprise*. London: Allen & Unwin.

Engwall, Lars (2006). Global Enterprises in Fields of Global Governance. In: Djelic, Marie-Laure; Sahlin-Andersson, Kerstin. *Transnational Governance: Institutional Dynamics of Regulation*. Cambridge, UK: Cambridge University Press, 161–179.

Falkner, Robert (2010). Business and Global Climate Governance. In: Ougaard, Morten; Leander, Anna. *Business and Global Governance*. New York: Routledge, 99–117.

Foster, John Bellamy (2012). The Planetary Rift and the New Human Exemptionalism: A Political-Economic Critique of Ecological Modernization Theory. *Organization & Environment* 25 (3): 211–237.

Fuchs, Doris (2007). Transnational Corporations and the Effectiveness of Private Governance. In: Schirm, Stefan. *Globalization: State of the Art and Perspectives*. London: Routledge, 122–142.

Gereffi, Gary; Garcia-Johnson, Ronie; Sasser, Erika (2001). The NGO-Industrial Complex. *Foreign Policy*, July 1, 56–65.

Glasbergen, Pieter (2007). Setting the Scene: The Partnership Paradigm in the Making. In: Glasbergen, Pieter; Biermann, Frank; Mol, Arthur P. J. *Partnerships, Governance and Sustainable Development: Reflections on Theory and Practice*. Cheltenham: Edward Elgar, 1–27.

Global Environment Facility (2012). *Private Sector Engagement in Climate Change Adaptation. GEF/LDCF.SCCF.12/Inf.06*. Washington, DC: Global Environment Facility Secretariat.

Global Methane Initiative (2013). *About the Initiative*. Available at: www.globalmethane.org/about/index.aspx (accessed November 4, 2013).

Gond, Jean-Pascal; Kang, Nahee; Moon, Jeremy (2011). The Government of Self-Regulation: On the Comparative Dynamics of Corporate Social Responsibility. *Economy and Society* 40 (4): 640–671.

Green, Jessica F. (2010). Private Standards in the Climate Regime: The Greenhouse Gas Protocol. *Business and Politics* 12 (3): Article 3.

Greenhouse Gas Protocol (2002). *Greenhouse Gas Protocol Newsletter Issue 5*. Geneva; Washington, DC: World Business Council for Sustainable Development and World Resources Institute.

Greenhouse Gas Protocol (2003). *Greenhouse Gas Protocol Newsletter Issue 8*. Geneva; Washington, DC: World Business Council for Sustainable Development and World Resources Institute.

Greenhouse Gas Protocol (2004). *A Corporate Accounting and Reporting Standard: Revised Edition*. Geneva; Washington, DC: World Business Council for Sustainable Development and World Resources Institute.

Greenhouse Gas Protocol (2005a). *Greenhouse Gas Protocol Newsletter Issue 14*. Geneva; Washington, DC: World Business Council for Sustainable Development and World Resources Institute.

Greenhouse Gas Protocol (2005b). *Greenhouse Gas Protocol Newsletter Issue 17*. Geneva; Washington, DC: World Business Council for Sustainable Development and World Resources Institute.

Greenhouse Gas Protocol (2006). *Mexico GHG Program Becomes Permanent. Greenhouse Gas Protocol Newsletter Issue 20*. Geneva; Washington, DC: World Business Council for Sustainable Development and World Resources Institute.

Greenhouse Gas Protocol (2007). *Philippine Greenhouse Gas Program Launched in Manila. Greenhouse Gas Protocol Newsletter Issue 21*. Geneva; Washington, DC: World Business Council for Sustainable Development and World Resources Institute.

Greenhouse Gas Protocol (2008). *Greenhouse Gas Protocol Newsletter Issue 25*. Geneva; Washington, DC: World Business Council for Sustainable Development and World Resources Institute.

Greenhouse Gas Protocol (2009). *Top Companies in Brazil Report Greenhouse Gas Emissions for the First Time. Greenhouse Gas Protocol Newsletter Issue 28*. Geneva; Washington, DC: World Business Council for Sustainable Development and World Resources Institute.

Greenhouse Gas Protocol (2011a). *Chinese Companies Pilot-Test a New Energy-GHG Conversion Software. Greenhouse Gas Protocol Newsletter Issue 32*. Geneva; Washington, DC: World Business Council for Sustainable Development and World Resources Institute.

Greenhouse Gas Protocol (2011b). *Corporate Value Chain (Scope 3) Accounting and Reporting Standard: Supplement to the GHG Protocol Corporate Accounting and Reporting Standard*. Geneva; Washington, DC: World Business Council for Sustainable Development and World Resources Institute.

Greenhouse Gas Protocol (2011c). *New Initiative Announced to Help ICT Industry Measure Carbon Footprint. Greenhouse Gas Protocol Newsletter Issue 31*. Geneva; Washington, DC: World Business Council for Sustainable Development and World Resources Institute.

Greenhouse Gas Protocol (2012a). *The Foundation for Sustainable Climate Strategies*. Geneva; Washington, DC: World Business Council for Sustainable Development and World Resources Institute.

Greenhouse Gas Protocol (2012b). *Launch of the GHG Protocol Product Life Cycle and Corporate Value Chain Standards. Greenhouse Gas Protocol Newsletter Issue 33*. Geneva; Washington, DC: World Business Council for Sustainable Development and World Resources Institute.

Greenhouse Gas Protocol (2013a). *About the GHG Protocol*. Available at: www.ghgprotocol.org/about-ghgp (accessed August 19, 2013).

Greenhouse Gas Protocol (2013b). *All Tools*. Available at: www.ghgprotocol.org/calculation-tools/all-tools (accessed November 27, 2013).

Greenhouse Gas Protocol (2013c). *Corporate Standard*. Available at: www.ghgprotocol.org/standards/corporate-standard (accessed November 13, 2013).

Greenhouse Gas Protocol (2013d). *GHG Protocol Capacity Building Initiatives*. Available at: www.ghgprotocol.org/node/176 (accessed December 9, 2013).

Greenhouse Gas Protocol (2013e). *India GHG Program Launch. Greenhouse Gas Protocol Newsletter Issue 37*. Geneva; Washington, DC: World Business Council for Sustainable Development and World Resources Institute.

Greenhouse Gas Protocol (2013f). *Our Team*. Available at: www.ghgprotocol.org/our-team (accessed November 12, 2013).

Greenhouse Gas Protocol (2013g). *Required Greenhouse Gases in Inventories: Accounting and Reporting Standard Amendment*. Geneva; Washington, DC: World Business Council for Sustainable Development and World Resources Institute.

Greenhouse Gas Protocol (2013h). *Survey on Scope 3 Implementation. Greenhouse Gas Protocol Newsletter Issue 36*. Geneva; Washington, DC: World Business Council for Sustainable Development.

Grover, Katherine Sye (2008). *Development of International Standards by Non-State Actors: Assessing the Impact of the GHG Protocol Initiative*. Paper presented at the Meeting of the Midwest Political Science Association, held in Chicago from April 3–6.

Harmes, Adam (2011). The Limits of Carbon Disclosure: Theorizing the Business Case for Investor Environmentalism. *Global Environmental Politics* 11 (2): 98–119.

Haufler, Virginia (2001). *A Public Role for the Private Sector: Industry Self-Regulation in a Global Economy*. Washington, DC: Carnegie Endowment for International Peace.

Hoffman, Andrew J. (2005). Climate Change Strategy: The Business Logic behind Voluntary Greenhouse Gas Reductions. *California Management Review* 47 (3): 21–46.

Hoffmann, Matthew (2011). *Climate Governance at the Crossroads: Experimenting With a Global Response After Kyoto*. Oxford: Oxford University Press.

Huang, Anny Y.; Weber, Christopher L.; Matthews, Scott H. (2009). Categorization of Scope 3 Emissions for Streamlined Enterprise Carbon Footprinting. *Environmental Science & Technology* 43 (22): 8509–8515.

Ietto-Gillies, Grazia (2012). *Transnational Corporations and International Production: Concepts, Theories and Effects*. Cheltenham: Edward Elgar.

International Energy Agency (2009). *Energy Technology Transitions for Industry: Strategies for the Next Industrial Revolution*. Paris: International Energy Agency.

International Finance Corporation (2011). *Climate Finance: Engaging the Private Sector*. Washington, DC: International Finance Corporation.

International Institute for Sustainable Development (2012). *Global Business Day Bulletin: A Summary Report of the Doha Global Business Day*. New York: International Institute for Sustainable Development Reporting Services.

International Organization for Standardization (2006). *ISO 14064-1: Specification with Guidance at the Organization Level for Quantification and Reporting of Greenhouse Gas Emissions and Removals*. Geneva: ISO Central Secretariat.

IPCC (2014). *Climate Change 2014. Mitigation of Climate Change. Contribution of Working Group III to the Fifth Assessment Report of the Intergovernmental Panel on Climate Change*. Cambridge, UK: Cambridge University Press.

Jackson, Rachel; Knight, Alan (2011). *The Carbon We're Not Counting: Accounting for Scope 3 Emissions*. London: Association of Chartered Certified Accountants.

Jänicke, Martin; Jacob, Klaus (2004). Lead Markets for Environmental Innovations: A New Role for the Nation State. *Global Environmental Politics* 4 (1): 29–46.

Jenkins, Rhys Owen (1987). *Transnational Corporations and Uneven Development: The Internationalization of Capital and the Third World*. London: Methuen.

Jones, Charles A.; Levy, David L. (2009). Business Strategies and Climate Change. In: Selin, Henrik; Van Deveer, Stacy D. *Changing Climates in North American Politics*. Cambridge, MA: MIT Press, 219–240.

King, Andrew A.; Lenox, Michael J. (2000). Industry Self-Regulation Without Sanctions: The Chemical Industry's Responsible Care Program. *Academy of Management Journal* 43 (4): 698–716.

Knox-Hayes, Janelle; Levy, David L. (2011). The Politics of Carbon Disclosure as Climate Governance. *Strategic Organization* 9 (1): 1–9.

Koenig-Archibugi, Mathias (2004). Transnational Corporations and Public Accountability. *Government and Opposition* 39 (2): 234–259.

Kolk, Ans (2008). Developments in Corporate Responses to Climate Change within the Past Decade. In: Hansjürgens, Bernd; Antes, Ralf. *Economics and Management of Climate Change: Risks: Mitigation and Adaptation*. New York: Springer, 221–230.

Kolk, Ans; Levy, David L. (2001). Winds of Change: Corporate Strategy, Climate Change and Oil Multinationals. *European Management Journal* 19 (5): 501–509.

Kolk, Ans; Levy, David L.; Pinkse, Jonatan (2008). Corporate Responses in an Emerging Climate Regime: The Institutionalization and Commensuration of Carbon Disclosure. *European Accounting Review* 17 (4): 719–745.

Kolk, Ans; Tulder, Rob van (2002). The Effectiveness of Self-Regulation: Corporate Codes of Conduct and Child Labour. *European Management Journal* 20 (3): 260–271.

Kolk, Ans; Tulder, Rob van (2005). Setting New Global Rules? TNCs and Codes of Conduct. *Transnational Corporations* 14 (3): 1–27.

Kourula, Arno; Halme, Minna (2008). Types of Corporate Responsibility and Engagement With NGOs: An Exploration of Business and Societal Outcomes. *Corporate Governance* 8 (4): 557–570.

Lash, Jonathan; Wellington, Fred (2007). Competitive Advantage on a Warming Planet. *Harvard Business Review* 85 (3): 94–102.

Levy, David L.; Egan, Daniel (2003). A Neo-Gramscian Approach to Corporate Political Strategy: Conflict and Accomodation in the Climate Change Negotiations. *Journal of Management Studies* 40 (4): 803–830.

Levy, David L.; Newell, Peter, (eds). (2005a). *The Business of Global Environmental Governance*. Cambridge, MA: MIT Press.

Levy, David L.; Newell, Peter (2005b). Introduction: The Business of Global Environmental Governance. In: Levy, David L.; Newell, Peter. *The Business of Global Environmental Governance*. Cambridge, MA: MIT Press, 1–17.

Lipschutz, Ronnie D.; Rowe, James K., (eds). (2005). *Globalization, Governmentality and Global Politics: Regulation for the Rest of Us?* New York: Routledge.

Mazurkiewicz, Piotr (2005). Corporate Self-Regulation and Multi-stakeholder Dialogue. In: Croci, Edoardo. *The Handbook of Environmental Voluntary Agreements: Design, Implementation and Evaluation Issues*. Dordrecht: Springer, 31–45.

Mol, Arthur P. J. (2001). *Globalization and Environmental Reform: The Ecological Modernization of the Global Economy*. Cambridge, MA: MIT Press.

Morgenstern, Richard D.; Pizer, William A., (eds). (2007). *Reality Check: The Nature and Performance of Voluntary Environmental Programs in the United States, Europe, and Japan*. Washington, DC: RFF Press.

Newell, Peter (2000). Environmental NGOs and Globalization: The Governance of TNCs. In: Cohen, Robin; Rai, Shirin M. *Global Social Movements*. London: Athlone Press, 117–132.

Newell, Peter; Paterson, Matthew (1998). A Climate for Business: Global Warming, the State and Capital. *Review of International Political Economy* 5 (4): 679–703.

OECD (1999). *Voluntary Approaches for Environmental Policy: An Assessment*. Paris: OECD Publishing.

Okereke, Chukwumerije; Küng, Kristina (2013). Climate Policy and Business Climate Strategies. *Management of Environmental Quality* 24 (3): 286–310.

Okereke, Chukwumerije; Wittneben, Bettina; Bowen, Frances (2012). Climate Change: Challenging Business, Transforming Politics. *Business & Society* 51 (1): 7–30.

Ozawa-Meida, Leticia; Fransen, Taryn; Jiménez-Ambriz, Rosa María (2008). The Mexico Greenhouse Gas Program: Corporate Response to Climate Change Initiatives in a 'Non-Annex-I' Country. In: Sullivan, Rory. *Corporate Responses to Climate Change: Achieving Emissions Reductions Through Regulation, Self-Regulation and Economic Incentives*. Sheffield: Greenleaf Publishing.

Pattberg, Philipp (2006). The Influence of Global Business Regulation: Beyond Good Corporate Conduct. *Business and Society Review* 111 (3): 241–268.

Pattberg, Philipp; Biermann, Frank; Chan, Sander; Mert, Aysem, (eds). (2012). *Public-Private Partnerships for Sustainable Development: Emergence, Influence and Legitimacy*. Cheltenham: Edward Elgar.

Pattberg, Philipp; Stripple, Johannes (2008). Beyond the Public and Private Divide: Remapping Transnational Climate Governance in the 21st Century. *International Environmental Agreements* 8 (4): 367–388.

Peters, Glen P. (2010). Carbon Footprints and Embodied Carbon at Multiple Scales. *Current Opinion in Environmental Sustainability* 2 (4): 245–250.

Pinkse, Jonatan; Kolk, Ans (2009). *International Business and Global Climate Change*. London: Routledge.

Porter, Michael E.; Kramer, Mark R. (2006). Strategy and Society: The Link between Competitive Advantage and Corporate Social Responsibility. *Harvard Business Review*, December 1, 78–92.

Porter, Michael E.; van der Linde, Claas (1995). Toward a New Conception of the Environmental-Competitiveness Issue. *Journal of Economic Perspectives* 9 (4): 97–118.

Prather, Michael J.; Hsu, Juno (2008). NF_3, the Greenhouse Gas Missing From Kyoto. *Geographical Research Letters* 35 (12): L12810.

Pulver, Simone (2005). Organising Business: Industry NGOs in the Climate Debates. In: Begg, Kathryn; Van der Woerd, Frans; Levy, David L. *The Business of Climate Change: Corporate Responses to Kyoto*. Sheffield: Greenleaf Publishing, 47–60.

Rittberger, Volker; Nettesheim, Martin; Huckel, Carmen; Göbel, Thorsten (2008). Introduction: Changing Patterns of Authority. In: Rittberger, Volker; Nettesheim, Martin. *Authority in the Global Political Economy*. Basingstoke: Palgrave, 1–9.

Ruggie, John G. (2003). Taking Embedded Liberalism Global: The Corporate Connection. In: Held, David; König-Archibugi, Mathias. *Taming Globalization: Frontiers of Governance*. Cambridge: Polity Press, 93–129.

Ruggie, John G. (2007). Global Markets and Global Governance: The Prospects for Convergence. In: Bernstein, Steven; Pauly, Louis W. *Global Liberalism and Political*

Order: Toward a New Grand Compromise? Albany, NY: State University of New York Press, 23–50.

Sahlin-Andersson, Kerstin (2004). Emergent Cross-Sectional Soft Regulations: Dynamics at Play in the Global Compact Initiative. In: Mörth, Ulrike. *Soft Law in Governance and Regulation: An Interdisciplinary Analysis*. Cheltenham: Elgar, 129–152.

Sahlin-Andersson, Kerstin (2006). Corporate Social Responsibility: A Trend and a Movement, But of What and for What? *Corporate Governance* 6 (5): 595–608.

Southworth, Katie (2009). Corporate Voluntary Action: A Valuable But Incomplete Solution to Climate Change and Energy Security Challenges. *Policy and Society* 27 (4): 329–350.

Stoner, James A. F.; Wankel, Charles, (eds). (2012). *Managing Climate Change Business Risks and Consequences: Leadership for Global Sustainability*. New York: Palgrave.

Strange, Susan (1996). *The Retreat of the State: The Diffusion of Power in the World Economy*. Cambridge, UK: Cambridge University Press.

Strasser, Kurt A., (ed.). (2011). *Myths and Realities of Business Environmentalism: Good Works, Good Business or Greenwash?* Cheltenham: Edward Elgar.

Sullivan, Rory, (ed.). (2008a). *Corporate Responses to Climate Change: Achieving Emissions Reductions Through Regulation, Self-Regulation and Economic Incentives*. Sheffield: Greenleaf Publishing.

Sullivan, Rory (2008b). Do Voluntary Approaches Have a Role to Play in the Response to Climate Change? In: Sullivan, Rory. *Corporate Responses to Climate Change: Achieving Emissions Reductions Through Regulation, Self-Regulation and Economic Incentives*. Sheffield: Greenleaf Publishers, 320–333.

Sullivan, Rory; Crossley, Rachel; Kozak, Jennifer (2008). Corporate Greenhouse Gas Emissions Management: The State of Play. In: Sullivan, Rory. *Corporate Responses to Climate Change: Achieving Emissions Reductions Through Regulation, Self-Regulation and Economic Incentives*. Sheffield: Greenleaf Publishing, 9–25.

Sundin, Heidi; Ranganathan, Janet (2002). Managing Business Greenhouse Gas Emissions: The Greenhouse Gas Protocol – A Strategic and Operational Tool. *Corporate Environmental Strategy* 9 (2): 137–144.

Talbot, David; Boiral, Olivier (2013). Can We Trust Corporates GHG Inventories? An Investigation Among Canada's Large Final Emitters. *Energy Policy* 63: 1075–1085.

Thalmann, Philippe; Baranzini, Andrea (2004). An Overview of the Economics of Voluntary Approaches in Climate Policy. In: Baranzini, Andrea; Thalmann, Philippe. *Voluntary Approaches in Climate Policy*. Cheltenham: Edward Elgar, 1–30.

UNFCCC (2008). *Investment and Financial Flows to Address Climate Change: An Update*. *FCCC/TP/2008/7*. Bonn: UNFCCC Secretariat.

UNFCCC (2012). *Doha Amendment to the Kyoto Protocol: Adoption of Amendment to the Protocol*. C.N.*718*.*2012*.*TREATIES-XXVII*.*7*.C. Bonn: UNFCCC Secretariat.

United Nations Environment Programme; World Resources Institute (2012). *Submission to the UNFCCC under the Durban Platform for Enhanced Action on 'Options and Ways for Further Increasing the Level of Ambition'*. Nairobi; Washington, DC: United Nations Environment Programme and World Resources Institute.

United Nations Global Compact (2013). *Overview of the UN Global Compact*. Available at: www.unglobalcompact.org/AboutTheGC/index.html (accessed October 4, 2013).

Utting, Peter (2012). Activism, Business Regulation and Development. In: Reed, Darryl; Utting, Peter; Mukherjee-Reed, Ananya. *Business Regulation and Non-State Actors: Whose Standards? Whose Development?* New York: Routledge, 38–53.

van Asselt, Harro; Zelli, Fariborz (2014). Connect the Dots: Managing the Fragmentation of Global Climate Governance. *Environmental Economics and Policy Studies* 16 (2): 137–155.

Vogel, David (2005). *The Market for Virtue: The Potential and Limits of Corporate Social Responsibility*. Washington, DC: Brookings Institution Press.

Vogel, David (2010). The Private Regulation of Global Corporate Conduct: Achievements and Limitations. *Business & Society* 49 (1): 68–87.

World Business Council for Sustainable Development (2012). *Energy and Climate: COP 18 Report: Doha Delivers a Doha Climate Gateway – So What?* Geneva: World Business Council for Sustainable Development.

World Business Council for Sustainable Development (2013). *Climate Solutions – Key Messages: WBCSD at the UNFCCC Warsaw Climate Change Conference (COP 19)*. Available at: www.wbcsd.org/work-program/focus-areas/energy-and-climate/climate solutions2013/cs2013keymessa.aspx (accessed December 11, 2013).

World Resources Institute (2002). *Working 9 to 5 on Climate Change: An Office Guide*. Washington, DC: World Resources Institute.

World Resources Institute (2006). *Hot Climate, Cool Commerce: A Service Sector Guide to Greenhouse Gas Management*. Washington, DC: World Resources Institute.

World Resources Institute (2013). *Measurement and Performance Tracking Workshop*. Available at: www.wri.org/event/measurement-and-performance-tracking-workshop (accessed November 4, 2013).

York, Richard; Rosa, Eugene A. (2003). Key Challenges to Ecological Modernization Theory: Institutional Efficacy, Case Study Evidence, Units of Analysis, and the Pace of Eco-Efficiency. *Organization & Environment* 16 (3): 273–288.

Notes

1 NF_3 is an inorganic gas that is used as an etchant in microelectronics, primarily in the manufacturing process of flat panel displays and solar cells. It has a global warming potential that is about 17,200 times higher than that of CO_2 when compared over a time period of 100 years (Prather and Hsu 2008).

2 The Fortune Global 500 is an annual ranking of the 500 biggest corporations in the world measured by revenue that is compiled and published by *Fortune* magazine.

3 Personal interview conducted on December 2, 2012 with David Rich, *Senior Associate* at the World Resources Institute, during an Expert Workshop on the tools and methodology of the Greenhouse Gas Protocol convened by the World Resources Institute in Doha on the sidelines of the 18th Conference of the Parties to the UNFCCC from November 26 to December 8, 2012.

4 Personal interview conducted on December 5, 2012 with Thierry Berthoud, *Managing Director for Energy and Climate* of the World Business Council for Sustainable Development, during the 18th Conference of the Parties to the UNFCCC held in Doha from November 26 to December 8, 2012.

5 Personal interview conducted on December 5, 2012 with Thierry Berthoud, *Managing Director for Energy and Climate* of the World Business Council for Sustainable Development, during the 18th Conference of the Parties to the UNFCCC held in Doha from November 26 to December 8, 2012.

6 Personal interview conducted on December 2, 2012 with David Rich, *Senior Associate* at the World Resources Institute, during an Expert Workshop on the tools and methodology of the Greenhouse Gas Protocol convened by the World Resources Institute in Doha on the sidelines of the 18th Conference of the Parties to the UNFCCC from November 26 to December 8, 2012.

7 Personal interviews conducted on December 5, 2012 with Beatriz Kiss, Greenhouse Gas Protocol Trainer in Brazil and on December 6, 2012 with two Greenhouse Gas Protocol Trainers from the Asian region (who wished to remain anonymous), during the 18th Conference of the Parties to the UNFCCC held in Doha from November 26 to December 8, 2012.

7 Conclusions

Summary

This book has explored the interplay of the ICLEI network, the Gold Standard, and the Greenhouse Gas Protocol with the international climate regime. While it is beyond doubt that the rapid expansion of transnational climate initiatives has made the landscape of global climate governance multifaceted and multi-layered, this study questions the widespread assertion that the growing significance of sub- and non-state actors in global (climate) politics leads to the decline of state-based forms of governance. The overall finding of this book is that the international climate regime remains the center of the global response to climate change around which different types of sub- and non-state actors revolve and upon which their initiatives are built. This concluding chapter begins by briefly recapitulating the starting point, primary research question, and key focus of this book. Then, I compare across the three case studies conducted in the previous chapters and assess the findings within the analytical framework, before I highlight the study's main conclusions. After that, I discuss the theoretical implications of this book for the debate on the concept of authority in global climate governance. Finally, I emphasize the study's practical relevance and point to a number of questions that warrant discussion in future research.

Starting point

The present study started from the observation that the past two decades of international climate negotiations have delivered only limited results to cope with the climate change problem. In order to close this policy gap, several multilateral and transnational governance initiatives have emerged outside the auspices of the UNFCCC with the aim of tackling climate change in novel ways at various levels of decision-making. In this study, I concentrated the analysis on transnational initiatives launched by different types of sub- and non-state actors operating in the policy domain of climate change, namely transnational city networks, private certification schemes, and business self-regulation. As discussed at length in the second chapter, the great variety of newly emerging climate governance arrangements has considerably increased the institutional complexity in the field of global climate politics. This has been described as the 'fragmented governance architecture' (Biermann *et al.* 2010: 15), the 'regime complex for climate change' (Keohane and Victor 2011), the 'polycentric system for coping with global climate change' (Ostrom 2010: 555), the 'multi-level and multi-arena nature of climate governance' (Bulkeley and Newell 2010: 13), and the 'experimental climate governance system' (Hoffmann 2011: 80). Most relevant for this book, numerous authors contend that sub- and non-state actors have adopted various roles and functions in global climate governance that previously rested rather exclusively with national governments and international institutions (e.g. Jagers and Stripple 2003; Betsill and Bulkeley 2006; Pattberg 2007; Bäckstrand 2008; Andonova, Betsill, and Bulkeley 2009; Bulkeley and Newell 2010; Hoffmann 2011; Pattberg 2012; Green 2014). More specifically, some of these scholars even assert that the emergence of transnational governance arrangements has generated a 'shift in the centre of gravity in climate governance away from traditional state-centric multilateral processes to multilevel governance whereby diverse, decentralised initiatives (…) form the basis for the global response to climate change' (Bernstein *et al.* 2010: 171). Building upon new concepts of authority in world politics, this group of scholars hold that the increasing importance of local governments, civil society networks, business associations, and other groups of actors concerned with the problem of climate change has led to the development of authority structures beyond national governments and state-based international regimes. With this claim, they challenge classical approaches to international politics and traditional understandings of authority in world politics. In this book, I have taken up this thread and put forward the argument that scholars have thus far made only little effort to thoroughly analyze the *vertical* institutional interplay between the various transnational climate governance arrangements and the intergovernmental level. For that reason, the present study has addressed this issue and takes a significant step towards bridging this gap in the state of research on contemporary global climate governance.

Primary research question

With this in mind, the study was concerned with the increasing involvement of sub- and non-state actors in global affairs and aimed to figure out what the emergence of transnational climate governance arrangements implies for global climate policy-making. Thereby, the discussion of different theoretical approaches to the concept of authority in world politics was used as a theoretical background for the empirical analysis of the relationship between transnational climate initiatives and the existing modes of inter-state cooperation clustered around the UNFCCC. The primary research question addressed in this book was how the various newly emerging transnational climate initiatives launched by sub-national, non-profit, and business actors relate to the international climate regime. In order to systematically analyze this question, I developed an analytical framework in which I introduced three perspectives on the relationship between transnational climate governance arrangements and the intergovernmental level. Using this framework, I empirically investigated whether transnational climate initiatives created by actors other than the nation-state (i) *conflict*, (ii) *complement*, or (iii) *depend on* the existing modes of inter-state cooperation in the policy domain of climate change. Hence, in a nutshell, this book has dealt with the topical issue of the growing importance of sub- and non-state actors in global climate governance to generate findings that advance the general theory about the concept of authority in world politics.

Key focus of the study

In the past decades, scholars of world politics have dedicated increasing attention to the development of new 'spheres of authority' in global affairs that have emerged beyond the nation-state and state-based international regimes (Rosenau 1997; 1999; 2007). This is particularly evident in the field of global climate governance, where several authors have highlighted the gradual loss of authority by national governments and international institutions with the emergence of various climate initiatives developed by sub- and non-state actors. Drawing on this literature, the present study focused in particular on the issue of what the development of transnational climate governance arrangements entails for the dispersion of authority in global climate governance. By this means, the book aimed to go one step further than many of the previous studies that often simply assume that the authority of the nation-state and state-based international regimes is eroding due to the increasing significance of sub- and non-state actors in different domains of global affairs. Indeed, the numerous case studies on individual climate initiatives launched by cities, provinces, civil society groups, environmental organizations, and business associations have surely consolidated our knowledge about these actors in the global response to climate change. Nevertheless, I contend in this study that the role and function of transnational governance arrangements in global climate governance cannot satisfactorily be evaluated without taking into account their interplay with the norms and rules anchored in international climate agreements. Thus, by building upon different theoretical approaches to the concept of authority in world politics, the study moves beyond the current literature on the emergence of transnational climate governance arrangements and aims at contributing to a better theoretical and empirical understanding of the consequences associated with the proliferation of these arrangements for global (climate) policy-making.

Cross-case comparison

After having recapitulated the general idea of this book, I now proceed with the cross-case comparison in order to extract common patterns across the three cases under investigation. Although each case study is to some extent unique, a number of fundamental features can be identified that characterize the relationship between transnational climate initiatives and the intergovernmental level. Next, I return to the three conceptual assumptions outlined in the research design and assess the case studies within the analytical framework of this book. After that, I highlight the key conclusions that can be drawn from the empirical analysis and briefly refer to the generalizability of the cases studied in the preceding chapters.

Assessing the case studies within the analytical framework

The empirical analysis in this book was guided by three conceptual assumptions regarding the interrelationship between transnational climate governance arrangements and the intergovernmental level. The first conceptual assumption portrayed a *conflictive* relationship and suggested that transnational climate initiatives weaken the norms and rules of the international climate regime. Concerning this assumption, it can be noted that no convincing evidence was found that transnational governance arrangements are in conflict with existing modes of inter-state cooperation. The case studies on the ICLEI network and the Gold Standard have not delivered any indications that these initiatives propagate norms and rules opposed to those stipulated in international climate agreements or seek to establish their own rules and procedures as alternatives to the intergovernmental level. In the third case study, there were weak indications that the Greenhouse Gas Protocol could theoretically conflict with the norms and rules of the international climate regime. In particular, some authors surmised that individual corporations might have exploited their dominant position in the creation of the Greenhouse Gas Protocol guidelines in order to prevent more stringent regulations established at the intergovernmental level. However, the case study on the Greenhouse Gas Protocol did not support this proposition.

The second conceptual assumption portrayed a *complementary* relationship and implied that transnational governance initiatives strengthen the norms and rules of the international climate regime. With regard to this assumption, it can be stated that all three case studies suggest that transnational governance arrangements contribute in different ways to achieving the ultimate objective of the UNFCCC. The ICLEI network has supported the development of local climate policies, which have led to quantifiable GHG emission reductions. The Gold Standard has certified numerous carbon offset projects delivering significant sustainable development benefits to emerging economies and developing countries. And the Greenhouse Gas Protocol has filled a regulatory gap in global climate policy-making by providing the means for private companies to comprehensively measure and manage their GHG emissions. In light of these empirical results, it can be argued that transnational governance arrangements help promote and implement the norms and rules agreed upon by nation-states in international climate negotiations and hence may be viewed as complementary to the intergovernmental level. Interestingly, the three case studies also showed that the activities of transnational governance arrangements, in certain respects, go beyond the norms and rules set out in international climate agreements. The GHG emission reductions attained by the ICLEI network were partly realized before the Kyoto Protocol came into force and were also achieved in countries not obligated to reduce their GHG emissions. Moreover, the methodologies developed by the Gold Standard for the evaluation of voluntary carbon offset projects might, in the long run, improve the validation and verification processes applied in the compliance offset market. In addition, large corporations from countries without specific emission reduction targets increasingly use the tools for the measurement and reporting of GHG emissions provided by the Greenhouse Gas Protocol. These findings underline the fact that transnational governance arrangements are indispensable and innovative parts of the global response to climate change.

The third conceptual assumption portrayed a *dependency* relationship and supposed that transnational governance initiatives rely on the norms and rules of the international climate regime. Relating to this assumption, the case studies have provided strong evidence that the effective operation of transnational climate governance arrangements is highly dependent on a particular institutional context in which key regulatory decisions are made. The ICLEI members, for instance, rely on external funding to implement climate projects in their communities. In the absence of a wide-ranging international climate treaty, the financial support for local climate actions remains uncertain and scarce. As a consequence, the activities of the ICLEI network are first and foremost oriented towards the intergovernmental level in order to raise the global level of ambition. Similarly, the demand for carbon offset projects under the Clean Development Mechanism certified by the Gold Standard is dependent on a functioning global offsetting scheme. The uncertain future of the Clean Development Mechanism raises serious problems for the Gold Standard and makes it difficult for the private certification scheme to achieve its self-proclaimed objectives. Furthermore, the Gold Standard for the voluntary carbon market is largely modeled on the rules and procedures of the Clean Development Mechanism and employs many of the methodologies developed for the compliance offset market. This underscores the great similarity between the voluntary offset market and the Clean Development Mechanism. Accordingly, the Gold Standard for the voluntary offset market is also adversely affected by the current crisis of the Clean Development Mechanism, particularly concerning the declining demand for high-quality carbon offsets. For these reasons, the Gold Standard Foundation strongly advocates a reform of the compliance offset market and pushes for new measures to introduce an efficient global offsetting scheme. Finally, the adoption of the Greenhouse Gas Protocol also depends on the right incentive structure created by nation-states for the corporate sector to take action on climate change. Due to the lack of significant progress in the international climate negotiations, the guidelines and training courses offered by the Greenhouse Gas Protocol do not encourage many companies to conduct reliable and complete inventories of their GHG emissions. Representatives of the Greenhouse Gas Protocol have therefore recently urged national delegates to adopt more stringent GHG emission reduction targets and to set up a coherent UNFCCC-led cap and trade system.

Thus, to sum up, the empirical analysis in this book has demonstrated that transnational governance arrangements cannot be treated as alternatives to existing modes of inter-state cooperation. Rather, the various climate initiatives launched by different types of sub- and non-state actors may be seen as complementary to the intergovernmental level. Their impact on policy outcomes, however, relies on the existence of an international regulatory environment created by nation-states in international climate negotiations. The table below provides an overview of the main findings from the three case studies (see Table 7.1). On the basis of the previous general assessment of the case studies within the analytical framework of the book, three main conclusions can be derived that will be highlighted in the following paragraphs.

The role and function of sub- and non-state actors in global climate governance

The first conclusion that can be drawn from the empirical analysis is that national governments and international institutions are not the only relevant actors in the global response to climate change. In this study, it has become obvious that sub-national, non-profit, and business actors have all adopted important roles and functions in global climate governance. To begin with the first case study, the ICLEI network has initiated several projects and programs to tackle climate change at the local level and employed different strategies of internal governing to steer its members towards the reduction of GHG emissions. More recently, ICLEI has put emphasis on the development of self-regulatory instruments mainly to enhance the ability of its member cities and municipalities to access the sources of international carbon financing for local climate actions. Beyond that, the ICLEI network is actively involved in the various meetings and conferences of the UNFCCC to persuade national governments to commit themselves to more stringent GHG emission reduction targets. In the second case study, it has been shown that the Gold Standard has developed strict criteria for the evaluation of carbon offset projects in the Clean Development Mechanism and in this way enhanced the environmental and social integrity of the market-based instrument. It has also established guidelines and developed new verification and validation methodologies to ensure the credibility of the voluntary carbon market. In addition, the Gold Standard Foundation is increasingly engaged in the UNFCCC conferences to induce nation-states to adopt a functioning global offsetting scheme. And the third case study has demonstrated that the Greenhouse Gas Protocol has provided a widely used guidance document for conducting corporate GHG emission inventories. To support the broad application of this standard, the Greenhouse Gas Protocol Team has collaborated closely with different industry groups, published numerous calculation tools as well as additional guidelines, and developed specific training courses and capacity building programs. As the two other climate initiatives, representatives of the Greenhouse Gas Protocol have also participated in UNFCCC conferences and repeatedly called for a clear and stable international policy framework. In general terms, these findings underscore the broad range of instruments and capacities at the disposal of sub- and non-state actors to address the climate change problem.

Most relevant for the focus of this study, it has become apparent that the three transnational governance arrangements reviewed here are all involved in rule-setting activities. This can be illustrated by a number of examples from the case

Table 7.1 Overview of the main findings from the analysis of the relationship between different transnational climate initiatives and the international climate regime

Conceptual assumptions	*Transnational climate initiatives*		
	The ICLEI Network	**The Gold Standard**	**The Greenhouse Gas Protocol**
Conflictive relationship	No indication	No indication	Only weak theoretical indications
Complementary relationship	The ICLEI network develops local climate policies, which have led to quantifiable GHG emission reductions	The Gold Standard certifies carbon offset projects, which deliver significant sustainable development benefits to less-developed countries	The Greenhouse Gas Protocol provides the means for companies to comprehensively measure and manage their GHG emissions
	The emission reductions were partly realized before an international regulatory framework came into force and have also been achieved in countries without reduction obligations	The Gold Standard Foundation develops innovative methodologies that might improve the validation and verification processes in the compliance offset market	Corporations from countries without emission reduction obligations measure and report their emissions by using the tools of the Greenhouse Gas Protocol
Dependency relationship	The ICLEI members largely rely on external funding from their national governments and international institutions to implement climate projects in their communities	The demand for carbon offset projects under the Clean Development Mechanism certified by the Gold Standard is dependent on a functioning global offsetting scheme	The adoption of the Greenhouse Gas Protocol depends on the right incentive structure for the corporate sector to take action on climate change
	In the absence of an ambitious international climate agreement, the financial support for local climate actions will remain uncertain and scarce	The Gold Standard for the voluntary market is also adversely affected by the current crisis of the Clean Development Mechanism, particularly the declining demand for high-quality carbon offsets	Due to the lack of progress in the international climate negotiations, the Greenhouse Gas Protocol will not encourage many companies to conduct reliable and complete GHG inventories
	As a consequence, the activities of the ICLEI network are first and foremost oriented towards the intergovernmental level in order to raise the global level of ambition	For these reasons, the Gold Standard Foundation strongly advocates a reform of the compliance offset market and pushes for new measures to introduce an efficient global offsetting scheme	Representatives of the Greenhouse Gas Protocol have therefore urged national delegates to adopt more stringent emission reduction targets and to set up a coherent UNFCCC-led cap and trade system

studies. The ICLEI network has designed a Five-Milestone Approach that includes the definition of concrete GHG emission reduction targets for its constituents. It also developed standards for local GHG inventories and introduced programs for the actual reporting of local climate actions. With these and other instruments, the ICLEI network aims at guiding urban actors when they cope with climate change in their communities. The Gold Standard has created strict guidelines for the implementation of climate change mitigation projects and is concerned with the development of new methodologies for the verification and validation of individual project activities. As indicated above, these rules and procedures seek to improve the quality of the carbon offset projects in both the voluntary and compliance offset markets. And the Greenhouse Gas Protocol has established standardized rules and procedures for GHG accounting and reporting by the corporate sector. The tools of the Greenhouse Gas Protocol provide the necessary basis for individual corporations to measure and manage their GHG emissions. These instances support the general premise that the capacity to set rules and standards in the policy domain of climate change no longer resides exclusively with national governments and international institutions (e.g. Bäckstrand 2008: 77; Andonova, Betsill, and Bulkeley 2009: 65; Bulkeley and Newell 2010: 56).

Furthermore, the case studies have shown that the transnational climate initiatives analyzed in this book use so-called 'soft' forms of governance to persuade their constituents to comply with their rules. In contrast to traditional command-and-control approaches that usually build on binding agreements, economic incentives, or sanctions, the various newly emerging transnational governance arrangements employ mostly non-hierarchical forms of steering (e.g. Risse 2004). Above all, it has become clear that the guidelines and standards set by transnational governance initiatives have gained prominence and are followed by other actors operating in the issue area of climate change. As laid out in the previous chapters, numerous local governments participate in the self-regulatory programs developed by the ICLEI network; the Gold Standard is regarded as a high-quality carbon offset standard and has been widely adopted by participants in carbon offset markets; and the guidelines of the Greenhouse Gas Protocol are now perceived as the common language and practice of corporate GHG measurement and management. This is evidence that the guidelines and standards developed by different types of sub- and non-state actors enjoy a high level of recognition among other actors. It can therefore be argued that sub- and non-state actors have assumed a new form of rule-making authority in the field of global climate politics.

Transnational initiatives as pioneers in the global response to climate change

The second major conclusion of this study implies that the three transnational governance arrangements to some extent reach further than the norms and rules of the international climate regime. As the case studies have demonstrated, transnational governance initiatives occasionally set guidelines and standards that are more ambitious than those contained in international climate agreements. Moreover, it has become apparent that sub- and non-state actors create novel means to cope with climate change. The ICLEI network, for instance, started its activities to tackle climate change before the adoption of an international regulatory framework, and has implemented projects and programs in countries that do not have legally binding obligations to reduce their GHG emissions. Recently, the local climate actions supported by the ICLEI network have also been integrated into national climate programs of developing countries to reduce GHG emissions. Accordingly, the activities of the ICLEI network could make international climate agreements more attractive for nation-states in future international climate negotiations. In a similar vein, the Gold Standard has established stricter requirements than the current international regulatory regime for the eligibility of climate change mitigation projects. In particular, it assigns its label only to those project activities that generate significant sustainable development benefits in the project host countries. Additionally, it also supports the development of innovative methodologies for the evaluation of climate change mitigation projects, particularly for the voluntary carbon market. These innovations might sooner or later help advance the rules and procedures for the evaluation of project activities under the Clean Development Mechanism and improve the regulatory structure of the compliance offset market. And the guidelines of the Greenhouse Gas Protocol are utilized not only by companies from industrialized countries that have to meet certain GHG emission reduction targets, but increasingly also by large companies from emerging economies and developing countries. Thereby, the Greenhouse Gas Protocol Team supports these companies in their endeavor to comply with the rules and procedures for GHG measurement and management. The Greenhouse Gas Protocol's two founding organizations have furthermore undertaken various efforts to enhance the GHG accounting and reporting capacities of corporations in several less-developed countries. Until now, these countries have rejected any concrete obligations in the international climate regime. The actions taken by companies to measure and manage their GHG emissions with the support of the Greenhouse Gas Protocol could hence possibly motivate their national governments to accept legally binding GHG emission controls in an upcoming commitment period.

Thus, the analysis suggests that sub- and non-state actors can be conceptualized as pioneers in the global response to climate change, whose actions might encourage nation-states to take more determined steps towards addressing this issue (Hoffmann 2011; Stewart, Oppenheimer, and Rudyk 2013). More precisely, their initiatives could increase the confidence level of national governments to adopt concrete measures to reduce GHG emissions and by this means stimulate progress in the international climate negotiations. This indicates that the activities of sub- and non-state actors can be seen as a crucial precursor to stringent international policy action, since they broaden the scope of the available solutions to cope with climate change.

The shadow of the international climate regime

The third core conclusion of this book is that transnational climate initiatives are in need of an international regulatory framework in order to effectively contribute to the global response to climate change. In the first case study, it has been shown that ICLEI members strongly rely on external funding to implement climate projects in their communities. In the absence of a wide-ranging international climate treaty, cities and municipalities do not receive adequate financial support for their local climate actions. Therefore, in the past few years, the ICLEI network has directed its activities increasingly at the international climate change conferences in order to prompt national governments to enter into a far-reaching international climate treaty. Likewise, the second case study has demonstrated that the Gold Standard builds upon the regulatory framework of the compliance offset market and uses the rules and procedures adopted by the Clean Development Mechanism's Executive Board for the evaluation of carbon offset projects. Moreover, it has become obvious that the demand for climate change mitigation projects certified by the Gold Standard depends heavily on the existence of a functioning global offsetting scheme. Without the establishment of such an instrument by nation-states at the intergovernmental level, the Gold Standard will continue to run into major difficulties. As a result, Gold Standard representatives have sought to convince national governments to introduce an effective international market-based mechanism. Finally, in the third case study, it has become apparent that the Greenhouse Gas Protocol also greatly depends on political signals from the international climate change conferences. Only if stringent GHG emission controls are likely to be adopted at the intergovernmental level will private corporations put substantial effort into GHG measurement and management. For that reason, staff members of the Greenhouse Gas Protocol Team have called for clear guidelines to be adopted in international climate negotiations. This is further illustrated by the period around the 2009 Copenhagen Climate Change Summit. In the years ahead of this widely noticed conference when nation-states planned the adoption of a new legally binding international climate agreement, there was considerable increase in business self-regulation because companies anticipated the introduction of stricter regulations and sought to gain first-mover advantages (Green 2014: 166-167). In particular, the firms that participated in self-regulatory initiatives intended to prepare for future GHG emission controls and hoped to get a head start in a newly established market-based mechanism or cap and trade system. However, after it turned out that the conference failed to deliver a new multilateral treaty, many self-regulatory business initiatives lost much of their spark and companies went for the short-term profit instead of further investing in pre-compliance action. This demonstrates once again that transnational governance arrangements obviously relate their climate-related actions to the targets and timetables stipulated in international climate agreements.

Taking these findings into account, the argument can be put forward that transnational climate governance arrangements operate in the 'shadow' of the international climate regime (Stripple and Lövbrand 2010: 175-176; Bulkeley *et al.* 2012: 603; Lederer 2012: 528). In fact, the findings from this study suggest that the principles, norms, rules, and decision-making procedures established at the intergovernmental level have a significant and often overlooked impact on the initiatives launched by sub- and non-state actors. It has become evident that international climate agreements are of eminent importance for effectively dealing with climate change at various levels of decision-making. Put differently, multilateral treaty-making continues to be more important than many scholars and policy-makers suppose. This insight resembles findings gained by other research projects in the field of international relations and related disciplines (e.g. Conzelmann and Wolf 2008; Bäckstrand *et al.* 2010; Börzel and Risse 2010; Mayer and Gereffi 2010; Christoff and Eckersley 2013). In general terms, it can be stated that transnational governance initiatives require the maintenance of a rule-based framework negotiated by nation-states in multilateral settings. Thus, while sub- and non-state actors certainly have great potential to make a significant contribution towards addressing the problem of climate change, the analysis in this book reveals that the prospects for tangible reductions of GHG emissions through their activities remain restricted in the absence of adequate norms and rules created by nation-states in international climate negotiations.

Generalizability

After having highlighted the main conclusions of the analysis in this book, I now discuss to what extent the results can be transferred to the broader population of transnational climate governance arrangements. It is in the nature of the case study methodology that the researcher has to generalize from a relatively small sample to a larger group of cases (Gerring 2004). This process of generalization involves the problem that the findings drawn from the cases under investigation do not necessarily apply to the broader unstudied population of cases (Lieberson 1991). Furthermore, when conducting qualitative case studies, researchers are faced with the problem that it is difficult to control for the effect of variables not included in the underlying research design. For that reason, the findings obtained from case studies must generally be treated with caution and cannot easily be generalized (Collier, Seawright, and Munck 2010). In this study, I took two measures to address these inherent shortcomings of the qualitative case study methodology. First, I aimed at selecting cases that are representative of a number of transnational governance arrangements by covering the wide spectrum of arrangements that have emerged over the past few years. The intention behind this was to examine three typical instances of transnational governance initiatives, which allow for conclusions that are not idiosyncratic to the cases investigated in this book (Seawright and Gerring 2008; Rohlfing 2012). Second, I employed the method of structured, focused comparison in order to guide and standardize data collection and to remain focused when confronted with a huge amount of information regarding the particular transnational governance arrangement under consideration (George 1979; George and Bennett 2005: 67–72). This method can be understood as an analytical instrument for theory development in qualitative small-N research, which stipulates a systematic procedure for the empirical analysis in order to arrive at general conclusions (Mahoney 2004).

On this basis, I contend that the three cases analyzed in this book can be approached as illustrative instances of the relationship between climate initiatives launched by sub- and non-state actors and the international climate regime. More specifically, although the findings of the present study may not hold true for a number of specific transnational climate governance arrangements, I put forward the argument that the conclusions derived from the preceding chapters extend beyond the three cases under investigation and can indeed be applied to several other transnational climate initiatives. Yet, it is clear that more research needs to be conducted to examine whether and to what extent the findings apply to the wider population of unstudied cases. Therefore, the conclusions of this book are meant to be conceived as a first in-depth empirical examination of the relationship between transnational climate initiatives and the international climate regime, which lays the groundwork for future studies on this topic.

Theoretical implications

In the previous section, I assessed the case studies within the analytical framework and derived three main conclusions. Next, I revert to the theoretical background of the book and discuss the study's theoretical implications for the debate on the concept of authority in world politics. In particular, I evaluate which theories are called into question and which are reinforced through the empirical analysis carried out in this book. Hence, the following paragraphs situate the case studies within the larger context of the field of international relations theory.

Multiple loci of authority in global climate governance

On the one hand, the analysis in this study has shown that transnational governance arrangements have attained several authoritative functions in the policy domain of climate change. As indicated above, the ICLEI network exercises authority over its members by stipulating concrete emission reduction targets, developing standards for local GHG inventories, and introducing programs to systematically report local climate actions. The Gold Standard has gained authority in carbon markets through the development of strict criteria for the evaluation of carbon offset projects and the advancement of methodologies to verify and validate project activities in both the voluntary and compliance offset markets. And the Greenhouse Gas Protocol has acquired authority in the field of corporate-level GHG accounting and reporting because its rules and procedures are widely recognized by relevant actors, including individual companies, business associations, national government agencies, and international organizations. These findings suggest that sub- and non-state actors have adopted governance capacities, which have traditionally been assigned to nation-states and international institutions. More precisely, the case studies have demonstrated that different types of sub- and non-state actors have developed rules and standards that are voluntarily accepted by others, which Jessica Green describes as 'private entrepreneurial authority' (Green 2010; 2014). This underlines the fact that 'there are multiple loci of authority rather than a single locus that rests with the state' (Green 2014: 164). It is clear that these insights challenge classical approaches to international politics, which assume that state-based forms of governance constitute the only source of authority in world politics. This theoretical perspective is in urgent need of revision, since it neglects the various problem-solving and decision-making functions performed by sub- and non-state actors in global affairs (e.g. Avant, Finnemore, and Sell 2010). What has also become apparent in the case studies is that the various newly emerging transnational climate governance arrangements do not operate as distinct spheres of authority. Instead, the analysis has shown that the initiatives launched by different types of sub- and non-state actors are inextricably linked to existing modes of inter-state cooperation. This is in line with other scholars who have argued that clear boundaries between public and private forms of authority cannot be drawn and hence private authority structures should not be treated separately from public authority (e.g. Pattberg and Stripple 2008; Stripple and Lövbrand 2010; Bulkeley and Schroeder 2012). Based on the analysis in this book, it can thus be stated that transnational governance arrangements do not work independently of state-based forms of governance, while their rules and standards have become an integral part of the global response to climate change.

In short, it has become obvious that the increasing significance of sub- and non-state actors reveals the limitations of classical approaches to international politics and questions traditional concepts of authority in world politics. This underscores the relevance of alternative approaches to authority, which emphasize the rise of authority structures beyond the nation-state and state-based international regimes. In light of these insights, it can be acknowledged that a purely state-centric view no longer captures the dense institutional landscape in global policy-making.

The persistent authority of state-based forms of governance

On the other hand, however, the development of multiple loci of authority in global climate governance does not imply that we are witnessing a general shift of authority away from state-based forms of governance to transnational governance arrangements. In particular, the case studies have shown that the activities of the ICLEI network, the Gold Standard, and the Greenhouse Gas Protocol by no means limit the authority of national governments and international institutions. By contrast, the evidence provided in this study suggests that the impact of transnational climate governance arrangements relies on the continuous evolution of the norms and rules set out in international climate agreements (Bulkeley *et al.* 2012: 603). This indicates that the authority of nation-states and state-based international regimes is not challenged by the emergence of transnational governance arrangements, but is in fact considerably strengthened (Krasner 1995; Kahler and Lake 2004). What follows from this is that the changes in the distribution of authority in global climate governance cannot be understood as a simple zero-sum game (Büthe 2010: 21–23; Risse 2013: 255; Green 2014: 163–164). While the results of the present study clearly highlight the fact that transnational climate initiatives have become important elements in the global response to climate change, this does not signal a weakening of existing modes of inter-state cooperation. In other words, the recent development pertaining to the growing involvement of sub- and non-state actors in global policy-making should not be conceived as a one-sided relocation of authority from national governments and international institutions to transnational governance arrangements (Higgott, Underhill, and Bieler 2000; Zürn 2013). Accordingly, the term *shift* of authority seems inappropriate to capture the current trend in global climate politics. Instead, what can be observed is a *reconfiguration of authority* across various actors and multiple levels of decision-making, which apparently only reinforces the authority of state-based forms of governance.

To sum up, it has become clear that the increasing involvement of sub- and non-state actors in global affairs does not necessarily lead to a loss of authority at the expense of national governments or international institutions as much of the literature dealing with the concept of global governance implies. By contrast, the case studies have demonstrated that an international regulatory framework is of utmost significance for the effective operation of transnational climate initiatives launched by sub- and non-state actors. This suggests that the rise of transnational governance arrangements in global politics considerably enhances the centrality of existing modes of inter-state cooperation.

Seeking theoretical middle ground

Generally speaking, the present study has underscored that the development of authority structures beyond the nation-state and state-based international regimes has become a reality in global climate governance. Sub-national, non-profit, and business actors set rules and standards to govern their own behavior and that of others. This development is representative of the multilevel nature of climate policy-making that has recently attracted much scholarly attention. The emergence of transnational governance arrangements has evidently led to changes in the distribution of authority in the policy domain of climate change. At the same time, however, the analysis in this book has revealed that the activities launched by sub- and non-state actors are taking place within an international regulatory system that is key for their effectiveness (Newell, Pattberg, and Schroeder 2012: 368). These two central findings of this book imply that the theoretical picture regarding the concept of authority in world politics is more complex than widely assumed. Therefore, this study argues in favor of a theoretical middle ground between traditional and alternative understandings of authority in world politics as outlined in the third chapter of this book. Certainly, the empirical findings of this study raise serious questions about the appropriateness of classical theories of international politics to analyze contemporary global affairs. In particular, these approaches fail to take into account that sub- and non-state actors have become a key feature in various domains of global policy-making. Nevertheless, there are also several findings that indicate that classical approaches to international politics still have considerable explanatory power when studying the relationship between newly emerging transnational governance initiatives and state-based forms of governance (e.g. Drezner 2007). In fact, the empirical analysis in this book suggests that the international climate regime continues to be the most important site of global climate politics. With regard to Rosenau's argument regarding the emergence of new spheres of authority in world politics, it can hence be concluded that a number of new actors have indeed joined the nation-state and international institutions as relevant actors in global affairs. Yet, these actors obviously revolve around existing modes of inter-state cooperation and build their initiatives upon the norms and rules created by nation-states in international negotiations.

This general conclusion points to the need for a more nuanced perspective on the concept of authority in world politics. As stated above, there is no 'diachronic shift from government to governance' (Arts 2006: 196). Rather, what we observe is the development of a multirule system, in which different governance arrangements emerge and interact, but remain centered on state-based forms of regulation. Adherents of alternative approaches to the concept of authority certainly have a point when they argue that sub- and non-state actors, to an increasing extent, acquire problem-solving and decision-making capacities in world politics. However, the main premise of neo-realist and neo-liberal institutionalist scholars that nation-states and state-based international regimes remain the central part of the story cannot be dismissed altogether. With regard to the topic dealt with in this book, transnational governance arrangements can be viewed as important elements of the global response to climate change because they have adopted significant regulatory functions in global climate policy-making. Moreover, they work as pioneers and introduce new instruments to address the climate change problem. But their effective operation evidently depends on the existence of an overarching policy framework set up by nation-states at the intergovernmental level. As a result, despite the contributions of sub- and non-state actors to solving the problem of climate change, transnational climate initiatives cannot be praised to be an adequate replacement for the further evolution of the international climate regime. In fact, it would be highly problematic if the increasing importance of sub- and non-state actors in global affairs was taken as an excuse for preventing or delaying action by nation-states at the intergovernmental level. Hence, while this study has underscored that the international climate regime is not the only location where the problem of climate change is addressed, it has highlighted the persistent authority of state-based forms of governance.

Practical relevance

In a practical sense, this study has provided scholars and policy-makers with profound empirical knowledge about the largely neglected research question regarding the interplay between transnational governance arrangements and existing modes of inter-state cooperation. Ultimately, the empirical analysis conducted in this book has demonstrated that an international umbrella is essential for the activities of climate initiatives developed by different types of sub- and non-state actors. It has become evident that all three transnational climate initiatives analyzed in this book are not only closely linked to the

UNFCCC process, but are highly dependent on the regulatory framework created by nation-states in international climate negotiations. Nonetheless, the case studies have also shown that transnational governance arrangements can be perceived as innovative drivers for action that might under certain circumstances facilitate progress at the intergovernmental level. More specifically, the activities of transnational governance arrangements could to some extent render international climate agreements more feasible for national governments by demonstrating that real steps to mitigate climate change are indeed possible. This underscores that transnational climate initiatives are crucial for testing out new solutions to tackle the problem of climate change and hence potentially act as catalysts in the international climate negotiations (Hoffmann 2011).

Against this backdrop, this book aims to direct attention to the issue of how the existing modes of inter-state cooperation can be adjusted to enable sub- and non-state actors to more effectively contribute to the global response to climate change. This line of argument is embodied in the evolving literature on *orchestration* (e.g. Abbott and Snidal 2009; 2010; 2013; Abbott *et al.* 2015). The concept of orchestration has been defined as 'a process whereby states or intergovernmental organizations initiate, guide, broaden, and strengthen transnational governance by non-state and/or sub-state actors' (Hale and Roger 2014: 60–61). Building upon this concept, it can be argued that one promising and realistic option for increasing the overall effectiveness of the global response to climate change is to enhance the role of the UNFCCC Secretariat (e.g. Hale 2013; van Asselt and Zelli 2014). Compared with other intergovernmental treaty secretariats that enjoy relatively wide political leeway, the political influence of the UNFCCC Secretariat has traditionally been rather limited (Busch 2009). In the past few years, however, the UNFCCC Secretariat adopted a more active role and has begun to engage the different sub-groups of non-governmental organizations involved in the UNFCCC process into a policy dialogue. An illustrative instance in this regard is the UNFCCC Secretariat's *Momentum for Change Initiative* launched at the 2011 Conference of the Parties to the UNFCCC held in Durban (UNFCCC 2011). This program aims 'to highlight broad-ranging climate actions that are already achieving impacts on the ground, in addressing both climate change and wider economic, social and environmental issues' (UNFCCC 2014b). Furthermore, in mid-2013, the UNFCCC Secretariat compiled and published a list of individual cooperative climate measures, which comprises several projects conducted by sub-national governments and proactive businesses (UNFCCC 2014a).

These examples indicate that the UNFCCC Secretariat already acts as an orchestrator of the various climate initiatives developed by sub- and non-state actors. In principle, this approach could further be expanded in order to allow transnational governance arrangements to reach a significant impact in global climate governance. The main challenge thereby is to design the UNFCCC process in such a way that the activities of sub- and non-state actors 'become not substitutes or even complements to a global treaty, but stepping stones on the path to a higher climate ambition that an effective treaty will require' (Hale 2013: 2). While these ideas are still preliminary, they bear important policy implications. In every domain of world politics where collective action dilemmas have to be overcome and the interests of nation-states diverge, international organizations and intergovernmental treaty secretariats can contribute to solving transboundary problems by coordinating and steering the initiatives of sub- and non-state actors towards coherence and good practice (e.g. Abbott and Snidal 2013). More specifically, when international negotiations get stuck in gridlock (as is currently the case in several issue areas of world politics), international bureaucracies might turn to sub- and non-state actors to mobilize advocacy, create demonstration effects, or otherwise pressure national governments for initiating progress in multilateral treaty-making (cf. Abbott 2014).

Thus, there is a great potential for increased collaboration between sub- and non-state actors and international institutions, including both fully fledged international organizations and relatively small intergovernmental treaty secretariats. With regard to the issue of climate change, it has been acknowledged that a novel way of thinking is possible about the role of the UNFCCC Secretariat. In particular, this study recommends strengthening the UNFCCC Secretariat and opening up the UNFCCC process for the initiatives of sub- and non-state actors in order to push the international climate negotiations forward.

Outlook

The analysis conducted in this book has identified an important direction for further research. While several scholars concerned with global environmental politics conceptualize the emergence of authority structures beyond the nation-state and international institutions as a simultaneous loss of authority on the part of state-based forms of governance, this book finds that the changes in the distribution of authority in world politics should not be viewed as a zero-sum shift of authority to sub- and non-state actors. Indeed, in the past decades, we have seen that many transnational governance initiatives have acquired several important regulatory functions in global affairs. However, as argued above, this development is best described as a constant reconfiguration of authority that in fact reaffirms the centrality of existing modes of inter-state cooperation. Consequently, it is necessary to further unpack the concept of authority and explore the various interlinkages between the different spheres of authority in global politics, instead of inquiring whether one actor gains authority at the expense of another. In fact, this book is an early contribution to the study of the relationship between transnational governance arrangements and existing modes of inter-state cooperation. In this regard, the present study raises a number of questions, which ought to be central in future studies in the field of global (climate) politics.

A first research area touched upon in this study is how the initiatives of sub- and non-state actors could unlock progress in the various deadlocked international negotiation forums (e.g. Hale, Held, and Young 2013). While the case studies have underscored that transnational governance arrangements acquire various authoritative functions and act as pioneers, further inquiries are warranted to investigate the concrete pathways through which their activities might unfold a catalytic effect on the intergovernmental level (e.g. Hoffmann 2011; Bulkeley and Cástan Broto 2013; Bulkeley *et al.* 2014). With regard to the policy domain of climate change, it would be particularly fruitful to examine to what extent the activities of sub- and non-state actors can alter the political conditions for achieving a comprehensive international agreement on collective action to address climate change (Hoffmann 2013; 2014).

A second and related research field arising from the present analysis is how international institutions operate as mediators, enablers, and coordinators of the initiatives developed by sub- and non-state actors in various domains of global policy-making (e.g. Joachim, Reinalda, and Verbeek 2008; Biermann and Siebenhüner 2009; Bauer and Weinlich 2011). Empirical studies are needed to assess how international organizations and other international institutions attain authority to collaborate with different types of sub- and non-state actors in order to achieve common goals and provide public goods. Concerning the issue area of climate change, future research should in particular examine to what extent the UNFCCC Secretariat or other bodies, such as the United Nations Environment Programme and the World Bank, orchestrate transnational governance initiatives and sometimes even '*bypass* recalcitrant national governments by directly engaging sub-state and societal actors at multiple levels of authority and scales' (Abbott 2014: 57, emphasis in original).

And a third, again related, research topic that emerges from this study is how national interests continue to shape the political response to transboundary problems (e.g. Sprinz and Vaahtoranta 1994; Barrett 2003; Dimitrov 2013). Notwithstanding the emergence of authority structures beyond state-based forms of governance, it is clear that '[n]ation-states still aggregate territorial interests and put them forward in international negotiations' (Zürn 2013: 411). Relating to the issue of climate change, the most important decisions on emission reduction goals and the mechanisms to achieve them continue to be taken by national governments at the intergovernmental level. As a consequence, key conflicts will be further played out in the international climate regime, such as the North–South conflict as well as power struggles between pushers and draggers of international regulatory action (Depledge and Yamin 2009; Hurrell and Sengupta 2012; Terhalle and Depledge 2013). Further research is hence needed to shed light on the ongoing negotiation process as nation-states prepare for the 21st Conference of the Parties to the UNFCCC held in Paris in late 2015.

In conclusion, while these broadly defined research agendas illustrate how much work remains to be done, the present study offers several entry points and hopefully some motivation for scholars to address the related intriguing and important questions.

References

Abbott, Kenneth W. (2014). Strengthening the Transnational Regime Complex for Climate Change. *Transnational Environmental Law* 3 (1): 57–88.

Abbott, Kenneth W.; Genschel, Philipp; Snidal, Duncan; Zangl, Bernhard, (eds). (2015). *International Organizations as Orchestrators*. Cambridge, MA: Cambridge University Press.

Abbott, Kenneth W.; Snidal, Duncan (2009). Strengthening International Regulation Through Transnational New Governance: Overcoming the Orchestration Deficit. *Vanderbilt Journal of Transnational Law* 42 (2): 501–578.

Abbott, Kenneth W.; Snidal, Duncan (2010). International Regulation Without International Government: Improving IO Performance through Orchestration. *Review of International Organizations* 5 (3): 315–344.

Abbott, Kenneth W.; Snidal, Duncan (2013). Taking Responsive Regulation Transnational: Strategies for International Organizations. *Regulation & Governance* 7 (1): 95–113.

Andonova, Liliana B.; Betsill, Michele; Bulkeley, Harriet (2009). Transnational Climate Governance. *Global Environmental Politics* 9 (2): 52–73.

Arts, Bas (2006). Non-State Actors in Global Environmental Governance: New Arrangements Beyond the State In: Koenig-Archibugi, Mathias; Zürn, Michael. *New Modes of Governance in the Global System: Exploring Publicness, Delegation and Inclusiveness.* Houndsmills: Palgrave, 177–200.

Avant, Deborah D.; Finnemore, Martha; Sell, Susan K., (eds). (2010). *Who Governs the Globe?* Cambridge, UK: Cambridge University Press.

Bäckstrand, Karin (2008). Accountability of Networked Climate Governance: The Rise of Transnational Climate Partnerships. *Global Environmental Politics* 8 (3): 74–102.

Bäckstrand, Karin; Khan, Jamil; Kronsell, Annica; Lövbrand, Eva, (eds). (2010). *Environmental Politics and Deliberative Democracy: Examining the Promise of New Modes of Governance.* Cheltenham: Edward Elgar.

Barrett, Scott (2003). *Environment and Statecraft: The Strategy of Environmental Treaty-Making.* Oxford: Oxford University Press.

Bauer, Steffen; Weinlich, Silke (2011). International Bureaucracies: Organizing World Politics. In: Reinalda, Bob. *The Ashgate Research Companion to Non-State Actors.* Farnham: Ashgate, 251–262.

Bernstein, Steven; Betsill, Michele; Hoffmann, Matthew; Paterson, Matthew (2010). A Tale of Two Copenhagens: Carbon Markets and Climate Governance. *Millennium: Journal of International Studies* 39 (1): 161–173.

Betsill, Michele; Bulkeley, Harriet (2006). Cities and the Multilevel Governance of Global Climate Change. *Global Governance* 12 (2): 141–159.

Biermann, Frank; Siebenhüner, Bernd, (eds). (2009). *Managers of Global Change: The Influence of International Environmental Bureaucracies.* Cambridge, MA: MIT Press.

Biermann, Frank; Zelli, Fariborz; Pattberg, Philipp; van Asselt, Harro (2010). The Architecture of Global Climate Governance. In: Biermann, Frank; Pattberg, Philipp; Zelli, Fariborz. *Global Climate Governance Beyond 2012. Architecture, Agency and Adaptation.* Cambridge, UK: Cambridge University Press, 15–24.

Börzel, Tanja A.; Risse, Thomas (2010). Governance Without a State: Can It Work? *Regulation & Governance* 4 (2): 113–134.

Bulkeley, Harriet; Andonova, Liliana; Bäckstrand, Karin; Betsill, Michele; Compagnon, Daniel; Duffy, Rosaleen; Kolk, Ans; Hoffmann, Matthew; Levy, David; Newell, Peter; Milledge, Tori; Paterson, Matthew; Pattberg, Philipp; VanDeveer, Stacy D. (2012). Governing Climate Change Transnationally: Assessing the Evidence From a Database of Sixty Initiatives. *Environment and Planning C–Government and Policy* 30 (4): 591–612.

Bulkeley, Harriet; Andonova, Liliana; Betsill, Michele; Compagnon, Daniel; Hale, Thomas; Hoffmann, Matthew; Newell, Peter; Paterson, Matthew; Roger, Charles; VanDeveer, Stacy D. (2014). *Transnational Climate Change Governance.* New York: Cambridge University Press.

Bulkeley, Harriet; Cástan Broto, Vanesa (2013). Urban Governance and Climate-Change Experiments. In: Mieg, Harald A.; Töpfer, Klaus. *Institutional and Social Innovation for Sustainable Urban Development*. New York: Routledge, 72–87.

Bulkeley, Harriet; Newell, Peter (2010). *Governing Climate Change*. London: Routledge.

Bulkeley, Harriet; Schroeder, Heike (2012). Beyond State/Non-State Divides: Global Cities and the Governing of Climate Change. *European Journal of International Relations* 18 (4): 743–766.

Busch, Per-Olof (2009). The Climate Secretariat: Making a Living in a Straitjacket. In: Biermann, Frank; Siebenhüner, Bernd. *Managers of Global Change: The Influence of International Environmental Bureaucracies*. Cambridge, MA: MIT Press, 245–264.

Büthe, Tim (2010). Private Regulation in the Global Economy: A (P)Review. *Business and Politics* 12 (3): Article 2.

Christoff, Peter; Eckersley, Robyn (2013). *Globalization and the Environment*. Lanham: Rowman & Littlefield.

Collier, David; Seawright, Jason; Munck, Gerardo L. (2010). The Quest for Standards: King, Keohane and Verba's Designing Social Inquiry. In: Collier, David; Brady, Henry E. *Rethinking Social Inquiry: Diverse Tools, Shared Standards*. Lanham, MD: Rowman & Littlefield, 21–50.

Conzelmann, Thomas; Wolf, Klaus Dieter (2008). The Potential and Limits of Governance by Private Codes of Conduct. In: Graz, Jean-Christophe; Nölke, Andreas. *Transnational Private Governance and Its Limits*. London: Routledge, 98–114.

Depledge, Joanna; Yamin, Farhana (2009). The Global Climate-Change Regime: A Defence. In: Helm, Dieter; Hepburn, Cameron. *The Economics and Politics of Climate Change*. Oxford: Oxford University Press, 433–453.

Dimitrov, Radoslav S. (2013). International Negotiations. In: Falkner, Robert. *The Handbook of Global Climate and Environment Policy*. Chichester: Wiley-Blackwell, 339–357.

Drezner, Daniel W. (2007). *All Politics Is Global: Explaining International Regulatory Regimes*. Princeton, NJ: Princeton University Press.

George, Alexander L. (1979). Case Studies and Theory Development: The Method of Structured, Focused Comparison. In: Lauren, Paul Gordon. *Diplomacy: New Approaches in History, Theory, and Policy*. New York: Free Press, 43–68.

George, Alexander L.; Bennett, Andrew (2005). *Case Studies and Theory Development in the Social Sciences*. Cambridge, MA: MIT Press.

Gerring, John (2004). What Is a Case Study and What Is It Good For? *American Political Science Review* 98 (2): 341–354.

Green, Jessica F. (2010). Private Standards in the Climate Regime: The Greenhouse Gas Protocol. *Business and Politics* 12 (3): Article 3.

Green, Jessica F. (2014). *Rethinking Private Authority: Agents and Entrepreneurs in Global Environmental Governance*. Princeton, NJ: Princeton University Press.

Hale, Thomas (2013). *How the UNFCCC Can Drive Climate Ambition in Advance of a Treaty: Record, Review, Reinforce, Recruit*. Oxford: Blavatnik School of Government.

Hale, Thomas; Held, David; Young, Kevin (2013). *Gridlock: Why Global Cooperation Is Failing When We Need It Most*. Cambridge, UK: Polity Press.

Hale, Thomas; Roger, Charles (2014). Orchestration and Transnational Climate Governance. *Review of International Organizations* 9 (1): 59–82.

Higgott, Richard A.; Underhill, Geoffrey R. D.; Bieler, Andreas (2000). Introduction: Globalisation and Non-State Actors. In: Higgott, Richard A.; Underhill, Geoffrey R. D.; Bieler, Andreas. *Non-State Actors and Authority in the Global System*. London: Routledge, 1–12.

Hoffmann, Matthew (2011). *Climate Governance at the Crossroads: Experimenting With a Global Response After Kyoto*. Oxford: Oxford University Press.

Hoffmann, Matthew (2013). *Shifting the Center of Gravity in the Global Response to Climate Change*. Paper presented at the Annual Convention of the International Studies Association, held in San Francisco from April 3–6.

Hoffmann, Matthew (2014). *Can Climate Governance Experiments Save the UN Climate Negotiations?* Paper presented at the Annual Convention of the International Studies Association, held in Toronto from March 26–29.

Hurrell, Andrew; Sengupta, Sandeep (2012). Emerging Powers, North-South Relations and Global Climate Politics. *International Affairs* 88 (3): 463–484.

Jagers, Sverker C.; Stripple, Johannes (2003). Climate Governance Beyond the State. *Global Governance* 9 (3): 385–399.

Joachim, Jutta M.; Reinalda, Bob; Verbeek, Bertjan, (eds). (2008). *International Organizations and Implementation: Enforcers, Managers, Authorities?* London: Routledge.

Kahler, Miles; Lake, David A. (2004). Governance in a Global Economy: Political Authority in Transition. *Political Science & Politics* 37 (3): 409–414.

Keohane, Robert O.; Victor, David G. (2011). The Regime Complex for Climate Change. *Perspectives on Politics* 9 (1): 7–23.

Krasner, Stephen D. (1995). Power Politics, Institutions, and Transnational Relations. In: Risse-Kappen, Thomas. *Bringing Transnational Relations back in: Non-State Actors, Domestic Structures, and International Institutions*. Cambridge, UK: Cambridge University Press, 257–279.

Lederer, Markus (2012). Market Making Via Regulation: The Role of the State in Carbon Markets. *Regulation and Governance* 6 (4): 524–544.

Lieberson, Stanley (1991). Small Ns and Big Conclusions: An Examination of the Reasoning in Comparative Studies Based on a Small Number of Cases. *Social Forces* 70 (2): 307–320.

Mahoney, James (2004). Structured, Focused Comparison. In: Lewis-Beck, Michael; Bryman, Alan E.; Futing Liao, Tim. *Encyclopedia of Social Science Research Methods*. London: Sage, 1098.

Mayer, Frederick; Gereffi, Gary (2010). Regulation and Economic Globalization: Prospects and Limits of Private Governance. *Business and Politics* 12 (3): 1–25.

Newell, Peter; Pattberg, Philipp; Schroeder, Heike (2012). Multiactor Governance and the Environment. *Annual Review of Environment and Resources* 37: 365–387.

Ostrom, Elinor (2010). Polycentric Systems for Coping with Collective Action and Global Environmental Change. *Global Environmental Change* 20 (4): 550–557.

Pattberg, Philipp (2007). *Private Institutions and Global Governance: The New Politics of Environmental Sustainability*. Cheltenham: Edward Elgar.

Pattberg, Philipp (2012). The Role and Relevance of Networked Climate Governance. In: Biermann, Frank; Pattberg, Philipp; Zelli, Fariborz. *Global Climate Governance Beyond 2012: Architecture, Agency and Adaptation*. Cambridge, UK: Cambridge University Press, 146–164.

Pattberg, Philipp; Stripple, Johannes (2008). Beyond the Public and Private Divide: Remapping Transnational Climate Governance in the 21st Century. *International Environmental Agreements* 8 (4): 367–388.

Risse, Thomas (2004). Global Governance and Communicative Action. *Government and Opposition* 39 (2): 288–313.

Risse, Thomas (2013). Transnational Actors and World Politics. In: Carlsnaes, Walter;

Risse, Thomas; Simmons, Beth A. *Handbook of International Relations*. Los Angeles, CA: Sage, 426–452.

Rohlfing, Ingo (2012). *Case Studies and Causal Inference: An Integrative Framework*. Basingstoke: Palgrave.

Rosenau, James N. (1997). *Along the Domestic-Foreign Frontier: Exploring Governance in a Turbulent World*. Cambridge, UK: Cambridge University Press.

Rosenau, James N. (1999). Toward an Ontology for Global Governance. In: Hewson, Martin; Sinclair, Timothy J. *Approaches to Global Governance Theory*. Albany, NY: State University of New York Press, 287–301.

Rosenau, James N. (2007). Governing the Ungovernable: The Challenge of a Global Disaggregation of Authority. *Regulation & Governance* 1 (1): 88–97.

Seawright, Jason; Gerring, John (2008). Case Selection Techniques in Case Study Research: A Menu of Qualitative and Quantitative Options. *Political Research Quarterly* 61 (2): 294–308.

Sprinz, Detlef; Vaahtoranta, Tapani (1994). The Interest-Based Explanation of International Environmental-Policy. *International Organization* 48 (1): 77–105.

Stewart, Richard B.; Oppenheimer, Michael; Rudyk, Bryce (2013). A New Strategy for Global Climate Protection. *Climatic Change* 120 (1–2): 1–12.

Stripple, Johannes; Lövbrand, Eva (2010). Carbon Market Governance Beyond the Public-Private Divide. In: Biermann, Frank; Pattberg, Philipp; Zelli, Fariborz. *Global Climate Governance Beyond 2012*. Cambridge, UK: Cambridge University Press, 165–182.

Terhalle, Maximilian; Depledge, Joanna (2013). Great-Power Politics, Order Transition, and Climate Governance: Insights From International Relations Theory. *Climate Policy* 13 (5): 572–588.

UNFCCC (2011). *Momentum for Change: Launch Report*. Bonn: UNFCCC Secretariat.

UNFCCC (2014a). *Compilation of Information on Mitigation Benefits of Actions, Initiatives and Options to Enhance Mitigation Action: List of Selected Cooperative Initiatives*. Available at: http://unfccc.int/meetings/bonn_jun_2013/items/7655.php (accessed July 28, 2014).

UNFCCC (2014b). *Parternships between the UNFCCC Secretariat and the Private Sector*. Available at: https://unfccc.int/secretariat/partneships/items/6621.php (accessed August 11, 2014).

van Asselt, Harro; Zelli, Fariborz (2014). Connect the Dots: Managing the Fragmentation of Global Climate Governance. *Environmental Economics and Policy Studies* 16 (2): 137–155.

Zürn, Michael (2013). Globalization and Global Governance. In: Carlsnaes, Walter; Risse, Thomas; Simmons, Beth A. *Handbook of International Relations*. Los Angeles, CA: Sage, 401–425.

Appendix I

List of interviews conducted

The interviews were held at the 18th Conference of the Parties to the UNFCCC in Doha, from 26 November to 8 December 2012.

Yunus Arikan	Cities Climate Center Manager, ICLEI World Secretariat
Thierry Berthoud	Managing Director for Energy and Climate, World Business Council for Sustainable Development
Sven Braden	CARLO Foundation
Huey-Por Chang	Kaohsiung City, Taiwan
René Estermann	MyClimate
Beatriz Kiss	Greenhouse Gas Protocol Trainer *Note: Two other Greenhouse Gas Protocol Trainers from the Asian Region were interviewed, but are not named here as they wished to remain anonymous.*
Nancy Lago	Environmental Promotion Office, City of Buenos Aires
Axel Michaelowa	Perspectives
Simone Mori	Enel Foundation
Yuko Nishida	Bureau of Environment, Tokyo Metropolitan Government
Rodrigo Perpétuo	Deputy Secretary of International Relations, Belo Horizonte
Tanya Petersen	Director of Marketing and Communications, Gold Standard Foundation
Sunil Pote	City Engineer, Thane Municipal Corporation
David Rich	Senior Associate with the Greenhouse Gas Protocol, World Resources Institute
Adrian Rimmer	Chief Executive Officer, Gold Standard Foundation
Gino Van Begin	Secretary General, ICLEI World Secretariat
Marion Vieweg-Mersmann	Climate Analytics
Edgar Villasenor	Regional Director, ICLEI Mexico and Caribbean Secretariat

Appendix II

List of attended meetings

Measurement and performance tracking expert workshop organized by the World Resources Institute on new guidelines of the Greenhouse Gas Protocol held in parallel with the 18th Conference of the Parties to the UNFCCC in Doha December 2, 2012

Doha global business day that took place in conjunction with the 18th Conference of the Parties to the UNFCCC in Doha December 3, 2012

Gold Standard side-event at the 18th Conference of the Parties to the UNFCCC in Doha December 3, 2012

Informal environmental non-governmental organizations meetings at the 18th Conference of the Parties to the UNFCCC in Doha December 3 and 4, 2012

Informal business non-governmental organizations meeting at the 18th Conference of the Parties to the UNFCCC in Doha December 5, 2012

Informal local governments and municipal authorities meetings at the 18th Conference of the Parties to the UNFCCC in Doha December 5 and 6, 2012

ICLEI side-event at the 18th Conference of the Parties to the UNFCCC in Doha December 6, 2012

Sustainable innovation forum that took place in conjunction with the 18th Conference of the Parties to the UNFCCC in Doha December 6, 2012

Index